Karl Barth

Karl Barth

Theologian of Christian Witness

JOSEPH L. MANGINA

Westminster John Knox Press
LOUISVILLE • LONDON

© 2004 Joseph L. Mangina

All rights reserved. No part of this book may be reproduced or transmitted in any form or by any means, electronic or mechanical, including photocopying, recording, or by any information storage or retrieval system, without permission in writing from the publisher. For information, address Westminster John Knox Press, 100 Witherspoon Street, Louisville, Kentucky 40202-1396.

Published in the United States by Westminster John Knox Press, Louisville, Kentucky.

Published in Great Britain by Ashgate Publishing Limited.

Cover illustration: Karl Barth. Courtesy of Special Collections, Princeton Theological Seminary Libraries on behalf of *Karl Barth Stiftung* of Basel, Switzerland.
Cover design by Jennifer K. Cox.
Typeset by Express Typesetters Limited, Farnham.
Printed and bound in Great Britain by MPG Books, Bodmin, Cornwall.

04 05 06 07 08 09 10 11 12 13 – 10 9 8 7 6 5 4 3 2 1

Library of Congress Cataloging-in-Publication Data is on file at the Library of Congress, Washington, D.C.

ISBN 0-664-22893-3

Contents

Contents

Preface

Writing an introduction to Barth's theology is a daunting task. Among those friends who gave early encouragement to this project, and who also furnished some key ideas, are Reinhard Hütter, David Kelsey, and Kendall Soulen. Everyone I consulted stressed the importance of readability, especially for beginning students in theology. Everyone stressed that the book should help students get into the text of the *Church Dogmatics* as quickly as possible, so that they can form their own judgments; it is always more profitable to read Barth than to read about him. I hope the following pages attain these goals in at least a modest way.

I was able to begin the research and writing during a sojourn at the Center of Theological Inquiry, Princeton, New Jersey, in the spring and summer of 2002. Thanks are due to Wallace Alston, at that time Director of the Center, and to Robert Jenson, Senior Scholar in Residence, who patiently read my early drafts. Fellow CTI members also provided much support and encouragement as I worked my way through the *Dogmatics*. I am grateful for the many lunchtime conversations, sometimes about people's research, sometimes about food, or church politics, or whatever happened to be in the *New York Times* that morning. It is a good thing that theological companionship does not always have to involve talking about theology.

Besides Dr Jenson, those who read portions of the manuscript at various stages are George Coon, Garrett Green, Stanley Hauerwas, Reinhard Hütter, Patrick McManus, Rusty Reno, Robin Darling Young, Philip Ziegler, and the students in my Barth seminar in the spring of 2003. All provided insightful and helpful criticism, and saved me from more than a few errors. I am grateful for the able work of Amy Coon, George Coon, and Patrick McManus in preparing the bibliography.

Wycliffe College and the Toronto School of Theology are where I hang my hat as a theological teacher. George Sumner, Principal of Wycliffe, has not only encouraged this project from the beginning, but has been generous in providing some flexibility in my teaching schedule. One could hardly ask for a better 'dean'. Sarah Lloyd of Ashgate Publishing responded to my many e-mail queries with unfailing cheerfulness and efficiency, as she awaited a book that was very long in the coming. Also on the other side of the Atlantic, Professor John Webster of the University of Aberdeen made some helpful last-minute suggestions on matters of style and annotation.

My early-morning sessions at the computer were often interrupted by my daughter Frances, the apple of her father's eye. The pages that follow incorporate an excellent idea she had for 'Papa's book'. Finally, a word of thanks to my wife Elisa, *sine qua non*…. 'A good wife who can find? She is far more precious than jewels. The heart of her husband trusts in her' (Proverbs 31). I dedicate this work to her in love, gratitude, and affection.

Introduction

As recently as a quarter-century ago, the theology of Karl Barth was widely regarded as a thing of the past. He was thought to represent a particular movement in modern Protestantism, often referred to as neo-orthodoxy or the theology of crisis. This theology might, it was thought, have been appropriate in the early twentieth century, when the experience of depression and world war shook cultural confidence in human progress. But with the passing of that era, Barth's relevance seemed to decline accordingly. This was especially true in the English-speaking world, where his reputation as a dour Calvinist mainly concerned to deny all 'points of contact' between God and humankind has been hard to dispel.

It is striking, therefore, that the late years of the twentieth century saw a major renaissance in Barth studies. It became more and more clear that the *Church Dogmatics* represents one of the towering achievements of modern Christian theology, and that it must be reckoned with even by those who disagree with its premises. One reason for this is simply a matter of perspective: at half a century's remove, it is easier to see what Barth was trying to accomplish than was possible during his lifetime. A steady stream of books, articles, and dissertations continues to illuminate his intellectual development and his peculiar style of doing theology. All this increases the chances that students will actually encounter the pipe-smoking, Mozart-loving theologian from Basel, rather than the mythical creature often associated with the name 'Karl Barth'.

The rediscovery of Barth also reflects seismic shifts that have occurred in the intellectual landscape over the past few decades. In the years following World War Two, it was easy to dismiss him because his writing focused on a text (the Bible) read in the context of a specific tradition and community (that of the Christian church). This kind of approach simply did not seem terribly relevant in a world of rapid social change; moreover, it was said that Barth's traditionalism failed to reflect 'the' experience of modern persons. Such objections now seem curiously dated. In hindsight, one can see that the traditioned character of Barth's thought is what keeps it fresh and alive: he engages the perennial questions of Christian thought (God, Christ, Trinity, creation, sin, grace, the church) in a way that theologies merely seeking to be 'up to date' often do not. This is by no means to say that Barth ignored the context in which he was writing; his strong political awareness, not just in the Nazi era but in the time of the cold war, suggests quite otherwise. If he did not actually say that one should have the Bible in one hand and the daily newspaper in the other – a remark often attributed to him – the sentiment jibes with the overall spirit of his thought. But he was convinced that the best way for theology to be relevant was to stick to its last, insisting on the priority of God over all movements and ideological programmes. Barth remains interesting fifty years later because he never lost sight of God; this is still the best reason to read him.

If we are in a better position to appreciate Barth today, this also surely has something to do with the influence of postmodernism. At the time he was writing, the charge was often made that he rejected modernity outright (classic liberal theologians like Harnack feared this was the case) or that he went too far in his criticisms (the claim of neo-orthodox liberals such as Reinhold Niebuhr and Emil Brunner). In the current intellectual climate it is easier to see Barth's radicalism as being a virtue. His rejection of all claims to identify any secure starting-point for reason outside revelation bears a surface resemblance to the move toward non-foundationalism in philosophy. Moreover, his orientation to questions of language, and even his own powerful use of rhetoric, echoes the general turn toward language in twentieth-century thought – for example, in authors like Heidegger and Derrida. Thinkers who have interpreted Barth along such lines include Graham Ward, Walter Lowe, and William Stacey Johnson.[1] Others have reacted vehemently to this 'postmodern Barth', insisting that his real affinities are with the Enlightenment and the nineteenth century. On this reading, he is not so much anti-modern or postmodern as critically modern, venturing a distinctive Christian answer to questions rightly posed by Enlightenment thinkers. Among recent scholars who have pressed this interpretation are Bruce McCormack and Neil MacDonald.[2] To oversimplify matters, one might say that the first group highlights the postmodern element as a way of rescuing Barth from Barthians, who precisely miss the radical and subversive aspects of his thought; while the second group sees postmodernism itself as insufficiently radical, a retreat from the hard questions concerning reason and truth.

This debate itself serves as testimony to the sheer intellectual power and imagination that marks Barth's authorship. Seeking to bring him into conversation with Kant, Hegel, Wittgenstein, Heidegger, or Derrida is a worthwhile endeavour, and the reader who poses such questions will not go away disappointed. Yet it must be admitted that Barth himself would likely have been frustrated by the whole debate. One can imagine him borrowing a line from St Paul, arguing that neither modernity nor postmodernity matters, but the new creation (Galatians 6:15). The subject matter of Christian theology is *God*. The theological enterprise is a response to *God*'s action, a human attempt to bear witness to this unheard-of thing that has occurred in our history: that 'the Word became flesh, and lived among us' (John 1:14). To be fair, the participants in the discussion all know this; indeed, their explorations into Barth's intellectual roots and philosophical affinities are intended as contributions to theo-logy in the strict sense: Christian talk about God. Still, Barth would have cautioned that arguments about his relation to modern culture run the risk of distracting us from the activity that he regarded as most central: reflecting on the 'great disruption' that has come upon the world in the life, death, and resurrection of Jesus Christ. Human language is never adequate to the task of thinking about this surprising event. Theological discourse will always involve the breaking of words, the stretching of ordinary concepts, to say what needs to be said about God. If Barth commended study of his own work – and he was not shy about doing so – it was so that the theological student, or simply the interested reader whether Christian or non-Christian, might begin to gain a sense of what talk about God involves.

But where does the student of Barth begin? His theological corpus is so vast and complex as to seem daunting to the beginner. In my own teaching, I have found that students often approach Barth with trepidation, having been told that he is an extremely difficult 'read'. In most cases, they come away pleasantly surprised; Barth is long-winded, but he is not a highly technical writer. After a while, students become accustomed to his style, and even begin to enjoy those long rhetorical sweeps by which he seeks to lead his reader inexhorably toward the conclusion of the argument. I have had more than one student say that reading Barth converted them to the study of theology. (I employ the brief *Dogmatics in Outline* in my introductory course.) Reading Barth is not difficult, but it does take practice, and it helps to have a guide to show one the way.

This book aims to provide such a guide. At one level, I simply seek to provide orientation to the major themes and topics that dominate Barth's thought. Much of the book consists of simple exposition of the *Church Dogmatics*. Why the *Dogmatics*? Because it is not only the most mature statement of Barth's theology, but also the most widely-cited and influential. I hope that the summaries here provided will give the reader a basic grasp of how this gargantuan work coheres as a whole, what to look for, what puzzles the author is trying to solve. Most introductions to Barth end up following some such procedure, and I have seen no reason to be different for difference's sake. I do hope that the exposition will be lively, and not fall into the 'painfully boring' paraphrase that Hans Frei cited as the chief failing of works on Barth. Once the student has an overall sense of the *Dogmatics*, he or she will be in a position to approach other works in the corpus – essays, sermons, biblical commentaries, expositions of the creed; there is virtually no theological genre in which Barth did not write.

Besides sheer exposition, I have incorporated a number of other devices that I hope will be of use to the reader. The first chapter offers an overview of Barth's life and work. While it is possible to read the *Church Dogmatics* independently, and profit from it, one's appreciation is helped enormously if one is able to set it in the context of the author's fascinating life. This chapter also includes an overview of the *Dogmatics*, some remarks on nomenclature – how to refer to its various sections and subsections – and a few hints on how to approach the actual reading of the work. My goal is to wean the student from the secondary literature as quickly as possible, and to move her along toward an actual engagement with Barth.

The central chapters of the book address in turn the four major doctrines that make up the *Church Dogmatics*: revelation, God, creation, and atonement or reconciliation. (Chapter 6 deals not with a doctrine proper but with Barth's ecclesiology and ethics, key components in his understanding of the Christian life.) In each case, I begin by citing a 'basic move'. It is important to be clear about what basic moves are and are not. They are not to be understood as fixed principles or ideas, floating free of the biblical text. Rather, they are a way of noting some of the more important intellectual decisions Barth makes, as he seeks to discern the inherent pattern and order in the world of Scripture. The basic moves are, if you will, to be seen as theological responses to divine moves. Barth often thinks so counter-intuitively about God and God's relation to human beings that it is worth having these responses pointed out. Part of my goal is to draw attention to the radicality that marks so much of the *Church Dogmatics*, which can easily be missed on a first reading. Barth seeks to unsettle some of our deepest assumptions about what the word 'God' means; just so, he offers a way into the strange world of Scripture and the church's doctrinal tradition.

Another device I employ is more integral to the strategy of the book. Each chapter concludes with a section titled 'Barth in Dialogue', where I seek to bring him into conversation with some other theologian. While Barth was famous for going his own way in theology, he did not ignore the work of either his teachers or his contemporaries. Indeed, one could learn a great deal just by studying the debates he carried on with other thinkers, whether Schleiermacher, Harnack, Brunner, or Bultmann. To be sure, he did not value this dialogical aspect of theology for the reason usually given today: that a sheer plurality of perspectives is a good in and of itself. Truth is not something 'constructed' by a community. Rather, dialogue is demanded because theology is a matter of listening; listening first of all for the Word of God in Scripture, but also – in service of that activity – listening respectfully to the voices of others, who may hear something in the Word that we have missed. This point is closely related to Barth's insistence that Christian theology has no choice but to be ecumenical theology (I/2, 823). While the theologian is always grounded in some particular community or confessional tradition, he or she cannot write simply with that tradition in mind; good theology has the whole church in view. The conversations I offer at the end of each chapter are one way of honoring this conviction. They are also meant to dispel the myth that Barth is some kind of narrow Protestant scholastic, with little of value to offer theologians working in other traditions.

The voices canvassed therefore represent something of an ecumenical spectrum. The Christians in the group comprise two Lutherans (George Lindbeck and Robert Jenson), a Roman Catholic (Henri de Lubac), and a

Methodist (Stanley Hauerwas). The fifth interlocutor is a Jew, Michael Wyschogrod. With the exception of de Lubac, a younger contemporary of Barth, all belong to the theological generation that came to maturity in the years following the Second Vatican Council. Again excepting de Lubac, all were still active at the beginning of the twenty-first century. Individual thinkers were chosen because they had something important to say concerning the doctrine at hand. If one looks at the group as a whole, two things should be evident. First, for all their differences, all five authors advocate precisely the kind of biblically-textured, ecclesial theology Barth himself practised (although interestingly, only Robert Jenson has written a theological system of his own). Indeed, three of the thinkers – Hauerwas, Jenson, and Wyschogrod – have been directly and deeply influenced by Barth, while Lindbeck shows a strong indirect influence. Far from being a disadvantage, these commonalities should be seen as a strength of the method here employed. Real, vigorous disagreement is possible only within a context of shared assumptions. If thinkers are too far apart, they will simply talk past each other; or to change the metaphor, one must be playing the same game in order to compete at it. All the theologians discussed here have a healthy respect for Barth's theological achievement; each chooses to go his own way on a wide range of important matters.

The second thing one will notice about the dialogue partners is that, in one way or another, all press us to reflect on ecclesiological issues. Not only are they ecclesial theologians, but each makes the church – or in Wyschogrod's case, the people Israel – an explicit theme of reflection. This will be most obvious in chapters 3 and 6, where Wyschogrod's account of Israel and de Lubac's account of the church stand in some tension with Barth's thought. But ecclesiology is constantly present as a background question in the other chapters as well. This thematic is deeply consonant with Barth, the title of whose defining work, *Die Kirchliche Dogmatik*, might equally well be rendered 'ecclesial theology'.[3] I have tried not to press a particular constructive agenda here, but letting the ideas emerge in the course of the dialogues themselves. I will be happy if these discussions shed some light on contemporary ecumenical discussions, which so often turn on differing views of the nature and purpose of the church. Chapter 7 offers some concluding reflections on Barth's significance for Christian ecumenism.

The device of having dialogue partners is merely a means to the book's larger purpose: introducing the reader to the thought of Karl Barth. I will be happy if the pages that follow provide an entrée into the rich world of the *Church Dogmatics*. I will be more gratified still if they convey some of Barth's intellectual adventuresomeness, humour, and deep love of God. He explicitly rejected the mantle of 'great theologian', arguing that 'greatness' is not what Christians should strive for.[4] He was, of course, a great Christian theologian despite this disclaimer. It is entirely fitting that he appear as an entry in the present series.

Notes

1 See William Stacey Johnson, *The Mystery of God: Karl Barth and the Postmodern Foundations of Theology* (Louisville: Westminster/John Knox Press, 1997); Walter Lowe, *Theology and Difference: The Wound of Reason* (Bloomington: Indiana University Press, 1993); and Graham Ward, *Barth, Derrida and the Language of Theology* (Cambridge: Cambridge University Press, 1995). These works by no means exhaust the literature on the theme 'Barth and postmodernism'. For an overview, see Ward's essay in *The Cambridge Companion to Karl Barth*, ed. John Webster (Cambridge: Cambridge University Press, 2000).

2 Bruce L. McCormack, *Karl Barth's Critically Realistic Dialectical Theology: Its Genesis and Development, 1909–1936* (Oxford and New York: Oxford University Press, 1995); Neil B. MacDonald, *Karl Barth and the Strange New World within the Bible: Barth, Wittgenstein, and the Metadilemmas of the Enlightenment* (Carlisle: Paternoster Press, 2000). This is not to say that McCormack and MacDonald read Barth identically. Broadly speaking, the first emphasizes his affinities with the Kantian tradition, the second his ties to Hegel and to Wittgenstein.

3 It was George Hunsinger who first suggested to me this possibility for rendering the German phrase.

4 Karl Barth, *Evangelical Theology: An Introduction* (New York: Holt, Rinehart and Winston, 1963), 77.

To Elisa

'You will see rare beasts, and have unique adventures'

Christ on the Cross. Central panel of the Isenheim altarpiece, Matthias Grünewald.
© Musée d'Unterlinden Colmar, photo O. Zimmerman.

Chapter 1

The Laughter of the Angels:
On Reading Barth

A Theological Existence: Barth's Life

Karl Barth was born on 10 May 1886, in the Swiss city of Basel, the first of five children.[1] His mother, Anna Sartorius, was descended from a long line of clergymen and academics. His father, Johann Friedrich ('Fritz') Barth, had received his degree in theology from Tübingen, and represented what was then called 'positive' theology – a moderate form of conservative Protestantism.[2] At the time of Karl's birth he was an instructor at the College of Preachers in Basel, but soon thereafter accepted an invitation to teach at the University of Berne.

The Barths were bookish, outdoorsy – summer holidays were spent in the mountains or at the lake – and fond of music. Not only did young Karl take violin lessons, but he had the example of his father: 'I must have been five or six years old at the time … My father was musical and was fond of improvising on the piano … One day he was playing something by Mozart. I can still picture the scene. He began a couple of bars from *The Magic Flute* ("Tamino mine, what happiness"). They went right through me and into me, I don't know how, and I thought, "That's it!"'[3]

Karl settled early on a career in theology, and began the grand tour of universities typical for European students of the day. He studied first under his father's faculty at Berne, and then moved on to Berlin – where he heard the great church historian Adolf Harnack – and later Tübingen. But his great ambition was to study at the University of Marburg, then known as a breeding ground of theological liberalism. Understandably, Fritz Barth opposed this move. But in the end Karl overcame his father's objections. It was at Marburg that he attended the lectures of Wilhelm Herrmann, whose synthesis of Christian faith and neo-Kantian philosophy stood at the cutting edge of contemporary Protestant thought. Barth finished his studies in 1909, a convinced member of the Herrmann school.

Following university, Barth spent a valuable year as assistant editor at *Die Christliche Welt*, an influential liberal journal, and then moved on to an assistant pastorship at Geneva (where he preached from Calvin's pulpit). In 1911 he accepted a call to be pastor of the Reformed Church in Safenwil, an industrial town in the region known as the Aargau. Just before accepting this post, Barth became engaged to eighteen-year-old Nelly Hoffmann, who had been a pupil in his confirmation class at Geneva. They were married on 27 March 1913.

No sooner had Barth arrived in Safenwil than he found himself embroiled in a bitter dispute between factory workers and owners. With startling swiftness he aligned himself with the cause of the workers – a move that alienated many in his congregation, and earned him the title 'the Red Pastor'. By 1915 he had become an active Religious Socialist. Yet the labour struggle was not the only challenge Barth faced. Week by week, he found that he was expected to mount the pulpit and say something about God. This was a task for which his high-culture university training had not prepared him. Liberal theologians were convinced that to talk about the highest achievements of the human spirit – religion, morality, culture, value – *was* to talk about God. Barth came to believe otherwise. Talk about God was something different, something startling and strange and new. How is the preacher to fulfill the congregation's expectation that he will preach God's Word, when all he has at his disposal are mere human words? Looking back on this period, Barth often cited his terror at preaching as a major factor in his break with liberalism.

Matters became even more pressing when war broke out in 1914, and each side claimed to be defending the cause of 'God' and 'Christian civilization'. Barth now found the equation of these two to be blasphemous. An important event in this period was a declaration signed by ninety-three intellectuals in support of German war policy. Among the signers were many of his former theological teachers. He entered on an intense period of intellectual questioning, much of it in dialogue with his close friend Eduard Thurneysen, the pastor in the village just across the valley. While the guns pounded away on the Western front, Barth and Thurneysen sat, smoked their pipes, and debated the current situation in both theology and politics (both men were involved in the Religious Socialist movement). At one point Thurneysen remarked that what was needed was something 'quite different' (*ganz anders*), a phrase that could also be construed as 'totally other'. Looking for inspiration where they could find it, the two men decided to undertake a fresh and serious reading of the Bible.[4]

The fruits of these labours became evident in an extraordinary series of lectures and addresses Barth delivered in the years following 1915. Most striking of all was the book he now began to write: a commentary on Paul's letter to the Romans. The first edition of *Der Römerbrief* appeared in 1918, followed by a much revised second edition in 1921. It was this second edition that made Barth famous. What, according to Paul, is Christianity all about? Not, said Barth, the upward human striving toward morality and religion – the answer he would have given in his liberal days. Rather, the apostle proclaims a God who is 'totally other' than anything in our imagination or experience. Far from being the reliable guarantor of our values, Paul's God is the God who smashes idols – especially idols with names like 'religion' and 'Christian culture'. God is not man, Barth said in a thousand variations. God is *God*. The phrase became something of a motto for his theological revolution.

A Roman Catholic observer of the day said that *The Epistle to the Romans* 'fell like a bomb on the playground of the theologians'.[5] The theological establishment saw it partly as an expression of brash youth, partly as an invitation to barbarism; Barth seemed to be rejecting all that was enlightened and progressive in the modern world. But some of his contemporaries responded with enthusiasm. Quite to his surprise, he found himself the leader of a small movement. It included Eduard Thurneysen, Emil Brunner, Rudolf Bultmann, Friedrich Gogarten, and Paul Tillich, along with a host of lesser-known figures. For a few years these theologians formed a loosely-configured school, identified by its flagship journal *Zwischen den Zeiten* ('Between the Times'). By the early 1930s it became clear that, while all opposed the older liberalism, they could not agree on a common constructive programme. The group fell into disarray, though Barth and Thurneysen remained lifelong friends and allies.

In 1921 Barth accepted his first teaching post: an honorary professorship in Reformed Theology that had just been established at Göttingen, outside the regular faculty. While the post was proffered on the basis of the Romans commentary, those who expected Barth to continue hurling bombshells would be disappointed. In Göttingen, he devoted himself to mastering the classical tradition of Christian theology – he had not prepared to be an academic – and to working out his approach to doctrinal questions. It was in Göttingen that Barth delivered his first series of lectures in dogmatics.[6] In 1925 he moved to the University of Münster, where his course on prolegomena – questions concerning revelation and theological method – formed the basis for a *Christian Dogmatics in Outline* (1927). While this work was planned to be the first in a projected series, Barth never got beyond the first volume. In 1932 he would make a fresh start with his *Church Dogmatics*.

In Münster, the Protestant faculty was an island in a sea of intellectually and culturally vital Roman Catholicism. This was Barth's first serious exposure to Catholic thought. In a gesture unusual for the time, he invited the Jesuit theologian Ernst Pryzywara to participate in his seminar.[7] It was also in Münster that Barth began his long collaboration with Charlotte von Kirschbaum, known to generations of his students as 'Lollo'. Though content to remain in Barth's shadow, Kirschbaum made a profound and lasting impact on his thought.[8] She was the virtual co-author of many of the famous passages in small print, where Barth does his exegesis and engages in debate with other thinkers. She contributed decisively to his account of the male–female relation in his treatment of human nature in *CD* III/2.

In 1930 Barth moved on to the University of Bonn, where he enjoyed generally good relations with his Protestant colleagues (including Ernst Wolf, who became a close friend and theological companion). Barth's deepening appreciation for medieval theology led to the publication of *Fides*

Quaerens Intellectum, a study of St Anselm's proof for the existence of God in his *Proslogion*.[9] His work on Anselm may not have occasioned the doctrine of revelation one finds in the *Church Dogmatics*, as he later implied; he certainly found Anselm a welcome ally in his quest for 'faith seeking understanding'.

As a Swiss citizen, Barth had refrained from participating in German politics throughout the 1920s; also his academic responsibilities left him little time for such involvement. All this changed when the National Socialist party assumed power in January 1933. Barth was an early critic of the 'German Christians', the group that saw the hand of God at work in Adolf Hitler and the Nazi movement. His famous pamphlet *Theological Existence Today!* (1933) became a manifesto for the Protestant opposition to Hitler. In 1934 Barth served as chief author of the Barmen Declaration, in which the Confessing Church affirmed the sole lordship of Jesus Christ in opposition to the new idolatry:

> Jesus Christ, as he is attested to us in Holy Scripture, is the one Word of God whom we have to hear, and whom we have to trust and obey in life and in death.
>
> We reject the false doctrine that the church could and should recognize as a source of its proclamation, beyond and besides this one Word of God, yet other events, powers, historic figures, and truths as God's revelation.[10]

Barth's activities in the Confessing Church spelled the beginning of the end of his time in Germany. In 1935 an oath of loyalty to Hitler became mandatory for all civil servants, including university professors. Barth agreed to sign only if he could add a proviso: 'I could be loyal to the Führer only within my responsibilities as an Evangelical Christian'.[11] But the die had been cast. Barth was banned from speaking, dismissed from his teaching post, and eventually placed on a train headed for Switzerland. His parting exhortation to his students was 'exegesis, exegesis and yet more exegesis! Keep to the Word, to the scripture that has been given us.'[12]

On returning to Switzerland in June, 1935, Barth accepted a chair in theology at the University of Basel. He remained in close contact with colleagues still active in Germany (including his young friend Dietrich Bonhoeffer), and sought to popularize the cause of the Confessing Church to the outside world. He also resumed work on the *Church Dogmatics*. In 1938 he was invited to deliver the prestigious Gifford Lectures on natural theology at the University of Aberdeen, Scotland – an irony, in that Barth had denounced natural theology as a hopeless project in a 1934 pamphlet directed at Emil Brunner, titled *Nein!* He justified his acceptance on the grounds that this theology can only benefit from a direct encounter with its chief rival, the Reformers' doctrine of God's unmerited grace.[13]

After the war Barth travelled twice to Germany to teach at Bonn, the University from which he had been dismissed in 1935. Standing literally amid the bombed-out ruins, he delivered the lectures that would become *Dogmatics in Outline*. It is one of the small masterpieces of modern Christian thought.[14] The postwar years also saw Barth actively engaged with the ecumenical movement, both as severe critic and active participant. He was a chief architect of the report 'Jesus Christ, the Hope of the World', which set the agenda for the Second Assembly of the World Council of Churches in 1954. He also urged the Assembly to address the church's relation to Israel and the Jews, the first and and most wounding of divisions within God's people.

In the 1940s and 1950s, Barth became notorious for refusing to join the crusade against Communism – for example, criticizing the NATO decision to re-arm West Germany, and inveighing against Christian support of nuclear weapons. While Barth opposed Communism, he believed Western reaction to it to be overblown, hypocritical, and often counterproductive. (He was equally suspicious of left-wing movements such as his friend Josef Hromádka's Christian Peace Conference.)[15] He also encouraged Christians in Soviet-bloc countries like Czechoslovakia and East Germany not to become lost in envy for the West, but to seek creative forms of witness in their own societies.[16] He walked a fine line in the political realm, arguing that believers had a duty to be involved in politics even while avoiding rigid ideological commitments.

In 1951 Barth set about writing his doctrine of reconciliation, a massive account of the person and work of Jesus Christ. The work was in some ways a response to the influential theology of Rudolf Bultmann, whom Barth had known since their days as students of Wilhelm Herrmann. He believed that Bultmann's existentialism was not that different from Herrmann's stress on human religiosity. Far more satisfying was his dialogue with Roman Catholic theology, a source of fascination for Barth since his time at Münster. He felt better understood by Catholic critics such as Hans Urs von Balthasar and Hans Küng than by many of his fellow Protestants. Unfortunately, illness prevented his accepting an invitation to be an observer at the Second Vatican Council (1962–65). But he later spent an entire summer mastering the major conciliar documents – these were the days when even Protestant theologians could read Latin – before travelling to Rome for discussions with the Council fathers. The little book *Ad Limina Apostolorum* offers a delightful, sometimes moving account of this experience.[17]

Barth retired from teaching in 1962. That spring he made his first and only journey to the United States, lecturing in San Francisco, Chicago, and Princeton. He took time off to visit some of the major battlefields of the Civil War (he was an avid student of the conflict). These lectures were later published as *Evangelical Theology: An Introduction*. In 1967 he authorized the publication of a fragment of *Church Dogmatics* IV/4, dealing with the theology of baptism. The book contained one last bombshell for the theologians: a decisive rejection of the practice of infant baptism, on the grounds both that it is unscriptural and that it reduces the church to a pale reflection of the dominant culture.

Barth kept up an extraordinary pace in his retirement, teaching, writing, lecturing, and maintaining an extraordinarily rich and varied correspondence. Each day began with the playing of a piece by Mozart on the phonograph. It was in Mozart, Barth maintained, that one could catch a glimpse of God's joy in his creation, as well as of the joys and sorrows that make up creaturely existence. Barth's praise of Mozart nicely embodies his convictions about God's affirming Yes to humanity.[18] The God who is wholly other proves his divinity not by maintaining his distance, but by humbly willing to be God-with-us in the person of Jesus. This motif of 'the humanity of God' sounded more and more clearly in Barth's later writings, although – as I hope to show in the pages that follow – the theme is implicit in virtually everything he wrote.[19]

On 9 December, 1968, Barth worked for much of the day on a lecture he had been invited to deliver to an ecumenical group in Zürich. In that talk, he underscored the importance of listening to the great voices of Christian history; bold confession must be accompanied by attentiveness to the witness of the past.[20] His writing was interrupted by a phone call from his old friend, Eduard Thurneysen. Referring to the troubled political situation of the day, he assured Thurneysen that 'He [Jesus] will reign!' Barth died in his sleep some time that night. At his memorial service four days later, mourners packed Basel Cathedral to hear Scripture, sing hymns, and listen for God's Yes in the music of Mozart.

Radical Faith: The Liberal Inheritance

'Karl Barth's break with liberalism' is one of the most familiar phrases in all of modern Christian thought. Barth did break – and decisively – with the theology of his teachers. Yet to grasp what that means, it is important to have a sense of what the liberal theologians were trying to accomplish, and of the ways in which Barth carried on as well as criticized their legacy.

In the late eighteenth century, the prospects for theology among European intellectuals looked bleak. Enlightenment thinkers had declared Christianity to be largely irrelevant – partly because of its suspect historical claims, but more important, because the God of the Bible seemed inimical to the modern project. Whereas this God demands human obedience, the great claim of the Enlightenment was that human beings should learn to think for themselves (an idea classically expressed by Kant with his motto *sapere aude*, 'dare to know'). The choice seemed clear. One could choose to be Christian, rejecting the modern ideals of autonomy and freedom; or one could choose to be modern, in which case one needed to throw off the yoke of Christianity once and for all. One could not coherently be both modern and Christian.

The young Friedrich Schleiermacher dissented from this judgment. In his famous book *On Religion: Speeches to the Cultured Among Its Despisers*, Schleiermacher (1768–1836) argued that Christianity's critics failed to grasp the true nature of what they were rejecting. Christianity is a religion, and religion must be understood on its own terms. Schleiermacher was using the term 'religion' in a new way, and he was at pains to state what he did and did not mean by it. Religion does not mean intellectual adherence to certain doctrines; religion is prior to theology. Nor is it just a question of morality; Kant had been wrong to reduce Christ to the status of moral exemplar. Rather, religion is a matter of something Schleiermacher called 'piety'. What makes a person religious is not having thoughts about the divine, but experiencing the divine in one's own life. It means having one's personality integrated by the awe-inspiring source that underlies the universe – what religious people call God, but what others might simply call the Universe or the Sublime. Indeed, it is precisely religious experience that makes genuine selfhood possible. Religion alone answers the question 'Who am I?', which no amount of thinking or doing can answer for us.

Schleiermacher's romantic appeal to experience fit the mood of the day. By 1800, intellectuals were eager to move beyond Enlightenment rationalism to a celebration of that which lies beyond reason's purview. Romanticism meant on the one hand a turn inward, to the impulses and longings of the human heart; it also meant a turn outward to the particularities of language, culture, and history. Schleiermacher's idea of 'religion' captured both these aspects. While the *Speeches* were clearly an expression of inner longing, Schleiermacher made quite clear that there is no such thing as religion in general; this universal human impulse takes shape only in concrete, historically specific communities. As Christians, we find our religious experience mediated through the positive language and images of our own tradition.

The central figure in Schleiermacher's theology, therefore, was a historical person: Jesus of Nazareth. Loyalty to him is what defines Christianity as Christian. Schleiermacher had learned a profound devotion to Christ during his childhood among Moravian Pietists; in later years, he referred to himself as a 'Moravian of a higher order'. The Christological emphasis became if anything more pronounced in *The Christian Faith*, which offers a more traditional presentation of church doctrine than what we find in the *Speeches*. Here Schleiermacher argued that each human being is marked by an awareness of the sheer gifted contingency of one's life, which he called the 'feeling of absolute dependence' – not a specific emotion, but a fundamental orientation of the self toward reality, prior to all language and thought. All persons are religious, Schleiermacher maintained; all stand in a relation to that ultimate ground of things. For the Christian, however, this relation is actualized only through a relation to the person of Jesus. As the one whose consciousness of God remained perfectly unclouded by sin, Jesus is more than an example of the religious life; he is the Mediator, the Redeemer.

In subsequent forms of liberal Protestantism the tactics might vary, but the overall strategy would remain the same. Christianity is a form of religion; religion is not about abstract doctrines, but about matters of experience, value, or personal meaning; at the centre of this experience stands Jesus – not the incarnate Logos of classical Christian thought, but the human preacher and healer, a historical figure knowable by historical means. This last point especially must be underscored. For the liberal theologians, historical investigation was necessary for at least two reasons: (1) With respect to salvation, the gospel comes to us as creatures immersed in history; the Jesus of the gospels is in fact more relevant to our moral and religious existence than the Christ of church dogma. Historical research can help to recover a religiously 'useful' Saviour. (2) Historical inquiry is central to theology's claim to be scientific, and thus entitled to a place in the modern university. Religious faith is more than history, but it cannot be in conflict with historical knowledge. Moreover, by studying Christianity historically, we deepen our understanding of the human ideals and values it embodies.

Toward the end of the nineteenth century, the most influential progressive voice in German theology was Albrecht Ritschl (1822–89). For Ritschl, the historical core of Christianity consists in Jesus' proclamation of the kingdom – an ethical message that echoed in the life of the community he founded. This was a strongly Kantian version of Protestantism. What sets human beings apart from the rest of the cosmos is their capacity for personhood, for moral autonomy and culture; to be a Christian is to follow Jesus in that high calling. Ritschl's student Wilhelm Herrmann embraced much of this programme, but took the argument one step further. He felt that Ritschl had succumbed to a misguided attempt to make faith dependent on historical knowledge. Yes, the Jesus of history is important. But we must not attempt to *verify* his claims, as Ritschl seemed to do when he appealed to Jesus' influence on the early church. To Herrmann this sounded too much like a form of apologetics – stepping outside of faith in quest of some objective security. Standing within the tradition of Pietism, he radicalized the classic Pietist distinction between mere knowledge about God, or doctrine ('dead orthodoxy'), and a personal or saving relation to God. If liberal Protestantism can be described as the effort to unite faith with history, Herrmann came down decidedly on the side of faith.

Herrmann seems to have lived what he taught. He was a deeply religious man; indeed, he could be so disarmingly pious in the classroom that students complained of receiving a form of 'advanced confirmation instruction'.[21] Nonetheless, Herrmann's apparent naïveté belied a great intellectual sophistication. Marburg was the home of the philosophical movement known as neo-Kantianism, and Herrmann made creative use of Kant to argue for the independence of religion from all other realms of human activity, including science and ethics. For a good neo-Kantian religion cannot be justified from the observer's perspective; it can only be lived from within. In this sense, Herrmann believed he was returning to the deepest insights of

Schleiermacher himself. Indeed, he once told his students that Schleiermacher's *On Religion* was the most important work to have appeared since the writing of the New Testament.[22]

Among the students who sat at Herrmann's feet in the first decade of the twentieth century was Karl Barth. When Barth entered into pastoral ministry in 1909, he took his Marburg training with him. His sermons from the period reflect the liberal confidence that Christianity and Western culture form a sturdy synthesis. To be a Christian *is* to embrace humanity's upward progress from ignorance to enlightenment, from barbarism to culture. Far from being an obstacle to this calling, Christian faith in God and Jesus was in fact seen as essential to it. For in Jesus, we see what it means to be a 'person' in the fullest sense of the word.

There are aspects of Herrmann's teaching Barth would never reject: the assumption that historical knowledge has an important role to play in theology, but the rejection of it as a foundation; a sense of the utter originality and underived character of faith, as that which explodes our ordinary categories of understanding; a distrust of all apologetic strategies that would seek to deny this; above all, Herrmann's vibrant Christocentrism. During Barth's 1962 tour of the United States, a student asked him what had been the most momentous theological discovery of his long life. His answer was 'Jesus loves me, this I know, for the Bible tells me so.'[23] A naïve answer, but not inaccurate as a summary of the central message of the *Church Dogmatics*.

Nonetheless, Barth would eventually deem the liberal project to be fatally misguided. While the liberals could speak persuasively of matters like religion, history, ethics, and culture, their resources for talking about God were remarkably thin. The God of neo-Protestant thought seemed to function mainly as the guarantor of values that human beings have determined in advance. The paradigm assumes that God and the religious person exist in a relatively stable communion; it has difficulty entertaining the idea that God might be *opposed* to our values and ideals, not confirming the status quo, but invading and disrupting it.

From about 1915 onward, Barth began to deny that we have any easy recourse to the reality called 'God'. We do not, he insisted, have God in advance. Rather, God comes to us on his own terms, calling into being a new world we could not have imagined. Before Barth could reclaim anything from the liberal tradition, he would need to explore an aspect of the New Testament that liberalism had no way of accounting for: its radically eschatological character.

Action in Waiting: The Eschatological Turn

Barth's background in the German university was certainly important. Yet we must bear in mind that the immediate context of his break with liberalism was not academic, but pastoral and political. As he and Thurneysen looked for a fresh start in theology, the options available to them were all options within the movement to which they were both committed: that of Swiss Religious Socialism. The burning question was how to respond to the new situation brought on by the war, and more broadly by the revolutionary changes taking place in contemporary Europe.

The two towering figures who dominated Religious Socialism were Leonhard Ragaz and Herrmann Kutter. Ragaz (1868–1945) was the classic left-wing activist, seeing secular Social Democracy as the avante-garde of the kingdom of God. He believed the church should seek an active alliance with the Socialists, as well as pressing its own pacifist and social justice agenda in the world. Although equally committed to the labour movement, Kutter (1863–1931) was more inclined to let it unfold without interference by the church. God is the lord of history, and may even use secular Marxism as an instrument of his will; meanwhile, the church can best serve the coming kingdom by being itself. This approach stressed watching and waiting, and was bound to frustrate those who wanted a clear programme of action.

Barth had sympathy for both these positions. Eventually, however, he came to see Kutter's as the more profound. Later in life, he acknowledged that it was from Herrmann Kutter that 'I simply learned to speak the great word "God" once again seriously, responsibly, and forcibly'.[24] But by 1915, Barth was asking questions that could no longer be contained within the Religious Socialist framework. In a letter to Thurneysen in September of that year, he offered a point-by-point comparison of Kutter and Ragaz before concluding: 'The religious socialist thing (*Sache*) is out, taking God seriously begins ...'[25]

It was around this time that Barth made a momentous discovery, or possibly rediscovery: the work of Christoph Blumhardt (1858–1919) and of his father Johann Christoph Blumhardt (1805–80). The activity of the Blumhardts would have been familiar to anyone operating in the milieu of Religious Socialism. Inheritors of the tradition known as Würrtemberg Pietism, the Blumhardts found themselves dissatisfied with the usual Pietist focus on the salvation of individuals. They argued that the message of early Christianity was not salvation in some other world, but the the coming of God's new creation to this one: 'thy kingdom come!' The Blumhardts' profound sense of the social embodiment of the gospel led them into a ministry of physical and spiritual healing, first at Möttlingen and later at their centre in Bad Boll. In the case of Christoph Blumhardt, this outlook would lead him to champion the cause of democratic Socialism – a move that cost him his official position in the church. He would eventually be elected to the German parliament as a Social Democrat.

Barth's embrace of the Blumhardts did not, therefore, mean in any sense a repudiation of social Christianity, but an attempt to rethink the gospel in a more eschatological and God-centred framework. A meeting with Christoph Blumhardt in Bad Boll in April, 1915, left Barth profoundly impressed: 'The new element, the New Testament element, which appeared again in [Blumhardt's work] can be summed up in the one word: hope.'[26] It was an essentially anti-dualist faith, firmly rooted in the material world, while looking ahead with eager longing for the new creation. Barth exclaimed over the way in which 'the hurrying and the waiting, the worldly and the divine, the present and the future, met, were united, kept supplementing one another, seeking and finding one another'.[27]

Barth's encounter with Blumhardt seemed to shift his thinking into a whole new key. The change can be heard in the great address, 'The Strange New World Within the Bible', which Barth delivered in the autumn of 1916. We may, Barth tells us, read the Bible as a sourcebook on history, morality, or religion, and indeed all these things can be found within its pages. But to read it this way is to miss the most important thing it has to tell us:

> The key question is whether we have understanding for this different, new thing, or good will enough to meditate and enter upon it inwardly. Do we desire the presence of 'God'? Do we dare to go where we evidently are being led? That would be 'faith'! A new world projects itself into our old ordinary world. We may say, It is nothing; this is imagination, madness, this 'God'. But we may not deny nor prevent our being led by Bible 'history' far out beyond what is elsewhere called 'history' – into a *new* world, the world of God.[28]

Previously Barth had been concerned to define his 'position', whether academically or within the spectrum of Religious Socialist options. Having a position assumes that the object of study can be pinned down – that if we can just find the proper method or working principles, we will know what to do. But what if this assumption is false? What if our desire to have a position is itself a symptom of where theology has gone astray? In a lecture on Christian social responsibility at Tambach in 1919 – a lecture that made him famous overnight – Barth warned his listeners that his new emphasis on divine action did not constitute a standpoint. God's action is, precisely, God's:

> ... our attitude toward our situation is in fact an instant in a *movement*, comparable to the momentary picture of a bird in flight, and outside the context of the movement completely meaningless, incomprehensible and impossible. (*WGWM*, 282–3, rev.)

The 'movement' in question here is thus not some human programme of reform, but 'a movement from above, from a third dimension' (p. 283). While the theologian cannot help trying to describe the bird in flight, he will remind his readers that the bird in motion is different from what he tries to convey on paper. Above all, we must not identify the movement of God with religion:

> Our concern is with *God*, the movement originating in *God*, the motion which *he*

lends us – and it is not religion. Hallowed be *thy* name. *Thy* kingdom come. *Thy* will be done. The so-called 'religious experience' is a wholly derived, secondary, fragmentary form of the divine. (*WGWM*, 285)

The new life revealed in Jesus is not a new form of godliness. That is the reason why Paul and John are interested not in the personal life of the so-called historical Jesus but only in his resurrection. And that is the reason why the synoptic accounts of Jesus can be really understood only with Bengel's insight: *spirant resurrectionem* ['they breathe the resurrection']. Christ is the absolutely *new from above*; the way, the truth, and the life of God among men … (*WGWM*, 286)

Barth's eschatological turn after 1915 is a positive turn, toward God's action, toward resurrection, toward hope. Keeping this in mind is crucial, given the frequent stereotype that sees his early theology as 'pessimistic'. Nonetheless, it should already be clear that Barth's affirmations involve some important denials. The world of God is not human religion or morality. The movement of God from above is not a human standpoint, but the path of a bird in flight, which we can only trace. In the years immediately after the Great War, this critical element – reminding us that whenever we think we have God pinned down, we do not – became increasingly prominent in Barth's writing. The new world of God requires the destruction of our present world, or at least of this world as we imagine it to be.

It is in this period that Barth begins to invoke an image that will become emblematic of his whole theology: Mathias Grünewald's famous rendering of the crucifixion, the centrepiece of the Isenheim altar. The painting is organized around the gruesome, tortured figure of the Crucified. At the left of the cross stands the beloved disciple, cradling Mary in his arms. At the right stands John the Baptist, his hand directing the viewer's gaze to the crucified Lamb of God. Barth comments, 'It is this hand which is in evidence in the Bible' (65). Near this hand we see the words *Illum oportet crescere, me autem minui*; he must increase, while I must decrease (John 3:30). 'Reality' is here defined by God-in-Christ alone, in whose presence the religious person – even a prophet like John – is reduced to nothing:[29]

The prophet, the man of God, the seer and hearer, ceases to be, as that to which he unwaveringly points begins to be. The object, the reality, the Divine Himself takes on new meaning; and the meaning of piety as such, of the function of the church as such, falls away. We may call this the characteristic insight of the Bible.

Shall we dare turn our eyes in the direction of the pointing hand of Grünewald's John? We know whither it points. It points to Christ. But to Christ the crucified, we must immediately add. That is your direction, says the hand … The only source for the real, the immediate revelation of God is *death*. He brought *life* to light out of *death*. (*WGWM*, 76–7).

The language here foreshadows the second edition of *The Epistle to the Romans*. It is important that we spend a little time on this crucial text, before turning to the development of Barth's thought in the 1920s and 1930s.

Time and Eternity: *The Epistle to the Romans*

As mentioned earlier, Barth prepared two major editions of his *Epistle to the Romans*. It used to be standard for scholars to emphasize the differences between the two texts; more recently, the tendency has been to stress continuities, and to treat the differences as mainly rhetorical. The relation between the 1918 and 1921 *Romans* is an interesting question for Barth scholarship. Yet as it was the second edition that made the lasting impact, it will form the basis for our discussion here.[30]

To read *The Epistle to the Romans* is an unsettling experience on many levels. Barth seeks to dispel any illusion that we can approach Paul's text from a safely neutral stance. To engage the letter can only mean to engage its theme, its subject matter: the gospel of God (Romans 1:16–17). To interpret means to be seized by Paul's questions, to hear and see what he hears and sees. It means asking the question of God – or rather, allowing ourselves to be called into question *by* God. One of the key terms that recurs in the text is the word KRISIS, suggesting that in the Christ-event the very judgment of the world is taking place, and that being related to God is less a matter of spiritual 'nurture' than of a painful remaking at the hands of Another. Moreover, Barth does not just talk about this crisis; he seeks to evoke it. All of this contributes to the book's reading nothing at all like a commentary in the modern, academic style.

But that does not mean he writes no commentary at all. While the rhetoric of the book may have been a key to its impact, it nonetheless purports to be a work of exegesis. Against charges that *The Epistle to the Romans* had been an exercise in freestyle theologizing, and parrying attempts to derive a system or method from his book, Barth maintained that his only goal had been to expound the text of Paul. As he wrote in his famous 'Preface to the Second Edition':

> I know that I have laid myself open to the charge of imposing a meaning upon the text rather than extracting its meaning from it, and that my method implies this. My reply is that, if I have a system, it is limited to a recognition of what Kierkegaard has called the 'infinite qualitative distinction' between time and eternity, and to my regarding this as possessing negative as well as positive significance: 'God is in heaven, and thou art on earth.' The relation between such a God and such a man, and the relation between a man and such a God, is for me the theme of the Bible and the essence of philosophy. (*Romans*, 10)

Notice that Barth's primary concern here is to underscore a difference: 'God is in heaven, and thou art on earth.' While Kierkegaard provides a useful phrase for articulating this distinction, Barth employs his Idealist terminology to affirm the Old Testament faith in God as sovereign Lord and

Creator, and to underscore the blasphemy involved in any confusion between God and his creature. At one level, *The Epistle to the Romans* is nothing but one long rehearsal of the First Commandment: 'You will have no other Gods before me.'

Second, note that Barth speaks not only of a distinction, but of a relationship: 'The relation between such a God and such a man, and the relation between a man and such a God, is for me the theme of the Bible'. Barth was never interested in talking about God in abstraction from the human being. Scripture depicts a covenantal drama of which God is the initiator, but which also involves real human response, action, obedience. Despite widespread stereotypes that Barth – and especially the early Barth – has nothing good to say about humanity, here he already displays what might be called his 'covenantal imagination'.

The impression that *The Epistle to the Romans* dwells exclusively on themes of death and judgment may in fact simply be a function of its commentary form. The theme of 'ungodliness' is thus prevalent in his treatment of Romans 1:18 because it is a major concern of the text itself. Nor is it surprising that Barth should title his discussion of Romans 1:18–32 'The Night', given Paul's own dire picture of the human plight under the divine judgment. God *can* exercise sovereignty over a lost creation by withdrawing his favour from his creatures; God is no part of the world, and hence the world has no inherent claim on the divine presence. This conviction is integral to the Bible's overall picture of the divine freedom.

Barth assigned the name 'religion' to the human tendency to confuse Creator and creature. Given the overwhelmingly positive use of this category in neo-Protestantism, his equating of it with 'ungodliness' was shocking. He could even use the language of pathology here: religion is a disease, a sickness, a basic deformation of the human creature. Humanity wishes to construct a god out of its own resources; this is what makes religion so ungodly. Yet there is another side to the picture. For Barth, the universality of the religious impulse is also a symptom of humankind's inability to get rid of God – that is, the true God. While it gives us no direct access to deity (quite the contrary), religion does mark in a curious way the fact that the human being is made for covenant communion with its Lord. While religion is a mistake, it bears a kind of negative witness to the true state of affairs – that human beings are grasped by One who is 'wholly other'. This usage points ahead to Barth's complex approach to religion in the *Church Dogmatics*, where he argues that religion itself is not beyond hope of redemption.

There are certainly dualist images and motifs in the Romans commentary. In a famous mathematical image, Barth compared time and eternity to a circle intersected by a tangent line, the two figures touching at a single point. The point is there, but inhabitants of the circle can do nothing with it; it simply intrudes on their world from outside, remaining essentially alien and mysterious. In a similar riddle, Barth says that the revelation that occurred in

Jesus is like the crater left behind by the explosion of an enormous artillery shell. (The military imagery is hardly surprising in light of the war just concluded.) Again, we know *that* something monumental has happened, but the event offers no resources that would allow us to make sense of it. Much of what Barth does Christologically in this text is seek to undermine confidence in the 'historical Jesus', or Jesus reconstructed by the historians, as a source of religious knowledge. At this stage in his career, he considered the radical scepticism about Jesus in recent scholarship to be an ally in his programme. The fact that we can know almost nothing about Jesus means that we will focus all the more intently on the cross, which is where the real clue to his significance will be found.

Yet for all this, it must not be thought that Barth's conclusions in this commentary are entirely negative. To stress God's otherness is not to stress God's indifference or impotence with respect to the human situation. This is no Marcionite deity, too pure to interact with the material world, but a God who hides his face *so that* he may reveal himself as the world's Creator. This is what happens in Christ:

> But in Christ God speaks as he is, and punishes the No-God of all these falsehoods. He affirms himself by denying us as we are and the world as it is. In Christ God offers himself to be known as God beyond our trespass, beyond time and things and men; to be known as the redeemer of the prisoners, consequently, as the meaning of all that is – in fact, as the Creator. He acknowledges himself to be our God by creating and maintaining the distance by which we are separated from him; he displays his mercy by inaugurating his KRISIS and bringing us under judgment. (*Romans*, 40–41)

Judgment, then, is not an end in itself. While it is true that God must 'deny us as we are and the world as it is', this is only so that God may affirm us and the world as we will be. Like Paul's own text, Barth's commentary is marked by a powerful eschatological urgency. The cross is the establishment of God's righteousness – and just so the inauguration of the new creation, when all things will be made new. Thus in the context of Romans chapter 8, we hear not so much of KRISIS as of a radical hope for redemption:

> The whole creation *waits for the manifestation of the sons of God*. From this manifestation of redemption no hair of our head can be excluded. The vast ocean of reality, which now embraces and submerges the island of truth, subsides and is established so that only truth remains: the truth of reality itself! Time, immense and vast, from its first beginning to its furthest future, is eternity! ... It is not some other man that is redeemed, but I myself; not a fragment of me, but I in my totality. I am transformed, renewed, purified, made a participator of the divine nature and of the divine life, with God, by his side, and in him. This is adoption. (*Romans*, 313, rev.; emphasis in original)

Neither here in 1921 nor later in life does Barth conceive of eschatology in neatly linear or spatial terms. Redemption is neither simply future, nor already realized, nor located in a divine realm 'above' present experience. One can find elements of all of these in his writing. Redemption means the final dissolution of all barriers separating the creature from God; ultimately, it means a participation in God's own life. In Christ himself this inclusion is already true; this is why Barth can make the surprising statement that time 'from its first beginning to its furthest future' is eternity. When the eternal itself appears among us, time itself is taken up into eternity; there is no aspect of creation that remains untouched by God's apocalyptic action. No 'hair of our head can be excluded'. On the other hand, Barth makes clear that our adoption as God's children is not a possession we can lay hold of – this would bring it back into the realm of religion – but rather a promise to be grasped in hope. We do not 'have' our salvation; all we can do is point to the cross as the event where God lays hold of us, redeeming the totality of our lives not just in some distant future but somehow already, a hope that illumines the entire landscape: 'We too stand under the Cross, unable to do more than bear witness to the "Now" of eternity which is ours, to the Day of Jesus Christ, which is no day, but the Day of Days, before and behind and above the days of our life' (*Romans*, 313).

Barth has rightly been called a dialectical theologian, and these brief snippets from *The Epistle to the Romans* show us why. The life that is ours in Christ is ours only through his cross – and therefore through the death of the present fallen world. But if so, our language too must be 'broken' if it is to bear its peculiar witness. Thus Barth eschews straightforward propositional statements, which might suggest that we, as creatures, are simply in a position to speak the things of God. (Propositions are apt when we know what it is we're talking about. With God, this is not the case.) Instead, he employs a rhetoric of dialectical opposition: death and life, cross and resurrection, judgment and mercy, transcendence and immanence – language in motion to reflect a God in motion. God will not be pinned down. To pursue 'dialectical theology' is thus to acknowledge the inadequacy of our language, but at the same time to affirm the utter necessity of bearing witness. As Barth once put it in a terse formula: 'As theologians we ought to speak of God. We are human, however, and so cannot speak of God. We ought therefore to recognize both *our obligation and our inability* and by that very recognition give God the glory.'[31]

The Epistle to the Romans laid down certain principles from which Barth never wavered. His thinking continued to be marked by the use of dialectic. In subsequent writings he was less self-conscious about this than he was in the early 1920s; nonetheless, he offers constant reminders that as creatures we are not capable of talking about the Creator, that our speech about God is at best a response to God's address to us. Likewise, the relentless focus on the cross that we see in *Romans* remains a constant in Barth's theology. Cross and resurrection belong together; we must not focus on the cross apart from the eschatological future God is ushering in through it; yet we must also never forget that this future is achieved through a death – a reminder that the God who 'gives life to the dead' always acts beyond the bounds of the humanly possible.

To be sure, in *The Epistle to the Romans* Barth left himself open to certain misunderstandings. The emphasis on the cross was heard at the time (and has continued to be heard) simply as an echo of the cultural pessimism of the years following World War One. Because of this kind of reading, Barth would later vigorously deny that he was seeking a foundation for theology in experience – including the postwar experience of death and despair. No experience prepares us to receive God's revelation. The God disclosed in Jesus Christ is truly 'totally other' than the God we expect.

A more pressing issue had to do with the relation between time and eternity, a theme that runs like a red thread throughout the commentary; God is God, and not a human religious construct. God is in heaven and we are on earth. But does that mean heaven and earth nowhere intersect? Had Barth lapsed into a form of dualism, in which God's eternity floats free of a tragically fallen creation? Should we seek escape from time into an otherworldly realm beyond? A careful reading of the Romans commentary suggests that Barth's intentions were quite otherwise; indeed, he argues that the construction of a world 'beyond' is precisely one of the chief symptoms of religion itself. Nonetheless, the book left many people with the impression that he was more interested in proclaiming the evils of creation than the goodness of God. In later works he would not abandon the 'infinite qualitative distinction,' but he would try to make clearer that the *difference* between time and eternity is not to be viewed in terms of their mutual *distance*. For in Jesus Christ, time and eternity cohere as one.

Barth's work on Romans had left a large agenda of unanswered questions. In order to address them, he would now turn to a different style of doing theology: the discipline known as dogmatics.

Faith's Reasoning: Writing Dogmatics

In the introduction to his *Theology and Social Theory*, John Milbank writes that the 'pathos of modern theology is its false humility'.[32] This is one way of describing the overall situation of Christian doctrine since the Enlightenment. A symptom of this pathos is the penchant for translating Christianity into some supposedly more rational or meaningful idiom. John Locke's *The Reasonableness of Christianity* and Immanuel Kant's *Religion Within the Limits of Reason Alone* are both classics in this genre. The assumption here is that Christian teachings simply will not stand scrutiny with modern people; these teachings do indeed mean something, perhaps even something profound, but only within some larger frame of reference. A common form of this argument runs: 'Here is a picture of real humanity, provided by some form of philosophical analysis; while we can know what this real humanity is, humankind as such cannot actually achieve it; in Christian faith alone (or in Christian faith primarily) is such genuine humanity realized.' Forms of this argument can be found in a wide range of modern theologians, including Friedrich Schleiermacher, Paul Tillich, Rudolf Bultmann, and – on some though not all readings of his work – Karl Rahner.

Barth's theological revolution cut off this line of argument. Human experience as such does not provide an adequate context for theology. The Word of God *is* the adequate context for theology – and indeed, for making sense of human experience itself. Jesus Christ does not answer a question or problem that we pose, but radically calls us into question; by contrast, the liberal procedure of beginning with the subject appears quite confident that God is simply 'there', available for our inspection. In Barth's view, this meant that the liberal method was in fact quite conservative. 'Experience', after all, reflects what the subject already knows. Barth insisted on God's radical priority over human knowledge and experience in part as a means of resisting the ideological subversion of the church, or simply the universal human embrace of the familiar over the new.

From the very beginning, Barth's critics objected that his denial of an independent apologetic strategy implied a flight into sheer subjectivism. If the theologian appeals neither to universal reason, nor to some general experience of the divine, is he not tacitly conceding that Christianity is after all a private matter? – an irrational leap into the dark, which we embrace simply because it makes sense 'to us'. On this interpretation, Barth would represent an extreme form of the modern privatizing of religion. Unable to answer the Enlightenment challenge to be rational, Christianity would thus acknowledge defeat at the hands of its critics.

However, this reading ignores two central aspects of his work. First, Barth was not content to leave the Enlightenment to the Enlighteners. Indeed, one of his chief criticisms of Schleiermacher is that the appeal to religious experience leaves us without rational resources for conceptualizing God (or forces us to adopt alien criteria for doing so). Barth believed strongly that to repudiate reason simply means abandoning the church's claim to speak of God; apart from this, the community would have nothing interesting to say to the world. But to carry through on this insight, theology must be rescued from the unwarranted assumption that its rationality is on shaky ground, and that it must derive its concepts from history, philosophy, or some other discipline. Theology would recover its lost integrity when theologians learned once again to drink from the waters of revelation. Beginning there, they will discover that the gospel has an intrinsic rationality of its own, a set of norms and canons appropriate to its subject matter.

We will have much more to say about Barth's doctrine of revelation in the next chapter. For now, we need simply to note that by the time he came to write the *Church Dogmatics*, Barth had come to see God's self-utterance in Jesus Christ as the only possible basis for Christian theology. It is not that we first know what reality or rationality look like in advance, and then measure revelation against these pre-existing standards. No, God's speech itself furnishes the very conditions that make reasoning about God possible. We begin with faith – that is, with Jesus Christ – and only from there proceed to unpack faith's intelligibility. We believe first, and then try to understand what it is we believe. Or to put the matter in ecclesial terms: we stand in the believing community first, and then try to make sense of the One to whom the church bears witness.

'Faith seeking understanding': this is the procedure Barth claimed to have learned from St Anselm, in the famous proof for God's existence set forth in his *Proslogion*. In this work, Anselm attempts to prove God's existence by means of the definition, 'God is that greater than which nothing can be conceived.' Unlike the modern theologian, who tries to render the gospel more plausible through complex strategies of re-interpretation, Anselm prays for the insight needed to carry through on his proof. He does not make understanding God a condition of his faith. Rather, he asks God for the very wisdom he needs to grasp something of God's being – and if the desired wisdom fails to materialize, he will go on praying nonetheless. Intelligibility is a function of the subject matter, and does not stand or fall with the 'success' of the proof.

Why should not Anselm's *fides quaerens intellectum* provide a model, Barth asked, for the pursuit of theology in the twentieth century? It makes for an inherently humble conception of the theological enterprise. We never assume we have the truth about God in advance; rather, we pray for the right words, concepts, and propositions we need in order to understand God better. ('Theology as prayer' is a constantly recurring theme in the *Church Dogmatics*.) It surrounds dogmatics with an air of freedom. We do not have to worry about whether our discourse will be up to the task; indeed, we know that it will not. Instead, we trust that God will take our finite language and use it as witness, as a relatively adequate testimony to the things of God.

Finally, *fides quaerens intellectum* promises a conception of theology as rational (though not rationalistic). The world of God is not a dark night in which all cats are grey, but a coherent world, indeed a world of powerful and urgent beauty; a world that can be described. The theologian's task is to explicate revelation, not to explain it, or to show how it is possible. This means that reasoning about God will largely take the form of scriptural reasoning – an attempt to discern the inner rationale of the biblical witness. Even Anselm's seemingly abstract formula 'That greater than which nothing can be conceived', Barth argued, serves as a kind of shorthand for what the biblical witness has to say: that the Creator is incomparably high and majestic, and that his relation to the world is not limited or constrained by the world itself. Anselm's proof is really a kind of sophisticated exegesis. This does not mean it fails as a rational proof! It is simply that the power of demonstration lies not with us, but with God's own self-declaration in his Word.

There is much else we could say about Barth's picture of theology as a rational enterprise; a more detailed account must wait for the next chapter. We have said enough, however, to suggest what will be the agenda of the *Church Dogmatics*. It will take the form of an extended wrestling with questions raised by Christian faith and proclamation, based on a constant attentive listening to Scripture. As 'scriptural reasoning', it will be anything but a flat-footed biblicism. The latter is ruled out by the simple fact that the world of the Bible is a world in constant motion – for theology can never be other than the attempt to trace a bird in flight.

The Structure of the *Church Dogmatics*

The *Church Dogmatics* is a huge, sprawling, and complex work of the imagination. It has been compared to a Gothic cathedral, with its crossings and side chapels, pointed arches and rose windows, the whole bathed in a radiant light from above. (Metaphors of light and illumination are surprisingly common in Barth's writing, besides the hearing metaphors one would expect from a Protestant thinker.) In the rest of this chapter I will offer a basic tour of the edifice, along with some hints on how to approach reading the text.

Barth planned the *Church Dogmatics* to consist in five volumes, each treating one of the major doctrines of the faith: revelation, God, creation, reconciliation, and redemption. With the exception of the doctrine of redemption, which Barth did not live to complete, each of these will be the subject of an individual chapter in the present book. But it will not hurt to have a preview of the overall contents:

I   *The Doctrine of the Word of God* (in two parts)
    This is Barth's 'prolegomena', or account of what theology is and how it knows what it knows. *CD* I/1 begins with God's self-revelation as Trinity – the answer to the question 'how is it possible for human beings to know God?' The account of revelation spills over into *CD* I/2, which concludes with a look at the authority of Scripture, the place of Christian doctrine, and the task of theology itself.
II *The Doctrine of God* (in two parts)
    The whole doctrine is an account of God's being, following the consistent rule: God is as God acts. *CD* II/1 revisits the question of God's 'knowableness', and also describes the divine attributes or perfections (holiness, eternity, glory and so forth). *CD* II/2 sets forth the doctrine of God's electing grace in Jesus Christ. The volume concludes with an exploration of God's commandment, the first of several treatises on ethics.
III *The Doctrine of Creation* (in four parts)
    CD III/1 deals with God as Creator, including major expositions of the creation stories in the first two chapters of Genesis. In III/2 Barth sets

forth his theological anthropology or doctrine of the human person. *CD* III/3 addresses a miscellany of topics pertaining to creation, including providence, evil, and 'angelology'. The doctrine concludes with *CD* III/4 on the ethics of creation: what is required of us precisely in our relation to God as Creator.

IV *The Doctrine of Reconciliation* (in four parts)
This is a carefully structured volume. *CD* IV/1 describes reconciliation or atonement as a gracious divine action: the self-humbling of the Son of God. In *CD* IV/2 Barth describes this same action from its human side, as Jesus, and in him all human beings, is exalted to fellowship with God. *CD* IV/3 describes Jesus Christ as the God-man, present and powerful in human history. *CD* IV/4 presents the ethics of reconciliation, published in fragmentary form after Barth's death.

V *The Doctrine of Redemption* (never written)
Note that Barth reserves the term 'redemption' for eschatology, preferring 'reconciliation' for the person and work of Christ. While *CD* V never appeared, the topic of eschatology recurs so frequently in the *Dogmatics* that one can make educated guesses as to what Barth might have said here. One might consult the eschatological sections in the Göttingen lectures, or works such as *Dogmatics in Outline*.

In the present book, the word 'volume' refers to these large expositions of a single doctrine, while 'part-volume' refers to individual physical books (III/1, III/2, III/3, and so on). Within each volume we also encounter a few other structuring elements. Thus, Barth organizes doctrines by 'chapters'. For example, the doctrine of the Word falls into four 'chapters': (I) the Word of God as Criterion of Dogmatics, (II) Revelation, (III) Holy Scripture, and (IV) The Proclamation of the Church. Each chapter is further divided into 'paragraphs' – not what is normally meant by the word in English, but a self-contained section of text, ranging from perhaps fifty to two hundred pages. The paragraph is an especially important unit, in that Barth introduces each one with a thesis or *Leitsatz*; these are of great help in tracing the argument that follows. Here is the *Leitsatz* that introduces paragraph 54 in *CD* III/4:

> As God the Creator calls man to himself, he also directs him to his fellow-man. The divine command affirms in particular that in the encounter of man and woman, in the relationship between parents and children and outwards from near to distant neighbours, man may affirm, honour, and enjoy the other with himself and himself with the other. (III/4, 116)

Not surprisingly, the table of contents of III/4 reveals that paragraph 54 has three subsections: (1) Man and Woman, (2) Parents and Children, and (3) Near and Distant Neighbours. Throughout the present book, subsections will be designated as follows: §54.2, 'Parents and Children', and so forth.

Open any given volume, and one will immediately notice a feature for which the *Dogmatics* is famous: the passages in small print, known as 'excursus' (the singular and plural forms are identical) ranging anywhere from a few lines to forty or fifty pages. Barth sometimes uses them like footnotes, to refer to a source or to make a brief aside in his exposition. But they are also where he does much of his biblical exegesis – at great and sometimes exhausting length – conducts arguments with other theologians and philosophers, and even comments (albeit rarely) on current events. Barth is famous for his rejection of apologetics, but this must be taken with a grain of salt. The small print is where he carries on *ad hoc* apologetics. Thus in the course of discussing the significance of the neighbour for our humanity in III/2, Barth offers a long, in many ways sympathetic exposition of Friedrich Nietzsche – his purpose being to show how *in*human Nietzsche's programme is in its disregard for the other.

It is possible to skip the excursus the first time through a given section of *CD*; the main text contains all the major argumentative 'moves'. But, in fact, the small print is often the most sheerly fun and engaging material in the entire work. Some practiced readers of Barth have been known to read only the excursus, a guilty pleasure.

Reading the *Church Dogmatics*

While acquaintance with the structure of the *Dogmatics* is useful, it does not prepare one for the actual experience of reading the text. A main reason is that Barth does not adopt the familiar persona of the impartial academic. He writes not impartially, but as a partisan; he writes as one who is passionately engaged in the very subject matter under discussion. Barth seeks to foster this kind of engagement in the reader as well. He draws the reader into a movement of reflection, examining a theological puzzle from different angles, at times leading him or her down false roads (only so will we understand why they are false), always pressing us forward to some resolution of the problem at hand. Barth will never say in the manner of textbooks: 'Here are two ways of looking at the topic, take your choice.' The nature of what the church proclaims demands clarity. If anything frustrates him in modern theology, it is the tendency one sometimes sees to celebrate doubt and ambiguity for their own sake. Barth believes the Word of God to be an ultimate mystery, but he does not see it as opaque. Because God has spoken clearly in Jesus Christ, we can actually arrive at answers to theological questions. To be sure, our answers – being human – are always contestable; but the best way to see where we have gone wrong is to express our thinking as clearly as possible. This is a key reason why Barth wants to embrace the modern term *wissenschaftlich*, 'scientific', for Christian theology. All this makes for the curious blend of passion and objectivity one finds in his writing. As Hans Urs von Balthasar writes, Barth is 'passionately enthusiastic about the subject matter of theology, but he is impartial in the way he approaches so volatile a subject. Impartiality means being plunged into the object ... And Barth's object is God, as he has revealed himself in Jesus Christ, to which revelation Scripture bears witness.'[33]

Yet just to the extent that theology's object is God, it is forbidden from adopting an easy attitude of security or self-confidence. The mystery of God as attested in the Bible has a way of undoing us, as the ground suddenly gives way under our feet – Isaiah's 'woe is me, for I am lost!', Peter's 'Depart from me Lord, for I am a sinful man'. This conviction, too, has an effect on the way Barth writes. He frequently employs a discursive strategy of pulling the reader up short, reminding us that God remains the Lord and can never be mastered or comprehended: whoever thinks he knows what he is talking about where God is concerned must think again. This is the grain of truth in the idea that Barth is a theologian of 'crisis'. Yet it is only a grain of truth, because – especially in his mature theology – he never wants to give the impression of dwelling on the experience of doubt or despair as such. That would still be to begin with the human subject! If there is crisis here, it is the divine KRISIS or judgment: the fact that we come up short in the face of *this* mystery is good news. While we tend to associate the notion of 'mystery' with darkness, for Barth it is very much a function of God's essentially luminary character. 'The light shines in the darkness, and the darkness has never overcome it' (John 1:5).

Perhaps this is the place to say something about the extraordinary length of the *Church Dogmatics*, which virtually every commentator feels compelled to remark on. Why did Barth write so much? There is more to it than simply the fact of his being naturally verbose. Rather, the prolixity seems somehow integral to what he was trying to accomplish – not to offer a 'system' of theology, but to offer a commentary and reflection on divine action (Barth described the theological task as one of *nach-denken*, literally 'thinking after' the reality of God). Although a finite human discourse, theology is in principle unending because there is always more of God to be said. Thus Stanley Hauerwas rightly calls attention to some comments Barth makes in II/1, where he acknowledges that 'we have no last word to speak. We can only repeat ourselves. We can, therefore, only describe [God] again, and often, and in the last resort infinitely often' (II/1, 250).[34]

But as the reader will discover, the *Church Dogmatics* is also expansive because of the way Barth's mind works. He tends to think in long, spiralling arcs of reflection, a trait that at times lends his writing an almost musical, contrapuntal quality (though clearly not all his efforts are equally successful). This is also why the *Dogmatics* largely defies attempts at paraphrase. Rather than summarizing doctrine in the form of discrete propositions, Barth offers a densely-woven fabric of thought, always closely connected with the primary language of faith. Hans Frei has suggested that part of what Barth was trying to do was to help modern Christians regain fluency in their own language, a set of skills that had been eroded in modernity. To do this one cannot simply state results, but must show the reader how one can speak the language of faith with power and conviction.[35] Barth is prolix, we might say, because he is a natural teacher and catechist – and the best way to teach is by offering examples.

Barth liked to say that danger lurks in generalities, and conversely that the best way of approaching the universal is through the particular. This counsel applies to reading him as well. The best way to approach the *Dogmatics* is to study a given doctrine in detail. Once one grasps its inner logic, one can begin to trace the web of language and ideas that link it to other parts of the work. When one does this, one discovers that Barth's thinking is marked by a remarkable degree of internal consistency, even if as it resists systematic closure. In reading the doctrine of creation, for example, one will discover constant references back to the doctrine of election (because God chose to *be* the creator in an eternal decision to relate to us in covenant love) as well as anticipations of the doctrine of reconciliation (because the cross and resurrection of Jesus is the paradigm instance of God's faithfulness to his creatures). To grasp what Barth has to say on a given topic, it is never enough just to summarize passages taken out of context; one must consider how a statement fits within the overall fabric of his thought. The *Church Dogmatics* thus has a complex, self-referencing quality, not unlike Thomas' *Summa Theologiae*, although Barth's narrative and temporal style seems on the surface quite different from Thomas' more analytic procedure.

Early in the *Dogmatics*, Barth announces that he will not treat 'ethics' as a separate set of questions, but will integrate reflection on the moral life into theology itself: there is no in-principle separation between dogmatics and ethics. This integration is designed to defeat the twin dangers of legalism (where the moral life is considered apart from its grounding in divine grace) and antinomianism (where the new life in Christ is viewed apart from obligation and Christian responsibility in the public world). Barth seeks to avert these dangers by including a treatise on ethics within each volume of the *Dogmatics*. The first such treatise in a formal sense occurs in II/2, though the reader should not overlook the paragraph titled 'The Life of the Children of God' in I/2, which locates the Christian life within the 'Outpouring of the Holy Spirit' (chapter II, part 3). But it would be misleading to think that Barth 'does ethics' only in these particular chapters. In reading the *Dogmatics*, one should be on the lookout for implicit or explicit moral reflection that appears in the most unexpected contexts. Theology is not mere theory that is, as a second step, to be 'actualized' by us – a highly Pelagian conception. Rather, it is a response to God's grace, and therefore always has in view both the doctrinal question 'what shall we teach?' and the practical question 'what shall we do?'

A final comment on reading Barth: to grasp his thought, it is important to know something of his life. This point is not unrelated to what we have just been saying about the centrality of the ethical. Barth was by no means a sheltered academic, uninvolved in the wider life of the church, culture, or the life of his nation. (In World War Two, he performed active duty in the Swiss military auxiliary, besides his work aiding and abetting the resistance in Nazi-occupied Europe.) The *vita activa* and the *vita contemplativa* went hand in hand. To read the Busch biography, one is astonished that Barth was able to produce the sheer volume of writing he did, even as he remained active in public affairs and kept up a rich, wide-ranging correspondence. Not only the Busch volume, but the selections from Barth's letters available in English – only a fraction of his correspondence, much more of which can be found in the German *Gesamtausgabe* (complete works) – are valuable for conveying a sense of the man behind the imposing black volumes of the *Church Dogmatics*.[36] Barth rarely writes in the autobiographical mode, although there are a few passages in the *Dogmatics* where he reflects on his own course of intellectual development. Nonetheless, it is impossible to read the work without gaining the sense of a forceful personality – an impression magnified by the rhetorical character of the writing itself.

Some readers are put off by that personality, finding it arrogant and overbearing. I would urge people who have that reaction to Barth to stick with it, partly because the insistent tone is intended to help us see things we might otherwise miss, and partly because the personality itself is more complex than that. Besides polemics, the *Church Dogmatics* also contains passages marked by lyric beauty and religious awe. It also contains a good deal of humour, sometimes conveyed by the use of odd punctuation – the mock-emphatic (!), the anticlimax-conveying (…), the puzzled (?).[37] Here, too, style and substance converge, in so far as humour helps convey the sense of confidence mixed with humility that Barth saw as the appropriate response to divine grace. Dietrich Bonhoeffer listed Barth among those thinkers who display *hilaritas*, 'cheerfulness', a trait he defined as 'confidence in one's own work, boldness and defiance of the world and of popular opinion, a steadfast certainty that in one's own work one is showing the world something *good* (even if the world doesn't like it), and a high-spirited self-assurance'.[38] The Christian can manifest *hilaritas* because the gospel tells, not of a tyrannical deity, but of a God who joyfully wills his creatures to flourish. Since God's relation to us is completely free of envy, God is free to share himself with us without reserve. Moreover, God's affirming 'yes' is precisely what allows us human beings to go about our work with confidence, *hilaritas*. Our work is, after all, merely work; it is not what saves us. In the end, all our achievements pale before the divine love that is the one thing really worth celebrating.

Barth captures this insight in a characteristically humorous way, setting his own accomplishments as a theologian in their proper perspective:

The angels laugh at old Karl. They laugh at him because he tries to grasp the truth about God in a book of Dogmatics. They laugh at the fact that volume follows volume and each is thicker than the previous one. As they laugh, they say to one another, 'Look! Here he comes now with his little pushcart full of volumes of the *Dogmatics*!' – and they laugh about the men who write so much about Karl Barth instead of writing about the things he is trying to write about. Truly, the angels laugh.[39]

Notes

1 My account of Barth's life draws on the one indispensable source: Eberhard Busch's *Karl Barth: His Life From Letters and Autobiographical Texts* (Grand Rapids: Eerdmans, 1994).
2 McCormack, *Dialectical Theology*, 36.
3 Busch, *Life*, 15.
4 Barth's correspondence with Thurneysen is one of the best resources for tracing his early development. A selection in English is available in *Revolutionary Theology in the Making: Barth–Thurneysen Correspondence, 1914–1925*, ed. James Smart (Richmond: John Knox Press, 1964).
5 Karl Adam, writing in the Roman Catholic monthly *Das Hochland* in June 1926, 276–7.
6 These lectures are being published as part of the complete edition of Barth's works. See Barth, *Unterricht in der christlichen Religion* (Zürich: Theologischer Verlag, 1985–). The first volume has appeared in English translation as *Göttingen Dogmatics: Instruction in the Christian Religion*, vol. 1, trans. Geoffrey Bromiley (Grand Rapids: Eerdmans, 1991).
7 See Busch, *Life*, 177 ff.
8 On Charlotte von Kirschbaum, see Renate Köbler, *In the Shadow of Karl Barth: Charlotte von Kirschbaum*, trans. Keith Crim (Louisville, Kentucky: Westminster/John Knox Press, 1989). The reader may also wish to consult the third volume of the Barth–Thurneysen letters, which contains Charlotte von Kirschbaum's own correspondence with Thurneysen. See *Karl Barth–Eduard Thurneysen: Briefwechsel: Band 3 1930–1935*, ed. Caren Algner (Zürich: Theologischer Verlag, 2000).
9 Barth, *Fides Quaerens Intellectum: Anselm's Proof for the Existence of God in the Context of His Theological Scheme* (London: SCM Press, 1960).
10 The text of the Barmen Declaration may be found in Clifford Green, *Karl Barth: Theologian of Freedom* (London: Collins, 1989), 148–51.
11 Busch, *Life*, 255.
12 Busch, *Life*, 259.
13 These lectures were later published as *The Knowledge of God and the Service of God* (London: Hodder and Stoughton, 1938).
14 Barth, *Dogmatics in Outline*, trans. G. T. Thomson (London: SCM Press, 1949).
15 See Barth, *Letters 1961–1968*, ed. Jürgen Fangmeier and Hinrich Stoevesandt, trans Geoffrey Bromiley (Grand Rapids: Eerdmans, 1981), no. 68.
16 See Barth, 'Letter to a Pastor in the German Democratic Republic', in Karl Barth and Johannes Hamel, *How to Serve God in a Marxist Land* (New York: Association Press, 1959), 45–80.
17 Barth, *Ad Limina Apostolorum: An Appraisal of Vatican II* (Richmond: John Knox Press, 1968).
18 See Barth, *Wolfgang Amadeus Mozart*, trans. Clarence K. Pott, foreword by John Updike (Grand Rapids: Eerdmans, 1986); cf. III/3, 297–9. Other references to Mozart are scattered through the *Church Dogmatics*.
19 See, for example, *The Humanity of God*, trans. J. N. Thomas and Thomas Wieser (Atlanta: John Knox Press, 1960).
20 This talk was published as 'Starting Out, Turning Round, Confessing', in Barth, *Final Testimonies*, ed. Eberhard Busch, trans. Geoffrey Bromiley (Grand Rapids: Eerdmans, 1977).
21 Busch, *Life*, 45.

22 McCormack, *Dialectical Theology*, 57.

23 Martin Rumscheidt, 'Epilogue' to Barth, *Fragments Grave and Gay*, trans. Eric Mosbacher (London: Collins, 1971).

24 Barth, 'Concluding Unscientific Postscript on Schleiermacher', in *The Theology of Schleiermacher*, trans. Geoffrey Bromiley (Grand Rapids: Eerdmans, 1982), 263.

25 Smart, *Revolutionary Theology*, 31; I have borrowed the translation of Barth's concluding remark from Timothy Gorringe, *Karl Barth: Against Hegemony: Christian Theology in Context* (Oxford: Oxford University Press, 1999), 34.

26 Barth, 'Naumann and Blumhardt', in *The Beginnings of Dialectical Theology*, ed. James M. Robinson (Richmond, Virginia: John Knox Press, 1968), 41. See also Barth's chapter on the elder Blumhardt in *Protestant Theology in the Nineteenth Century: Its Background and History* (Valley Forge, PA: Judson Press, 1973).

27 Busch, *Life*, 85.

28 Barth, *The Word of God and the Word of Man*, trans. Douglas Horton (London: Hodder and Stoughton, 1978), 37, rev. Subsequently referred to as *WGWM*; further citations will be given in the text.

29 As Neil MacDonald aptly comments, there is no 'logical space' for John in Barth's reading of the picture. MacDonald, *Karl Barth and the Strange New World Within the Bible*, 376. MacDonald's discussion of the Grünewald painting's significance for Barth is exemplary. For a comprehensive account of the work itself, see Andrée Hayum, *The Isenheim Altarpiece: God's Medicine and the Painter's Vision* (Princeton: Princeton University Press, 1989).

30 Barth, *The Epistle to the Romans*, trans. Edwyn C. Hoskyns (London: Oxford University Press, 1933); hereafter cited as *Romans*. Besides the two editions of this commentary, Barth also published an *A Shorter Commentary on Romans* (Richmond: John Knox Press, 1959), based on lectures given in 1940–41.

31 Barth, WGWM, 186, rev.

32 John Milbank, *Theology and Social Theory* (Oxford: Basil Blackwell, 1990), 1.

33 Hans Urs von Balthasar, *Karl Barth* (San Francisco: Ignatius, 1992), 25.

34 Hauerwas makes this point in *With the Grain of the Universe: The Church's Witness and Natural Theology* (Grand Rapids: Brazos Press, 2001), 173 ff.

35 Hans Frei, *Types of Christian Theology*, eds George Hunsinger and William Placher (New Haven: Yale University Press, 1992), 159.

36 Karl-Barth-Stiftung, *Gesamtausgabe* (Zürich: EVZ, 1971–).

37 Alas, many of these typographical clues are left out of the English translation, which in general has the effect of flattening Barth's vigorous, colloquial style. If I could add one last piece of advice it might be: read the *Church Dogmatics* in German.

38 Dietrich Bonhoeffer, *Letters and Papers From Prison*, enlarged edition, ed. Eberhard Bethge (New York: Simon & Schuster/Touchstone, 1997), 229, revised; Bonhoeffer's emphasis.

39 Barth, quoted in Robert McAfee Brown, 'Introduction', in George Casalis, *Portrait of Karl Barth* (Garden City, New York: Doubleday and Company, 1963), 3.

Chapter 2

Speech and Mystery: Revelation

Rhetoric, then, can serve the gospel, but the gospel itself is not fundamentally a matter of rhetorical persuasion ... For the gospel has the effect of placing at issue the nature of argument itself. That is to say, since the gospel is God's own utterance, it is not and can never be subject to ratiocinative criteria that have been developed apart from it.
– J. Louis Martyn[1]

The Word of God ... is a rational and not an irrational event.
– Barth, *CD* I/1[2]

God Who Speaks

It is well known that Barth seeks to do theology 'according to revelation'. The first volume of the *Church Dogmatics* is, among other things, a doctrine of revelation, an inquiry into the event of God's self-disclosure to creatures. Yet the emphasis on revelation can also be quite misleading. Barth was above all interested in the covenant relationship that binds God with human beings. In the *Church Dogmatics* he employs a wide range of terms for describing that relationship: grace, election, covenant, fellowship, participation, light, life. The concept of revelation must be understood within this much larger matrix of divine–human sharing. Indeed, while Barth never retracts what he says about revelation in *CD* I, the term is far less prominent in later volumes of the *Dogmatics*.

To put it another way: revelation for Barth is not, finally, an attempt to address an epistemological problem – the problem of saying something about the transcendent, for example. The point of the doctrine is not what it says about human knowing, but what it says about *God*. And what the doctrine says is that God speaks. It is no accident that *CD* I bears the title 'The Doctrine of the Word of God'. The whole text is one long celebration of the fact that God speaks, and that as God speaks he opens himself to us, giving us a share in his life through Christ and the Spirit. Barth's doctrine of revelation therefore coincides with his doctrine of the Trinity – a doctrine he helped rediscover for modern theology, and whose imprint can be seen in ways large and small throughout the work.

Here, then, is our basic move: 'God speaks.' Like every other doctrine in the *Dogmatics*, the doctrine of the Word refers first of all to God's action. But the doctrine also concerns the human response to God's action. *CD* I falls into the genre known as theological method or, more grandly, 'prolegomena to dogmatics'. It tries to set out the ground rules and assumptions about how *we* should speak if we hope to engage in responsible Christian dogmatics. As such, the volume also includes Barth's theology of Holy Scripture, his thinking on the nature and limits of the church's authority, as well as his reflections on the doing of theology itself.

The Warrants for Theology

As a glance at the title page will indicate, Barth's doctrine of the Word constitutes a 'prolegomena to church dogmatics'. The genre of prolegomena – the term means 'things spoken before' – developed in modern Protestantism as a way of establishing the ground rules of the theological enterprise. This self-consciousness about theology was a new thing. Thomas Aquinas devotes just one question at the beginning of the *Summa Theologiae* to 'the nature and extent of sacred doctrine', including a brief mapping of the term 'God' with respect to our experience of the world (the so-called 'five ways'). John Calvin begins his *Institutes* by diving directly into the knowledge of God as Creator. Neither author feels he has to provide an extensive justification for what he is doing. The warrants for theology are complex and mostly unstated, reflecting material convictions about God, the world, and the plan of salvation. We 'do theology' because it is important to talk about God and because that is what the church does; these warrants are sufficient.

In the modern era, the warrants for theology are no longer obvious. Protestant thought after Kant can be seen as a series of attempts to answer the question 'What makes theology possible?' What sense does it make to talk about God in a world where rational proofs of God's existence no longer convince? How can we persuade our contemporaries that theology is not so much nonsense, but provides a means of access to the real? We have already seen how Schleiermacher tried to answer this question. What makes theology possible is something about us. We have no cognitive access to a realm beyond time and space – Kant was right about this – but we do have access to the human subject, and we know that this subject is deeply and irreducibly religious. Theology thus builds on a secure foundation, since the concept is necessary to account for our experience. While later thinkers would vary Schleiermacher's tactics, they embraced his overall strategy of beginning with the human subject.

At this point it is appropriate to mention the name of Ludwig Feuerbach, one of Barth's favourites among his nineteenth-century predecessors.[3] Feuerbach accepted the argument from the subject – only to set about subverting it. While he agreed with Schleiermacher, Hegel, and other Idealists when they argued that human self-awareness implies an awareness of God, he thought they had failed to grasp the radical implications of their own argument. Feuerbach maintained that the object of the religious quest is not some 'being' who stands over/against man. It is simply man himself, projecting his finite existence on the screen of eternity. How sad that we should exalt 'God' and despise ourselves, when the idea of 'God' has no other reality than what we invest in it! The old religion is a tragically alienated form of human consciousness. But the time for alienation is past: the logical outcome of Feuerbach's project is an utterly this-wordly faith, a post-Christian form of romantic humanism.

Feuerbach's reductive project is obviously unacceptable to anyone with orthodox Christian sensibilities. His usefulness, Barth believed, lay in his keen diagnosis of the suicidal logic at work in neo-Protestantism. Theologians like Schleiermacher and Ritschl certainly did not intend to reduce talk about God to talk about ourselves. The question is whether this conclusion can be avoided, so long as theology has no other basis for its claims than the human subject. The turn to the subject promised to refute Enlightenment atheism; but had it simply restated atheism in a far more potent form?

The early Barth delighted in modern anti-theologians like Feuerbach, Overbeck, and Nietzsche, in so far as they force theology to make an honest reckoning with itself. In the case of Feuerbach, the challenge was this: How can our human words really be talk about God, and not just a covert form of talk about ourselves? If all we have is religion, are we not resigned in the end to a purely anthropocentric interpretation of reality? In Barth's view, Feuerbach had discovered the weak point in the whole structure of liberal Protestantism. But this weak point also represented an opportunity: to offer an alternative account of theology that does not subject it to alien criteria, nor seek to reconstruct Christianity on the foundation of the human subject.

Barth did not arrive at a solution to his problem all at once; but when he did, the answer he gave was simple and uncompromising. There is no basis for proclamation other than that provided by the Word of God itself. The quest for the human conditions of talk about God is finally illusory. There are no such conditions. Revelation is possible because it occurs – or more concretely, because God is the Lord. In a sovereign act of mercy, God draws our fallen speech (which in itself can never be *other* than speech about ourselves!) into correspondence with his own self-utterance. Human language bears witness to the divine Word. That it should do so lies entirely in God's hands. Yet miraculously, this does happen. Revelation occurs. God speaks. Even more extraordinary, this speech is heard, as the Spirit awakens human beings to faith and obedience.

This is a radical answer to the question of speech about God, but it is important that we accent the radicalism in the right place. Clearly there are denials involved here. Barth vigorously contests that there are human points of contact for revelation, whether positive (such as a vestigial awareness of God in the soul) or negative (a sense of guilt or existential crisis). Nothing in our experience can account for the fact of our standing before God.

Nonetheless, the overall tone of Barth's doctrine is overwhelmingly positive. The radicalism is not that God is unknown, but that God is very well known – one might even say, too close for comfort. As Barth wrote to his brother Peter in 1932, 'Don't things get dangerous only *if* and *because* God is?'[4] Things are dangerous in the church, because the church has to do with God. But precisely because the church does have to do with God, it lives in the light of a great promise.

Barth is well aware that the appeal to revelation alone leaves theology in a highly vulnerable position, humanly speaking. The secular critic can always respond that an appeal to revelation fails to answer Feuerbach's challenge; might not talk of 'revelation' be itself a projection of human needs? Barth knows that he runs this risk, but is willing to take it, being convinced that a God who could be proved on some independent basis would not be the God of the gospel. We are not, he thinks, called to make compromises with atheism; we are simply called to bear witness to the Word we have received. This response has never seemed very satisfying to Barth's critics, who point to the church's long tradition of natural theology and apologetics (an issue I will take up again in the next chapter). For now, suffice to say both that Barth is radically opposed to natural theology, and that his relation to it is more complex than might first appear. That the good creation objectively testifies to its Creator he did not doubt; God does not leave himself without witnesses. The more pressing question is whether sinful human beings can turn this testimony to good use, developing arguments that proceed from the world to God. This Barth vehemently denied; given what revelation tells us about ourselves, we should not expect to find knowledge of God outside the sphere of revelation and the church.

And indeed, beginning with revelation implies acknowledging one's location within the church. Consider the thesis that appears on the very first page of the *Church Dogmatics*: 'As a theological discipline dogmatics is the scientific self-description of the Christian church with respect to the content of its distinctive talk about God' (I/1, 3).

Rather than being a dialogue with unbelief, theology is to be conceived of as an activity of the church – the practice by which the church tests the faithfulness of its witness. The church says and does all manner of things in God's name. Some of these things actually manage to point to God; others occlude God with their banality, blasphemy, or simple lack of appropriateness. In truth, the church often fails miserably in its task of witness. Dogmatics takes its starting point in revelation, but then proceeds to examine the language, doctrines, and teachings by which the church seeks to give voice to revelation. It is the practice by which the church seeks to assume responsibility for its speech, so that it may confess the gospel with a proper mix of confidence and humility. Dogmatics is nothing but *fides quaerens intellectum* ('faith seeking understanding'). In a very real sense, one might say that Barth seeks to answer Feuerbach by means of Anselm.

The Word Uttered: Divine Speech

The criterion that allows theology to engage in this task is revelation, or the Word of God. The word 'criterion' is important. Barth criticizes both liberal Protestantism and Roman Catholicism for substituting other norms in place of the Word. Thus neo-Protestantism had raised religious experience to the status of an independent norm, while Catholicism argues that revelation occurs through Scripture – as interpreted in light of dogma and the teaching magisterium of the church. Materially, Barth finds himself far closer to the Catholic position than to the neo-Protestant one. Yet even here, he denies that the church as such can determine the content of revelation. If the Word of God is the criterion over the church's teaching, and even over its biblical interpretation, it must itself be given free reign in relation to these practices. Where the Word of God is concerned, human beings are entirely in the position of recipients.

Barth seeks to secure the freedom of revelation by insisting on its character as an event – a term we will encounter again and again in the course of this study. God's revelation is ultimately identical with God himself. And God is simply not available for our inspection or control. The Word 'happens'. As Luther famously put it:

> [The gospel] is not an eternal, lasting, static doctrine, but like a moving shower of rain which strikes what it strikes and misses what it misses. Nor does it return or halt, but is followed by the sunshine and warmth which lick it up, etc. Hence our experience that in no place in the world has the gospel remained pure and simple beyond a man's memory, but has stood and increased so long as they have remained who brought it, and its light has then gone out ...[5]

The event–character of revelation is intrinsic to its character as God's sheerly original, miraculous action of self-giving. Because it is identical with God himself, the Word cannot be identified with any worldly object – except in so far as God graciously wills to meet us there, as he does in Jesus Christ.

To say that revelation is an event is not to say that it lacks cognitive content. The Word is quite particular and definite, precisely because the God who utters it is a particular person – not a misty experience of the sacred, but the God of Israel. The subject of revelation is the One who 'is called Yahweh in the Old Testament and θεός or, concretely, κύριος in the New Testament' (I/1, 295). This point is crucial. If revelation were mere eventfulness in the abstract, there would be no means of applying it as a criterion of the church's witness (except maybe to say that 'dynamic' is better than 'static' – but then Nazism was dynamic as well). Revelation as acknowledged in the church is the speech of *this* God. This is why Barth's seeming relativizing of Scripture and doctrine – they are not themselves God – must not be seen as an attempt to undermine the authority of Scripture. On the contrary, the church constantly needs to return to Scripture, just as it needs to be involved in the task of formulating pure doctrine. Only in this way can it maintain the clarity of its message as a witness to the true God, the God of Israel, as opposed to the many false gods of the nations. The particularity of God's identity is basic to Barth's thought, and it is closely related to theology's character as a rational enterprise.

An even better term than 'event', therefore, is 'activity', because the Word of God is God's personal utterance – indeed, it is identical with the speech by which he created and rules the world. 'God's Word means that God speaks' (I/1, 132). That God speaks is appropriate to God's character as person, as freely purposive and self-directing. 'The doubtful thing is not whether God is person', Barth writes, 'but whether we are' (I/1, 139). God's being is in fact the original and perfect instance of personhood, while we enjoy this status only derivatively and by God's gift. Yet precisely because God is person in the basic and original sense, his speech is effective. Commentators have often noted an affinity between Barth's conception of the Word and the modern philosophical notion of the 'speech act'.[6] God's speech *is* God's action. In manifesting himself to creatures, God exercises his lordship over them. This means that we can never approach revelation from a safely neutral attitude, as though it were up to us to decide what the next move might be. God's revelation does not fit inside the world as we know it. The Word is both world-disrupting and world-creating:

> The promise of the Word of God is not as such an empty pledge which always stands, as it were, confronting a person. It is the transposing of a person into the wholly new state of one who has accepted and appropriated the promise, so that irrespective of his attitude to it he no longer lives without this promise but with it. The claim of the Word of God is not as such a wish or command which remains outside the hearer without impinging on his existence. It is the claiming and commandeering of the human being. Whatever may be his attitude to God's claim, the person who hears the Word now finds himself in the sphere of the divine claim; he is claimed by God. (I/2, 152 rev.)

The Word of God thus has a concretely self-involving character, on both the divine and the human side of the relationship. Revelation is marked by an 'I–Thou' – the language is Martin Buber's, although Barth would already have grasped the basic point from his teacher Herrmann. This claim has often given rise to misunderstandings. Anglican theologian Austin Farrer once complained that he did not know what it means when 'Germans set their eyeballs and pronounce the terrific words "He speaks to thee" (Er redet dich an).'[7] Farrer protests that he has never had an experience like the one described. Barth would find the objection irrelevant, in so far as he is making a conceptual point and not (or at least not in the first instance) an observation about experience. While the Word of God is indeed God's personal address, the fact is that we never encounter it directly. It always comes hidden under some creaturely veil – a notion Barth is happy to import from Luther. In principle, God might choose to encounter us anywhere he wants: 'God may speak to us through Russian Communism, a flute concerto, a blossoming shrub, or a dead dog. We do well to listen to him if he really does' (I/1, 55). But that does not mean we should be off seeking God in these places. It is not a question of what God might do, but of what the church is commissioned to do. And what the church is commissioned to do is preach the Word on the basis of the biblical witness. Proclamation and Scripture are two of the three (and only three) 'forms of the Word of God'.

To say that Scripture and proclamation are forms of the Word is to say that they participate in the event of revelation, without being directly identical with revelation itself. In themselves they are merely human words – the Bible an odd collection of texts from the ancient world, proclamation a talk given by the pastor on Sunday morning. Like Grünewald's John the Baptist, both point beyond themselves to the indescribable reality of the Word itself. We misunderstand these human pointers if we take them to be revelation itself. Nonetheless, the two forms are indispensable. The canon reminds us of revelation as it took place once for all in the past, and summons us to expect it once again in the future. The Christian community gathers on Sunday to hear the Word, in the hope that this expectation will be realized. It should be clear from this that Barth intends no relativizing of either Scripture or proclamation. If in one sense they are merely witnesses, in another sense they are 'raised up' (*aufgehoben*) into the divine event of the Word itself (I/1, 117–18). We cannot bypass them, for God has tied the promise of revelation to these frail human vessels – a sign of the divine humility.

As witnesses, proclamation and the scriptural canon to which it is bound can only receive their character as revelation. This is not the case with the third form of the Word of God. 'If "written" and "proclaimed" denote the twofold concrete relation in which the Word of God is spoken to us, revelation denotes the Word of God itself in the act of its being spoken in time' (I/1, 118, rev.). Revelation is that to which the witnesses direct us. It is the Archimedean point from which God 'leverages' all of reality, the unimaginable event of God's entry into time and space. 'Revelation, *revelatio*, ἀποκάλυψις means the unveiling of what is veiled' (I/1, 118–19). And it has a name:

> Revelation in fact does not differ from the person of Jesus Christ nor from the reconciliation accomplished in him. To say revelation is to say, 'The Word became flesh' ... . When in the word revelation we say 'The Word was made flesh and dwelt among us,' then we are saying something which can have only an intertrinitarian basis in the will of the Father and the sending of the Son and the Holy Spirit ... so that it can be established only as knowledge of God from God, of light in light. (I/1, 119)

The life, death, and resurrection of Jesus Christ just *is* the revelation of God, the place where God emerges out of hiddenness into the light. And it is the ground of the other two forms of the Word. When God speaks to us today through Scripture and the church's preaching, this is what – or rather Whom – we encounter: the mystery of the Word made flesh.

'Mystery' is indeed the operative word here. Barth is emphatic that revelation does not abrogate, but confirms the difference between God and ourselves. The unveiling is always accompanied by a veiling. We never have to do with God except in some secular, worldly form, a form that disguises God – for example, the human language of Scripture and the church. 'The veil is thick. We do not have the Word of God otherwise than in the mystery of its secularity' (I/1, 165). We might protest that Jesus must be the exception to this rule; in him, do we not have to do with God in a direct way? Yet Barth would reply that just the opposite is the case. For the One who manifests himself at Easter is always the Crucified, God veiled under the forms of sin, death, 'the flesh'. That God should enter human reality as it is disclosed at the cross is precisely the mystery of revelation. Barth leans heavily on Luther at this point (cf. I/1, 167–8, 169–74). It must be stressed that while the theme of mystery is closely linked to God's inalienable subjectivity, his sheer 'otherness' in relation to us, this should not be read in terms of distance or non-involvement. Barth's God is intimately involved in the world – as the cross indicates. But he is there for us on his own mysterious terms, not as an object in the furtherance of our projects. This is a salutary reminder for theology, and indeed the mystery of the Word offers something of a 'theological warning against theology, a warning against the idea that its propositions or principles are certain in themselves like the supposed axioms of the mathematicians and physicists' (I/1, 165). Theology cannot conjure God; it can only pray that he will show himself.

The Word Repeated: Trinity

Barth's doctrine of revelation can be seen as being animated by three convictions, each of which he sees as grounded in the biblical witness itself. First, God is always prior, always Subject in his relation to creatures; God's revelation is identical with his lordship. Second, the actual content of revelation is Christological: 'Revelation in fact does not differ from the person of Jesus Christ nor from the reconciliation accomplished in him' (I/1, 119). Third, revelation does not render human beings passive, but engages them in a self-involving way as knowers, subjects, agents. It makes little sense to speak of God's self-unveiling unless there is someone there to receive it.

Think these convictions together, and one arrives at the doctrine of the Trinity. The central portion of *CD* I/1 (Chapter II, paras 8–18) is devoted to 'The Revelation of God', and structured according to the three trinitarian persons.

Why has Barth's Trinitarian turn proved among his most enduring legacies? Because he was able to show how the doctrine of the Trinity solves a host of theological problems. It helps us to read the biblical witness as a coherent whole, a testimony to the self-same God active in both Old and New Testaments. It helps make sense of God's relation to the world: God's engagement with his creation is wholly Trinitarian, in that the world is made in and for Christ (John 1:3) while human beings are destined for life in Christ and the Holy Spirit. Most of all, Barth was able to show that the doctrine of the Trinity – precisely in that it describes the shape of God's self-revealing action – is the doctrine that has the crucial task of identifying the God of the Bible. If revelation can be summarized in the sentence *Deus dixit* – 'God has spoken' – the logical next question is, Which God? *Who* has spoken? According to Barth, Scripture answers this question only as it addresses two equally important questions: *what* does God speak and *what happens* when God speaks? It is only in answering these three questions together that the church gives an account of its God:

> *God* reveals himself. He reveals himself *through himself*. He reveals *himself*. If we really want to understand revelation in terms of its subject, i.e., God, then the first thing we have to realize is that this subject, God, the Revealer, is identical with his act in revelation and also identical with its effect. It is from this fact ... that we learn we must begin the doctrine of revelation with the doctrine of the triune God. (*CD* I/1, 296; Barth's emphasis)

We might note that even to ask the question 'Which God?' indicates that Barth assumes Christendom is dead. As long as European societies remained nominally Christian, one did not have to ask which God one meant. While Christendom existed, how could one doubt that the God of cultural religion and the God of Christian faith are identical? Now, however, Barth is proposing that the church needs to learn (as it did in the third and fourth centuries) how to distinguish the God of Jesus Christ from the gods of pagan religion. Barth's insight that trinitarian doctrine is intrinsically tied to the question of God's identity has been widely accepted among contemporary theologians.

Yet why does the church confess God as triune in the first place? Barth's answer is, because this is simply how God reveals himself to us; revelation has an inherently trinitarian structure. When God speaks, he repeats or 'reiterates' himself in a complex act of self-differentiation. In speaking his Word, the hidden God discloses himself to us – already this is a miracle of grace – without thereby ceasing to be God. In sending his Spirit, the God so revealed makes himself a 'fact' of human knowledge or experience – another miracle, and again something God does without ceasing to be God. God is the Subject of revelation, and always in such a way that he remains Subject. God is the Revelation itself, the 'other' in whom he both knows himself and makes himself known to creatures. And God is the historical effectiveness of his revelation, the lively response evoked by this event. In short, God is

Father, Son, and Holy Spirit, and only in the occurrence of all three taken together does revelation happen.

Already from this brief description, it should be clear that Barth tends to emphasize the unity of the Trinity somewhat at the expense of the threeness, the distinctiveness or unique character of each person. Indeed, he disapproves of the word 'person' as a way of denoting what the Greeks called *hypostasis*. 'Person', he believed, had in modern times become too heavily freighted with the notion of individual consciousness. Say 'three persons' and people are liable to think you mean 'three agents', and from there it is not much of a step to 'three gods'. If there is a 'person' in the Trinity it is the one God: all three are together. Father, Son, and Holy Spirit are the three 'ways of being' in which God has his being *as* God (I/1, 359).[8] They are irreducible – Barth is no modalist – but they are irreducible precisely as repetitions of God as Lord, the 'one divine I' (I/1, 351).

Much of Barth's energy in his discussion of the Trinity is devoted to maintaining the intimate connection between 'God' and 'revelation'. 'The doctrine of the Trinity tells us … how far the One who reveals himself according to the witness of Scripture can in fact be our *God* and how far he can in fact be *our* God' (*CD* I/1, 382–3). If we affirm God's unity but deny that he truly reveals himself to us, we end up with a distant, unloving deity – a God who is not 'our' God, and therefore not the God to whom Scripture bears witness. This is the heresy known as modalism, amounting finally to a 'denial of God' (I/1: 382). On the other hand, if we affirm the Father, Jesus, and the Spirit without a clear grasp that here we have to do with the one Lord, we end up with a deity who does our bidding: 'All subordinationism rests on the intention of making the One who reveals himself there the kind of subject we ourselves are, a creature whose Thouness has limits we can survey, grasp and master, which can be objectified, in face of which the I can assert itself' (I/1, 381). Subordinationism finally means the denial of revelation, the denial that our relation to God comes only on God's initiative and as his gift.

Revelation, then, has a trinitarian structure; we know God only in his self-disclosure as Father, Son, and Holy Spirit. Yet the three persons do not have identical roles in the revelatory act. Only the Son becomes incarnate. At the centre of revelation is the history of Jesus, not of the Father or the Spirit – although, conversely, we will fail to grasp who Jesus is if we ignore either the Father's mystery or the Spirit's work of personal disclosure. Why is this important? Because one sometimes hears it said that a Christocentric emphasis like Barth's needs to be 'balanced' by attention to the other two persons. The statement fails to take account of how Trinitarian talk arises in the first place. For Barth, knowledge of all three persons is generated by the divine action that takes place in Christ; Barth is trinitarian *because* he is Christocentric. Rightful attention to the Father and the Spirit there must be – but on the basis of the concrete enactment of revelation, not as a balancing of competing claims.

This is simply a reminder that for Barth, the church's doctrine of the Trinity is but an attempt to interpret the biblical witness. It is an essential commentary on the text, and is meant to send us back to a lively encounter with Scripture itself.

The Word Made Flesh: Incarnation

As we have seen, Barth unfolds the doctrine of the Trinity as the doctrine that specifies the 'who' of revelation – the identity of the God attested in the Bible. Having established this 'who', Barth now turns to the 'what' and the 'how'. The what is the incarnate Word of God itself, Jesus; the how is the Holy Spirit by whose activity human beings become knowers of God, active participants in the revelatory event. John Webster rightly says that Barth's 'lengthy exposition of Christology and pneumatology in paragraphs 15 and 16 ... are the first truly great piece of writing in the *Church Dogmatics*'.[9] The material fairly shimmers with the light of theological discovery.

What does it mean to say that the Son of God became incarnate in Jesus Christ? Let us begin, as many nineteenth-century thinkers did, with the reality of the communion that obtains between God and humanity. As persons are awakened and nurtured in the life of faith, they discover that their religious relation to God is something real, something actual. The next question one might pose is: how is such a thing possible? Given relatedness to God, what feature of the world or of human consciousness would account for it? This question – in Kantian terms, the question of the 'transcendental conditions' underlying religion – had been generally answered in terms of humanity's intrinsic orientation or aptitude for God. Human consciousness already participates in God to some degree; what happens in Jesus is the supreme realization of this prior possibility, so that when confronted with revelation a person can see it in the fulfilment of her inward longing.

It is just this overall form of argument that Barth sets out to demolish in 'The Incarnation of the Word' (I/2, paras 13–15). He denies that the incarnation falls in that class of realities that are 'possible' from the perspective of human experience. Jesus is not an instance of the general category 'Saviour' or 'Revealer of God', available to us in advance. His particular reality as true God and true human being is itself the ground of possibility of its actual occurrence. Barth begins the working out of this logic in paragraph 13, titled 'God's Freedom for Man'. The reversal of our usual ways of thinking about possibility and actuality has the effect of focusing our attention on the particular, unsubstitutable contours of Jesus' story. To grasp what is possible for God, one can only attend to the reality of God, to what has actually occurred in the history between God and humankind. This setting of actuality before possibility is one of the most characteristic features of Barth's thought. Note that he does not base this argument primarily on the darkening of human reason by sin – this might simply be one more way of focusing on ourselves – but rather on the 'majesty of God in his condescension to the creature' (I/2, 31). Grace, not sin, is the point of departure. While the discussion in these paragraphs is fairly abstract, the reader can hardly miss the tone of awe and wonder that marks Barth's Christology as a whole.

If the person of Jesus Christ plays havoc with our basic logical categories, then we might expect it to unsettle our temporal ones as well. Barth works out these dynamics in paragraph 14, 'The Time of Revelation', which wrestles with the relation of time to eternity in ways reminiscent of *The Epistle to the Romans*. We recall that, in the 1921 text, Barth has trouble articulating time's positive meaning; at the cross, eternity simply seems to negate time. But in *CD* I/2 he has a rich, substantive Christology at his disposal, permitting him not only to bring time and eternity together, but to narrate a story in which they coincide. Jesus himself is the reality of the coming together of time and eternity, man and God – a fact disclosed in the forty days he spent with his disciples after his resurrection. Indeed, we might say that this forty-day period is nothing less than the event of revelation in its purest form. Far from cancelling time, Christ renews it by his presence in the midst of time:

> The Word of God is. It is never 'not yet' or 'no longer'. It is not exposed to any becoming or, therefore, to any passing away, or therefore, to any change. The same holds also of the Word of God become flesh and therefore time. In every moment of his temporal existence, and also at every point previous or subsequent to his temporal existence, in which he becomes manifest as true God and true man and finds faith and witness, Jesus Christ is the same. The Word spoken from eternity raises the time into which it is uttered (without dissolving it as time), up into his own eternity as now his own time, and gives it part in the existence of God which is alone real, self-moved, self-dependent, and self-sufficient. (I/2, 52)

Barth's account of the Risen Crucified as 'fulfilled time', in whom past, present, and future find their genuine meaning and purpose, is among the more important imaginative turns in the *Church Dogmatics*. It displays his metaphysical cast of mind, while at the same time pointing to his consistent rooting in the biblical text: the coming together of time and eternity takes the form of a story, a description of the covenant fellowship shared between Jesus and his disciples. For Barth, time and eternity are not general ideas, but derive their meaning from this concrete fellowship – a fellowship that reaches out to embrace all of human history. The narrative of the forty days is the centre of the story, or rather the revelation of the centre. Bracketing it on either side is the 'time of expectation', the time that characterizes the witness of the Old Testament, and the 'time of recollection', the time marking the apostolic testimony to the risen Christ (§14.2–3).

Just as the doctrine of the Trinity answers the question 'Who is God?', Barth tells us, so Christological doctrine answers the question 'Who is Jesus Christ?' Ultimately Christology forms but a commentary on the Johannine confession that 'the Word became flesh'. Most of Barth's account of the incarnation is not directly exegetical, however, but takes the form of a respectful engagement with the the church's teaching tradition, the immediate point of departure being the Chalcedonian affirmation that Jesus is both 'truly God' and 'truly human'. Barth constantly urges on us the limitations of doctrines like this. They cannot explain the mystery of the incarnation, but can only bear witness to it. Nonetheless, he vigorously defends the necessity of doctrine. The modern notion that avoidance of doctrine reflects intellectual 'humility' is false; at best it is a form of laziness, at worst a sheer denial of the Word made flesh. By contrast, the Church Fathers' care in doctrinal definition embodies a genuine humility in face of the mystery attested in Scripture. As with the doctrine of the Trinity, Barth revels in the subtlety and intellectual power of classical Christology, even as he insists on thinking the problems through in his own way.

One particular notion from the tradition can help to clarify the basic thrust of Barth's Christology: the notion of *anhypostasia*. Briefly, the Fathers used this idea to make clear that Jesus' humanity has no independent reality (*hypostasis*) of its own, but depends entirely on the divine Logos for its existence. There is no man Jesus 'already there', waiting to be drawn into unity with the Son of God. The Son assumes human flesh, and *therefore* there is a man called Jesus. Moderns have often resisted the *anhypostasis*, seeing it as a denial that Jesus was a real person with will, consciousness, and passions of his own. Barth insists that this is not the point. Of course we must acknowledge that Jesus was 'a man', a particular human identity among others. Only so could he suffer and die for us. What is at stake, rather, is whether we see the salvation enacted in him as God's radical gift, or as a possibility that lies immanent in human nature. Barth's argument here follows that of Luther: only a high Christology can safeguard the utterly gratuitous character of grace. He joins Luther in acknowledging Mary to be *theotokos*, the mother of God. This reason-jarring affirmation is essential, Barth argues, if we wish to maintain the unity of Christ's person – though he is severely critical of later Mariology, seeing it as a (typically Catholic) deifying of the creature in its own right.

As traditional as Barth's Christology is in many ways, it everywhere bears his unmistakeable mark. Thus he insists – with very few precedents in the tradition – that the flesh assumed by Christ is not a pristine, Edenic 'human nature', but 'flesh' in the Pauline sense, humanity in its willful opposition to God. What then of Jesus' sinlessness? Barth of course affirms it; Christ saves us by being obedient to God where we were not. This does not mean, however, that we can picture Christ's sinlessness in abstractly moralizing terms (see the discussion in I/2, 151–5). Christ was obedient, but just so submitted himself to the judgment of God; he who knew no sin became a curse for our sake (Gal. 3:13). Here doctrine encounters its limits; we do not know what it means to say that Christ 'became sin', but in a profound sense can only bear witness to it. The mystery of revelation is identical with the mystery of atonement, and both are identical with the mystery of the Word made flesh. All these themes will be developed in greater detail in the doctrine of reconciliation.

Equally characteristic is the way in which Barth insists on the dialectical character of Christology, precisely as a means of safeguarding the mystery involved. His language is precise: Ἐγένετο, the event of the incarnation of the Word, of the *unio hypostatica*, has to be understood as a *completed* event, but also as a completed *event*' (I/2, 165; emphasis in original). Barth identifies the emphasis on the completed character of the union with Lutheranism, which sees the Son of God as radically one with the man Jesus of Nazareth. 'There is no other form or manifestation in heaven or on earth save the one child in the stable, the one man on the cross. This is the Word to which we must hearken, render faith and obedience, cling ever so closely' (I/2, 166). He identifies the emphasis on the act-character of the union with the Reformed tradition, which stresses that in the incarnation God always remains God, while the creature remains a creature. Whereas for the Lutherans the Word is simply identical with Jesus, for the Reformed the Word that is Jesus is always God's spoken Word, and so needs to be received again and again in new acts of faith and obedience. Thus Barth characterizes the Reformed interest as 'dynamic–noetic', in contrast to the 'ontic–static' interest of Lutheranism ('noetic', having to do with knowledge; 'ontic', having to do with being). He argues that there are strengths and weaknesses in both approaches, and that a genuinely Evangelical theology will not resolve the issue either way, but will keep the dialectic constantly in motion.

It is a typically Barthian performance, in the sense that Barth thinks that maintaining a dialectical relation between two extremes is better than hewing to the safe middle. It is clear, however, that the very insistence on dialectic at this point tilts the balance in the so-called 'dynamic–noetic' direction (and Barth knows himself well enough to realize that). The Word became flesh in Palestine in the years A.D. 1–30. He is never anything or anyone other than the man Jesus. But this same Word also *becomes* flesh whenever God speaks to us in the present. It is Barth's way of bringing the dialectic of veiling and unveiling into the very heart of Christology. Jesus Christ is himself event, himself the primordial act of God. The Catholic or Lutheran critic may wonder if this is a good way to interpret John 1:14, which after all says that the Word 'became' (ἐγένετο) not 'becomes' flesh. Barth will ask whether the completed character of the incarnation permits us to treat it as an ordinary historical fact, a datum of experience that we might comprehend, rather than God's startling intrusion into human life.

The mystery of the incarnation thus has the character of all mystery: it exceeds human comprehension. The sign of this incomprehensibility is the miracle of Jesus' conception by the Holy Spirit and birth of the Virgin Mary ('The Miracle of Christmas', §15.3). Here again, Barth seems to delight in affirming a dogma dismissed by modern Protestants as being superstitious (perhaps because, somewhat embarrassingly, it implies a nature miracle) or at any rate as non-essential. Barth retrieves the dogma, while at the same time seeking to find the proper place and weighting for it within theology. The Virgin Birth is not the mystery, the gift of God; Jesus Christ is. But the church has found it cannot tell his story rightly without taking seriously the miraculous character of his birth. Negatively, the miracle consists in the exclusion of human (and specifically male) agency in the incarnation. Positively, it consists in the no less astonishing fact that God has acted – and that his action evokes a glad human 'Yes' in the person of Mary:

> The virginity of Mary in the birth of the Lord is the denial, not of man in the presence of God, but of any power, attribute, or capacity in him for God. If he has this power – and Mary clearly has it – it means strictly and exclusively that he acquires it, that it is laid upon him. In this power of his for God he can as little understand himself as Mary in the story of the Annunciation could understand herself as the future mother of the Messiah. Only with her *Ecce ancilla Domini* ['behold the handmaid of the Lord'] can he understand himself as what, in a way inconceivable to himself, he has actually become in the sight of God and by His agency. (I/2, 188)

There is an important hermeneutical point at stake here as well. Barth argues that when we read Scripture, we need to consider the unity between form and content, between the human witness of the prophets and apostles and the God to whom they bear witness. Because we can distinguish these, we are free to engage in a certain amount of 'demythologizing'. Barth does not think we place ourselves outside the bounds of Christian faith if we question whether Elijah made an axe head float on the water, or whether the gospels always present a pure, unvarnished version of the events concerning Jesus. What matters is the overall shape and pattern of the text as a witness to the Word of God, not precise 'correspondence' to the historical.

On the other hand, we must not press the distinction between form and content too far. Precisely because the Bible *is* a form of the Word of God, we are commanded to seek this Word in the richly textured, contingent character of the world it describes, and not by seeking some direct means of access to the truth (via experience, historical inquiry, and so forth). Angels, demons, floating axe heads, and virgin births may not themselves be revelation, but neither is there revelation apart from things. Nor should the Enlightenment conviction that miracles violate 'scientific' understanding place undue constraints on our reading of the text. Our primary goal in reading is to understand Scripture as a unified witness to Jesus Christ. How this witness then relates to the so-called modern worldview is an interesting question, but it can never be answered once for all, and it is not the theologian's primary task in any case.

Word and Spirit: Pneumatology

God is revealed to us in Jesus Christ – the mystery of Easter. God is hidden even in the midst of his revelation – the mystery of Good Friday. Now we come to the third moment in the triad, for the God revealed in the midst of hiddenness is also acknowledged by human beings. Revelation is complete with Pentecost, the eschatological outpouring of the Holy Spirit.

The first thing that needs to be said about Barth's doctrine of the Spirit is that he has one. Insisting as he does on the utter objectivity of the Word, he has often been charged with ignoring the hearer of the Word, the human subject. The charge is misplaced.[10] The *Church Dogmatics* is replete with rich, evocative descriptions of human life under grace. Moreover, a little reflection will show why Barth's project requires him to take the transformative aspect of revelation seriously. If the Word remains locked in mute objectivity, then the divine speech act 'misfires', and God's lordship itself is called into question. Barth's quarrel with his liberal predecessors was never with their assertion that human beings stand in an active, knowing relation to God. It is not even with whether human beings are capable of God: Barth says of Mary that she 'clearly has' the power to receive the message of the Annunciation, and the same holds true of anyone who receives the Word in faith. Rather, the question is on what grounds one makes statements like this. Unlike most modern theologians, Barth refuses to privilege any static, structural aspect of human existence as the point of contact for revelation. Rather than appeal to anthropology, he directs us once again to the Trinity. The Word of God is a trinitarian event, and we are participants in it by virtue of the Holy Spirit, who is the 'subjective reality' of revelation and therefore its 'subjective possibility' as well. Only the Spirit can set us free for God – but the Spirit really does set us free (para. 16, 'The Freedom of Man for God').

Attention to Barth's pneumatology can help correct the misapprehension that there is no room for human experience in his thought. Already in I/1, we learn that the Word of God is humanly knowable, and that if this is so we must certainly affirm that it can be experienced.[11] In I/2, Barth makes the still more surprising claim that *religion* can serve as a vehicle for divine revelation. The point is unfortunately masked in the English translation, which titles paragraph 17 'The Revelation of God as the Abolition of Religion'. Barth did not write 'abolition', however, but *Aufhebung* – a complex term borrowed from Hegel, suggesting not just dissolution or suspension but elevation, reconstitution at a higher level. Viewed simply as a human activity religion is a dubious enterprise, a sign of human unbelief. This includes Christianity. Indeed, in a very real sense Christianity is the most culpable instance of religion, since it seeks to turn revelation itself into a human possession. Barth is not saying Christianity is 'better' than other religions; rather, he is making a severe judgment about the phenomenon of religion as a whole. But just as the individual sinner may be justified by faith, so the Spirit may sanctify even fallen religiosity. When Barth concludes that Christianity is, for all its flaws, the 'true religion', he makes it very clear that this is not by any inherent virtue it may possess, but solely by God's grace. Christianity – or more concretely, the church – is uniquely true among the religions because of the witness it bears; it alone directs people to the triune God.

For Barth, talk about the Spirit is never an end in itself. If the Spirit is 'the Lord and giver of life', good pneumatology should issue in descriptions of the life this Lord creates. Paragraph 18, 'The Life of the Children of God', is the first of many accounts of the Christian life that appear in the *Church Dogmatics*. In a sense, it brings revelation full circle. The doctrine of the Word is finally about God's love for the world – language Barth employs sparingly, and which is all the more telling when he does use it.[12] But to be God's adopted child means that one loves God in return.[13] The 'life of the children of God' is a life lived in love, praise, and service to the neighbour, all of which are part of the joyful witness to which Christians are called. While *CD* I does not include a formal treatment of ethics, the pneumatology in some ways offers a preview of ethical themes Barth will develop in volumes II, III, and IV.

The Church under the Word: Scripture and Dogmatics

The doctrine of revelation began, we recall, with the question about dogmatics itself: how is human speech about God possible? We now know the answer to this question. Speech about God is possible because God speaks the Word – because God is Father, Son, and Holy Spirit – because the Crucified manifested himself to his disciples at Easter. (We also know that these are all ways of saying the same thing.) Nothing gives us the confidence to proclaim other than the fact of God's being this God; but since this is who God is, we can and must proclaim.

Having established all this at massive length, Barth returns at the end of *CD* I to the question of dogmatics, approaching it now in a more practical way. What does it actually mean to pursue theology? What sort of a discipline is it? Are there particular rules, norms, and sources appropriate to this work? The last two chapters of the volume (chapter III on 'Holy Scripture' and chapter IV on 'The Proclamation of the Church') are the closest we come in the *Church Dogmatics* to an actual 'discourse on method'. While Barth is not afraid to speak of dogmatic 'method', the term should be approached with caution for two reasons. First, he never tires of reminding us that theology is not a closed, formal system of thought – which is not to say we should avoid consistency or discipline in our thinking. Barth is exquisitely systematic in terms of his overall unity of vision, and in the way he traces the interconnections among various doctrines. Nonetheless, he insists this unity should emerge from theology's subject matter rather than being arbitrarily imposed on it from without. The extent to which he himself follows this rule is, of course, for the reader to decide.

The second limit on method is the character of dogmatics as a practice of the church. The question 'How should we pursue dogmatics?' is completely abstract apart from the material question 'What is the church?' Indeed, what Barth gives us in these concluding sections of *CD* I is a preview of important themes in his ecclesiology, as a glance at the table of contents will indicate:

Chapter III – Holy Scripture
§19   The Word of God for the Church
§20   Authority in the Church
§21   Freedom in the Church
Chapter IV – The Proclamation of the Church
§22   The Mission of the Church
§23   Dogmatics as a Function of the Hearing Church
§24   Dogmatics as a Function of the Teaching Church

We might want to begin just by making some comments on this arrangement. Both Scripture and preaching are, as we have seen, forms of the Word of God, and in each case Barth begins by pointing to the divine eventfulness by which this is so: 'The Word of God is God himself in Holy Scripture' (thesis of para. 19; I/2, 743). 'The Word of God is God himself in the proclamation of the church of Jesus Christ' (thesis of para. 22; I/2, 457). These are both statements about divine action. Just so, they are statements about the church. We can go a step further and say that they are statements about the ontology of the church.[14] When God speaks today through the written word of the apostles and prophets, the church as a human community becomes what it is destined to be in the Spirit: a witness to Jesus Christ. Scripture is a testimony to Jesus Christ (the objective aspect of revelation) but it likewise fulfils its destiny only in the living activity of proclamation, animated by the Holy Spirit (the subjective aspect of revelation). This is one unified event, the-Spirit-testifying-to-Jesus-through-Scripture-and-proclamation, and it is the event in which the church lives and moves and has its being.

Barth has been strongly influenced by the Reformation understanding of the church as *creatura verbi*, a 'creation of the Word'. He advocates a vision of a community living in radical dependence on the written Word, continually testing its witness by this norm. Does this mean he construes authority in the church as *sola scriptura*, 'by Scripture alone'? In an ultimate sense, yes; there is no norm that stands above the attestation of Christ in Scripture, as the Barmen Declaration makes clear. Christ's authority implies biblical authority. At the same time, Barth is happy to acknowledge that while final authority resides in Scripture, this is not to the exclusion of other valid forms of authority. A 'naked' *sola scriptura* would be naive and self-deceiving (we never interpret the Bible in a vacuum) and would moreover evidence a lack of trust in the Spirit's guidance. Barth thus acknowledges that the church exercises a genuine, mediate authority of its own, embodied in such norms as canon, creeds, and confessions of faith. In this way the church participates indirectly in the authority of the Word itself.

And yet there are limits to the church's authority. Not only must the community always be open to correction by the Word of God; but in order to be that, it must not be overly bound by its own past. Even the early church's fixing of the canon of Scripture, Barth argues, must in principle be considered open to review. The Spirit might lead the world-wide church today to a different insight about the contents of the canon – though it is hard to imagine how agreement on this could ever be reached. In practice, Barth has a conservative view of the canon: these texts and these texts only serve as authoritative witnesses to Jesus Christ. The point he is making is a conceptual one: that the relative fixity of the canon does not represent a 'binding' of God to human decisions, but bears witness to the freedom of God's grace. And what applies to the canon applies even more strongly to later creeds, dogmas, and doctrines. For Barth church confessions do indeed achieve closure, establishing the boundary between faith and unbelief in particular historical moments. Moreover, he is willing to concede that confessions speak beyond their own time; the authority of texts like the Apostles' Creed or the Heidelberg Confession is attested by their fruitfulness in the church. Nonetheless, he seemed to think of such documents as a kind of self-consuming artifact. In so far as they bear genuine witness to Christ, they remind us of their own inadequacy:

> The *infallible* and thus unsurpassable and unalterable confession is the praise, that the church as the body eternally united with its head will present to its Lord in her own eternal perfection; it is therefore an eschatological concept, which corresponds to no realization in the here and now, to which all reality of church confession, all that we now know as dogma old or new, can only hasten. What we know as dogma is in principle *fallible* and therefore surpassable and alterable.[15]

This eschatological resistance to closure bears the marks of Barth's early study under Wilhelm Herrmann, who, we recall, posed a radical distinction between true religion and mere doctrines. The status of dogma and magisterial teaching continues to be an issue in dialogue between Rome and other Christian confessions. I will return to the question of the church's relation to the Word of God at the end of the chapter.

The counterpart of authority is freedom (para. 21, 'Freedom in the Church'). As we might expect, the church's freedom consists first of all in 'the freedom of the Word', the power of God at work through the biblical witness. Genuine freedom is a divine gift. But it is also a 'freedom under the Word', a human process of interpretation involving *explicatio* (clarifying the sense of the text), *meditatio* (theological reflection on the text), and *applicatio* (the application or use of the text in the life of the church). Barth's goal here is not to lay out a sequential method for reading Scripture, but to describe moments within a single, complex act of interpretation. Barth is emphatic that all members of the church are responsible for interpreting the Bible. The community that hands this task over to the biblical scholars is being slothful and immature, and just so unfaithful to Christ (I/2, 715). The picture Barth presents is that of a highly participatory local church, engaged in the task of hearing and interpreting the Word of God. Later volumes of the *Dogmatics* make clear that it is the congregation (*Gemeinde*) that stands at the heart of his ecclesiology.

It is against this background that Barth sets forth, finally, his understanding of dogmatics itself. What is the task of the theologian? It is no different from the task of the Christian preacher: the search for 'pure doctrine'. 'Doctrine' (*doctrina*) here means not the generating of theories, but concrete teaching intended to shape people's hearts and minds so that they may hear the Word of God. It represents a kind of disciplining of the Christian community with respect to the Word. Because it involves the orientation of the whole person to God, doctrine cannot be separated from the question of the Christian life, i.e. ethics (I/2, 782 ff.). Dogmatics is simply a formalized version of the church's ongoing search for clarity in its *doctrina*. Barth assumes that the church is often unclear about these matters. We constantly confuse the gospel with all manner of ideology, fantasy, and human self-will; dogmatics seeks to correct these tendencies by disciplining its thinking in light of revelation. It stands midway between the hearing church (the church in its receptive orientation toward the Word, paragraph 23) and the teaching church (the church in its active role as proclaimer of the gospel, paragraph 24). These are of course but the one Church, in its dual role as recipient of and witness to revelation.

Yet while dogmatics is a critical enterprise, it must not be thought of as primarily negative, much less an exercise in heresy-hunting. It stands in solidarity with the church, directing the church to the divine gift that stands at the heart of its life. The first thing the church ought to hear from the dogmatic theologian, Barth writes, is 'not a reminder of all the dangers to which it is exposed, but of the fact that without any merit or value of its own it is in good hands and therefore on the right road' (I/2, 809, trans. rev.). Or, as he would write thirty years later in *Evangelical Theology*, theology oriented toward the gospel 'can be nothing else but the most thankful and joyful science!'[16]

Barth in Dialogue: George Lindbeck on Religion, Language, and Culture

One of the more striking features of Barth's thought is his insistence on the radical priority of revelation as a source of Christian knowledge. There can be no two-source theory of revelation – the fatal 'and' by which the German Christians, for example, sought to link the Bible with Nazi ideology. And because revelation comes first, theology must maintain its independence in relation to other accounts of the real: philosophical, cultural, or experiential. As the church must look to Jesus Christ alone for salvation, so theology must take the form of a disciplined inquiry into the canonical testimony concerning him. It is in constantly testing and reappropriating the church's doctrine in light of Scripture that theology fulfils its specific task.

Among the standard criticisms of Barth is that his determined focus on revelation leads him into the swamps of irrationalism and fideism. Can theology truly be rational if it dispenses with norms available to any inquirer? Is not any appeal to revelation an admission that religion is in the end a private affair, and that Christianity must abandon all claims to truth? Such charges have been levelled by many critics and in many ways. Nonetheless, Barth certainly did not think he was being fideistic. It is striking to observe how consistently Barth returns to the theme of the essential rationality of the theological enterprise. His respect for the achievements of the Fathers and the scholastics – as well as Kant and Hegel! – was too strong for him to despise the use of concepts. Asked by a young Canadian student to describe the role of reason in his theology, he replied testily, 'I use it!'[17] More expansively, he shared these thoughts with a group of students:

> Concerning *reason*, I want to say this: I will have nothing to do with the distrust of reason. I have great trust in reason. I am not a rationalist, but I believe that the [sic] reason is a good gift of God and that we must make full use of it in theology. This is our praise of God, who has given us this gift to distinguish that two and two equals four instead of five. That is my rationalism! Some people want to make reason the abstract judge of all – and that is unreasonable![18]

In the early years of the twenty-first century, we have become familiar with the claim that knowledge does not have to be infallibly grounded to count as knowledge (reason as 'abstract judge of all'), and even that all significant thinking occurs inside a tradition. To be sure, one cannot simply appeal to postmodernism as an easy answer to questions about the truth of Christianity; Barth himself would be distinctly unhappy with such a move. Yet there are aspects of his theological practice that bear at least a surface resemblance to some form of postmodern and 'postliberal' theology. The parallels are striking enough to invite a comparison.

In the remainder of this chapter, we will examine the relation between Barth's thought and that of a particularly influential postliberal thinker: George Lindbeck, a Lutheran living and working in the United States. The advantage of this comparison is precisely that Lindbeck is not a philosopher, but a Christian theologian and historian of doctrine. While his speciality runs toward historical and ecumenical theology rather than dogmatics, he is nonetheless engaged in the same enterprise Barth is: seeking the reason implicit in Christian faith. Moreover, Lindbeck's best-known book, *The Nature of Doctrine*, concludes with a set of proposals on theological method

– proposals that make an indirect appeal to Barth's writings. While the book is not even a 'prolegomena to dogmatics', it does raise questions that have a direct bearing on the issues Barth deals with in *CD* I.

Like Barth, Lindbeck assumes that Christian theology is done in and for the church. More concretely, we can name three specific ecclesial contexts in which his work must be understood: (1) the Lutheran tradition, especially as defined by the Lutheran confessions of the sixteenth century; (2) the ecumenical movement – Lindbeck was an official Protestant observer at Vatican II, and was for years intensively engaged in Lutheran–Roman Catholic dialogue; (3) more broadly, Christian churches as they confront the challenge of living in a modern, post-Christian world, without benefit of the institutions of European Christendom. Lindbeck's own experience of growing up in a non-Christian culture (his parents were Lutheran missionaries in China in the years leading up to World War Two) was a key factor shaping his imagination on this last point.

The three ecclesial contexts I have named interact in complex ways. Thus, Lindbeck's understanding of what it means to be Lutheran is already ecumenical, in so far as he interprets the Lutheran confessions to be essentially irenic documents. Justification by faith was not intended to be a new doctrine, but a confirmation of the faith found in the ancient trinitarian and Christological creeds (given a prominent place in the Augsburg Confession). While Luther himself came to see the Papacy as the Antichrist, the founding *texts* of Lutheranism are by no means as pessimistic about unity with Rome. This 'evangelically catholic' reading of Lutheranism – indebted to theologians like Peter Brunner and Arthur Piepkorn – is clearly one that lends itself to a passion for Christian unity. Likewise, the church's diasporic existence in a post-Christendom world makes the question of her unity all the more pressing. If Christians are to present a credible witness to Jesus Christ, they have no choice but to try to overcome their division; hence the modern ecumenical movement had its roots in the Protestant missionary enterprise, where the scandal of disunity was painfully apparent. The classic ecumenism of the 'Faith and Order' movement is an expression of this spirit; it is the enterprise to which Lindbeck devoted much of his working life.

The three contexts examined help to underscore a further point. When Lindbeck says 'church', he always means concrete, empirically visible communities. This is true whether we are speaking of Pauline house churches, the monarchical episcopate of the fourth century, or the church in a Chinese mission compound. The notion of the church's visibility is deeply ingrained in Lindbeck's imagination. As a result, he has little difficulty making the shift to categories of sociology or cultural anthropology. For Lindbeck, there is a sense in which the church is simply a 'given' for thought. Here his philosophical and theological interests converge, for philosophically he shows debts to Aristotle and to Wittgenstein – each of them a highly 'material' thinker in his own way – while theologically he is a catholic Lutheran: the Word of God and its concrete expression in worship, word and sacrament belong together.

We need to make one last ecclesiological remark before moving on to questions of language and theological rationality. For Lindbeck, part of what it means to 'begin with the church' is to take the church seriously as a *culture* – in the terms Clifford Geertz has made famous, a 'semiotic system' marked by distinctive language, stories, rituals, and implicit understandings.[19] To be formed in a culture means knowing how to negotiate the complexities of everyday life using the semiotic tools at one's disposal. When the sign in front of me says STOP, I know to put my foot on the brake without having to think about it; the understanding comes with my immersion in this culture and its 'forms of life', to use Wittgenstein's phrase. The deeper one's immersion in a culture, the more expansive and subtle are the possibilities of communication within it. Being able to negotiate rush hour traffic by heeding signs and stop lights is one level of cultural understanding; debating politics, reading a Barbara Pym novel, or listening to a Mozart opera are considerably more demanding forms. Yet in whatever setting, the human being seems to be a cultural being 'all the way down'.

Lindbeck's project in *The Nature of Doctrine* is to explore the ramifications of religion as a culture – a semiotic system that not only helps us negotiate our way through the world, but that in a crucial sense *gives* us a world. Religions do what cultures in a more general sense do: endow our experience with structure and meaning. What sets them apart from other cultural expressions is that they perform this task on a cosmic scale. A religion, Lindbeck writes,

> ... is not primarily an array of beliefs about the true and the good (though it may involve these), or a symbolism expressive of basic attitudes, feelings, or sentiments (though these will be generated). ... Like a culture or language, it is a communal phenomenon that shapes the subjectivity of individuals rather than being primarily a manifestation of those subjectivities. It comprises a vocabulary of discursive and nondiscursive symbols together with a distinctive logic or grammar in terms of which this vocabulary can meaningfully be deployed. Lastly, just as a language ... is correlated with a form of life, and just as a culture has both cognitive and behavioral dimensions, so it is also in the case of a religious tradition. Its doctrines, cosmic stories or myths, and ethical directives are integrally related to the rituals it practices, the sentiments or experiences it evokes, the actions it recommends, and the institutional forms it develops.[20]

As the first line in the above quotation suggests, Lindbeck argues for the superiority of this cultural–linguistic picture over two other influential models of religion. The cognitivist model stresses the ways in which religious doctrines 'function as informative propositions', i.e. as statements of fact; thus, 'God is three persons in one nature' is analogous to sentences like 'Water boils at 100° C' or 'Germany invaded Poland on 1 September, 1939.' The strength of this model is its concern for matters of truth; its weakness is its intellectualism, and the fact that it is so far removed from the lived experience of religious life. This is not a problem with the experiential model, which stresses the priority of personal experience over doctrines: for the experientialist, a confession such as 'Christ is Lord!' helps articulate a pre-linguistic apprehension of the transcendent as mediated by Jesus. Weaknesses of this model are that it is deeply private, and that the very notion of 'pre-linguistic experience' has been roundly criticized by the philosophers. It also seems to have a hard time accounting for religious communities' claims that their teachings reflect 'the way things are' – beyond the vagaries of individual experience.[21]

But even if the cultural-linguistic model offers a superior account of religion, what makes it so important for Christian theology? One can easily imagine Barth's rising frustration as he worked his way through Lindbeck's *The Nature of Doctrine* (heaven's theological library being well-stocked). A great deal of the book has to do with how human beings construct meaning so as to make sense of their world. Religion as embodied in myths, rituals, and cosmic stories? Culture as an interpretive scheme for organizing experience, not unlike the *a priori* in Kant's theory of knowledge? If Barth were to read Lindbeck, I suspect he would focus not so much on questions of truth or religious relativism – central issues in the critical literature generated by Lindbeck's work – but on the conceptual centrality of the term *religion* itself. Is Lindbeck really proposing that an analysis of how religions 'work' can serve as an adequate basis for a Christian theology? Is he not in danger of replacing the liberal starting-point in individual experience with a new foundation in language and culture? In short, where is *God* in all this? Where is the triune revelation that takes priority over all things human, including the incurable human penchant for religious meaning?

These imagined Barthian challenges point up a major ambiguity in *The Nature of Doctrine*. Does the work propose to offer general theory of religion? Or is it a work of constructive Christian theology, making use of 'religious studies' categories only in service of theological ends? A careful reading of the text suggests that the latter is Lindbeck's intention. Indeed, the book is unintelligible apart from the theological interests that guide it – specifically, Lindbeck's ecumenical agenda of explaining how the doctrines of divided churches can converge while somehow remaining the same. Nonetheless, the book as it stands is a curious hybrid. *The Nature of Doctrine* is unmistakeably the work of a Christian theologian with strong views about how theology can and ought to be done; yet it stops short of being an actual performance within Christian theology.

Yet while Lindbeck remains oddly formalistic with regard to his own proposal, we need not be. A constructive theological reading of the text is possible. Consider a passage like the following:

> To become a Christian involves learning the story of Israel and of Jesus well
> enough to interpret and experience oneself and one's world in its terms. To

become a Christian involves learning the story of Israel and of Jesus well enough to interpret and experience oneself and one's world in its terms. A religion is above all an external word, a *verbum externum*, that molds and shapes the self and its world, rather than an expression or thematization of a preexisting self or of preconceptual experience. The *verbum internum* (traditionally equated by Christians with the act of the Holy Spirit) is also crucially important, but it would be understood in a theological use of the model as a capacity for hearing and accepting the true religion, the true external word, rather than ... as a common experience diversely articulated in different religions. (34)

The language of *verbum externum* and *verbum internum* places us squarely in the midst of medieval and Reformation debates about the mediation of grace. Luther ultimately found the assurance he needed not through introspection, but by turning to the *verbum externum* of the gospel – Christ available in the preached Word and the sacraments. In a sense, Lindbeck is simply seeking to replicate this turn in contemporary theology. Liberal theologies have, by and large, embraced an apologetic strategy of the *verbum internum*, appealing to our experience of a 'preexisting self or ... preconceptual experience'. Lindbeck not only finds this strategy philosophically unpersuasive – he doubts whether any such experience is possible – but more important, he finds it theologically reductive in the long run. The Christ who encounters us in the preached Word is Jesus the Jew, an agent in a particular story; his identity as rendered in canonical Scripture may be replaced by no other.

One feature that makes *The Nature of Doctrine* comparable with *Church Dogmatics* I/1 is that both make proposals about the use of Scripture in the church. For both Barth and Lindbeck, Scripture plays an essential and central role in the Christian life. Nonetheless, there is an important difference in emphasis. For Barth, what Scripture chiefly does is authorize proclamation: the act of preaching is the paradigmatic 'event' in which God communicates himself to us by his Word. Scripture and preaching are both forms of the Word of God, but only as they participate in the Word itself: Jesus Christ as God's self-revelation. Or to put it differently, they 'are' the Word of God only in so far as they also 'become' it. Barth thus honours the finite forms of the *verbum externum*, but constantly qualifies it by his Christocentric actualism.

Lindbeck has a rather different way of thinking about the Bible's role in the church. If Christianity is a semiotic system, then its normative 'code' is contained in the texts known as Holy Scripture – indeed, this is a formal feature of all the world-historical religions. Scripture is important not simply because it contains the information needed to be saved – the reductive cognitive account. Rather, it shapes our imaginations, giving us a set of categories by which to interpret ourselves and the world. And it does this in an almost imperial way, creating its own privileged domain of meaning. In words that have become indelibly associated with his thought, Lindbeck writes that 'a scriptural world is thus able to absorb the universe', supplying 'the interpretive framework within which believers seek to live their lives and understand reality' (117). It is not that the Bible needs to be brought into line with some external, fixed point of reference, such as religious experience or the structures of reason. On the contrary, reason, experience, and all else are to be subsumed under the 'strange new world within the Bible' – a phrase Lindbeck happily borrows from Barth – such that believers actually come to inhabit that world.

We have seen that in Barth's theology, the paradigm instance of Scripture's use is the event of preaching. Perhaps we could say that for Lindbeck it is the activity of catechesis – which, of course, has classically included instruction by sermons.[22] It is no accident that Lindbeck emphasizes *becoming* a Christian, learning to tell the stories of Israel and Jesus in such a way that they shape one's whole life. Such a concern is certainly not foreign to Barth's thought. In a well-known passage in IV/2, he recalled the Sunday school instruction he had received as a child, and how the songs composed by Pastor Abel Burckhardt rendered the biblical stories as 'things which might take place any day in Basel or its environs like any other important happenings' (IV/2, 112). The goal of theology is not theorizing, but Christian witness. There is indeed something of what Lindbeck calls 'intratextuality' in Barth's practice of dogmatics, a teaching and imparting of the skills needed to be a Christian through intensive immersion in the biblical world. It is worth recalling that in 1924 Barth named his first offical course of lectures 'Instruction in the Christian Religion'.[23] The title recalls that Calvin's *Insitutes*. While the label was ironically intended – the Lutheran faculty at Göttingen had forbidden Barth from advertising lectures in dogmatics – it nonetheless rings true. What else is the *Church Dogmatics* than a wide-ranging 'intratextual' exploration of the Christian religion?

However, Barth would certainly have raised two large objections to Lindbeck's project. The first has to do with the role of the church. Lindbeck implies, though he does not quite say, that formation in the language and practices of the church itself imparts grace or knowledge of God to the believer – not apart from faith, of course, but as a medium in which faith is received. That is, Lindbeck has an implicitly Catholic account of sacramental mediation. The *verbum externum* is not simply the mandated occasion for attending to the gospel Word, but is indirectly identical with it. Even if Barth held such a view in the 1930s, he moved away from it in later years, as can be seen in his discomfort with the notion of sacraments. He would have resisted any picture in which God's action and the church's action coincide; the church never 'has' God in advance, but can only pray for God to act – *veni Creator Spiritus!* By contrast, more sacramentally-minded Christians – Roman Catholics, Orthodox, and Anglicans among them – would deny that claims about ecclesial mediation set limits on the freedom or graciousness of God. The God who is wholly other may be said to confirm his freedom precisely in making himself available to us in the external means; nor is the church ever called to assert its own claims over against God, but humbly acknowledges the grace that has come to both the community and the world.

It could be argued that a properly 'thick' account of baptism and eucharist serves to guard against any valorizing of communal autonomy. One can imagine a vigorous debate among Catholics, Evangelicals, and Evangelical Catholics on just this issue.

But I suspect that most of Barth's ire would be directed not at Lindbeck's views on sacraments, but at the ambiguity that plagues the whole cultural–linguistic proposal. Is it merely a descriptive enterprise, an attempt to read the semiotic code that is Christianity? If so, then it is either entirely non-theological or (what is far worse) a theological account that sees 'the Christian religion' as a self-sustaining system, in which God or ultimate meaning is simply immanent. Without an account of God's prior action, the system of encoded human performance simply collapses in on itself. In the end, something like an account of revelation is needed to display how the human activity of interpreting Scripture is a response to God's action towards us. To use a very old-fashioned term, postliberal theology desperately needs an account of 'prevenient grace'.

Here we may return to the Reformers' notion of the *verbum externum*. It is true that Luther and Calvin saw this *verbum* embodied in word and sacrament. But the *verbum* also has a determinate content: the Word of God that is Jesus Christ. I suspect Lindbeck's program of catechetical theology might have intrigued Barth (both theologians share an interest in the fate of Christianity in a post-Christian world). But he would have assented to it only in so far as this theology actually takes the risk of being theological, of making actual assertions about God. A strength of postliberal theology is its conviction that the church's gospel is not reducible to generic religious experience. One of its weaknesses is that it is often tempted to substitute talk about the church and about Christian practices for God himself.[25] In the next chapter, we will examine how Barth averts this problem, as he moves on from his doctrine of revelation and the Trinity to an even more determinate set of claims about God.

Notes

1 J. Louis Martyn, *Galatians: A New Translation with Introduction and Commentary* (New York: Doubleday, 1997), 22; see also Martyn's discussion of Galatians 1:10–12.

2 *CD* I/1, 135.

3 See Barth's 1920 essay 'Ludwig Feuerbach', in *Theology and Church*, as well as the lecture that appears in his *Protestant Theology in the Nineteenth Century*.

4 Busch, *Life*, 91.

5 Luther, *Fastenpostille*, 1525, *W.A.* 17.11, 178. Cited in *CD* I/1, 49.

6 The classic work is J. L. Austin's *How To Do Things With Words* (Cambridge, MA: Harvard University Press, 1960).

7 Austin Farrer, *The Glass of Vision* (Westminster: Dacre Press, 1948), 8.

8 In the preface to the new (1975) translation of *CD* I/1, Thomas Torrance notes that the term *Seinsweise* might be better rendered as 'way of being' than as 'mode of being', the translation that appears in the text. 'Mode of being' unfortunately suggests 'modalism', i.e. the view that the threeness in God is merely an appearance. Barth is emphatically not

a modalist.

9   John Webster, *Barth* (London and New York: Continuum, 2000), 62.

10   See my book *Karl Barth on the Christian Life: The Practical Knowledge of God* (New York and Frankfurt a.M.: Peter Lang, 2001), for an extended refutation of the claim that Barth ignores human agency and affectivity.

11   See para. 6, 'The Knowability of the Word of God', and especially the section titled 'The Word of God and Experience'.

12   See, for example, I/1, 409 ff.

13   See especially §18.2, 'The Love of God'.

14   This actualist approach to ecclesiology has been the subject of much criticism. I will discuss the point further in chapter 6, below.

15   *KD* I/1, 737, present author's translation; cf. CD I/2, 657.

16   Barth, *Evangelical Theology: An Introduction*, 12.

17   See Barth, *Briefe 1961–1968*, eds Jürgen Fangmeier and Heinrich Stoevesandt (Zürich: Theologischer Verlag, 1975), 474; *Letters 1961–1968*, trans. Geoffrey W. Bromiley (Grand Rapids: Eerdmans, 1981), 294.

18   *Karl Barth's Table Talk*, ed. John D. Godsey (Edinburgh: Oliver and Boyd, 1963), 31, emphasis in original.

19   Clifford Geertz, *The Interpretation of Cultures: Selected Essays* (New York: Basic Books, 1973).

20   George A. Lindbeck, *The Nature of Doctrine: Religion and Theology in a Post* (Philadelphia: Westminster Press, 1984), 33. Subsequent references will be given in the text.

21   It is important to see that Lindbeck does not reject the claims of either truth or experience as crucial aspects of religion; he simply thinks the cultural–linguistic model can better accommodate these concerns than can its alternatives. See *Nature of Doctrine*, 34 ff.

22   Reinhard Hütter argues that as soon as one reads Lindbeck's postliberal project as normative theology, it ceases to be cultural ethnology, i.e. a mere description of Christian religious practice. Instead, the valid analogy is with catechesis: 'Lindbeck's postliberal method sooner resembles the catechesis of the early church: first a person is attracted by the witness of Christianity ... [and] is then socialized into this world by learning the configurations of language and action; and understands (learns) faith ever anew and ever more deeply by participating in its poietic pathos.' Hütter, *Suffering Divine Things* (Grand Rapids: Eerdmans, 2000), 62.

23   See Busch, *Life*, 155.

24   See Lindbeck's essay 'Barth and Textuality', *Theology Today* 43 (3), 1986.

25   Lindbeck's own thinking since *The Nature of Doctrine* has moved in the direction of an 'Israelology' – a constructive account of the church as people of God, more in continuity than in discontinuity with Israel. Clearly this theme cannot be treated while bracketing divine action! See 'Confession and Community: An Israel-like View of the Church', as well as the preface to the German edition of *The Nature of Doctrine*, found in Lindbeck, *The Church in a Postliberal Age*, ed. James J. Buckley (Grand Rapids: Eerdmans, 2002).

Chapter 3

Lord of the Covenant: God

Barth's doctrine of election [functions] as revelation: election reveals God, God's plan and mercy, not human decisions or salvation. Of course, human actors take part in this drama – 'the believing and disbelieving Jews' – but its Subject is God; God alone, his will, his wrath, and long-suffering mercy.[1]
– Katherine Sonderegger

If this letter reaches you in time, please try to get me something good to read over Christmas … And if you can get without difficulty Barth's *Doctrine of Predestination* (in sheets), or his *Doctrine of God*, please have them sent to me.[2]
– Dietrich Bonhoeffer, writing from prison in 1943

A 'Condescension Inconceivably Tender'

In *Church Dogmatics* I Barth argues that theology has no other basis than God's self-revelation as Father, Son, and Holy Spirit. Since the doctrine of revelation is materially already a doctrine of the Trinity, one might wonder if an explicit 'doctrine of God' is really needed. Barth has two good reasons for including such a doctrine. First, while the identity between God and his revelation is the first thing to be said about God, it is by no means the only thing. God not only reveals himself, God is; God's being can be known and understood. Indeed, discovering what it means to affirm that 'God is' is central to the whole enterprise of dogmatics. The doctrine of God is simply the place where we try to give an explicit account of that affirmation.

A second reason for the doctrine is the inherited agenda of questions Barth received from his predecessors. Beginning with the Church Fathers, and continuing through the medieval and Protestant scholastics, theologians had always wrestled with the question of the divine nature. Even when Barth thought he must depart from this tradition, he held it in high regard. He seemed to take special delight in the classical doctrines concerning God's being and attributes. Perhaps this is because these doctrines underscore the fact that God is fascinating and compelling for his own sake: God is of interest not because he is useful to us, but because God is supremely good, and true and indeed beautiful. These are conviction Barth shared with Christian thinkers such as Augustine and Jonathan Edwards.

Church Dogmatics II is divided into two substantial parts, related roughly as follows. *CD* II/1 offers an account of God as agent, 'the One who loves in freedom', whose being is identical with his activity; this part culminates in a discussion of the divine attributes or 'perfections'. *CD* II/2 goes on to explore a specific action performed by this agent – the act of electing grace; this part corresponds to older theological treatments of predestination, although Barth's departures from the tradition at this point are notable. Taken together, the two parts provide something like a 'character sketch' of the biblical God in relation to his human covenant partner. The God portrayed here is clearly no passionless Greek divinity, but the God of Abraham, Isaac, and Jacob, a God deeply and carnally involved in the finite world – 'the living God'.

Thomas Aquinas said that among the most apt names of God is 'He Who Is'.[3] Barth's doctrine is perhaps better captured in the title 'He Who Chooses' or 'He Who Elects'. The biblical God relentlessly separates light from darkness, good from evil, order from chaos. Compared with the actions of this God, the actions of human beings are distinctly secondary – though they do matter; it is no accident that Barth's doctrine of God concludes with a chapter on ethics! Yet while God calls forth genuine human action, he is in no way constrained by it. God is joyfully and utterly free. The freedom of God is no abstract power of choice, but a concrete freedom, a freedom with a definite content. Faithfulness to the biblical witness means tracing the way God himself has chosen.

And what has God chosen? To be completely and without reserve God for us in Jesus Christ. Thus the doctrine of election opens with this affirmation, among Barth's most famous:

> The doctrine of election is the sum of the gospel because of all words that can be said or heard it is the best: that God loves man; that God is for man too the One who loves in freedom. It is grounded in the knowledge of Jesus Christ because he is both the electing God and elected man in one. It is part of the doctrine of God because originally God's election of man is a predestination not merely of man but of himself. Its function is to bear basic testimony to eternal, free and unchanging grace as the beginning of all the ways and works of God. (II/2, 3)

God did not *have* to pour his grace out upon the world. Yet whatever might have been, the world we inhabit is one in which God has chosen to exercise his freedom in this specific way, entering into covenant fellowship with lost and sinful human beings. This 'condescension inconceivably tender', as Barth calls it – *eine unfassbar milde Herablassung* – shows us a God who not only loves his creatures, but is willing to pay the price such love entails (II/2, 121). This is the grace of which the gospel speaks. And it comes at the very beginning of the story, not as a hurried postscript at the end.

Barth's basic move in the doctrine of God is thus to affirm God's utter, sovereign priority over human beings – a sovereignty concretely determined as grace or covenant fellowship. Barth secures this picture of God in many ways. It comes partly through a constant recourse to the biblical witness (especially the case in II/2, with its long, sweeping exegetical excursus) and partly through techniques of dialectical description (especially evident in II/1, where the notions 'love' and 'freedom' constantly interpret one another). It is secured above all by a relentless Christological concentration. It is in *Jesus Christ* that God's love and freedom cohere. It is *Jesus Christ* who makes divine election good news, rather than a source of anxious worry. The resulting portrayal could never be mistaken for a god of the philosophers; the God of the gospel is the God who became flesh for our sake, in Jesus the Jew.

That last phrase is fraught with significance. The intensely biblical character of Barth's doctrine of God means that it is not merely Christocentric, but deeply rooted in the soil of the Old Testament. Stated simply, Barth discovered that he could not narrate God's identity without also speaking of the people Israel – not excluding European Jews under the Third Reich. Barth's identification of the triune God with the God of Israel, is among his most important legacies for contemporary Christian theology. We will return to this legacy in the last section of the chapter.

Grace as Knowledge

The doctrine of God, we have said, is about the being and action of God himself. It may therefore be surprising to learn that *CD* II/1 opens with an inquiry into the knowledge of God – a topic that would seem to belong to the doctrine of revelation. Yet Barth's beginning here is quite intentional. Once again, he seeks to remind us that God is not at our disposal. To talk about human knowledge of God (and there must be such knowledge, if the gospel is true) is to talk about the miracle by which God grants us knowledge of himself. As a corollary to this, Barth here offers his most extensive analysis of why natural theology is wrong – not just a theological mistake, but the very essence of unbelief. The discussion constitutes one of the great set-pieces in the entire *Church Dogmatics*.

In paragraph 25 Barth speaks of 'the fulfilment of the knowledge of God' by the Holy Spirit, describing its content as 'the existence of him whom we must fear above all things because we may love him above all things; who remains a mystery to us because he himself has made himself so clear and certain to us' (II/1, 3). The word 'fulfilment' or *Vollzug* suggests an action carried to completion. In typical fashion, we begin by analysing a gracious reality – God is known, God comes within the horizon of the creature's language and concepts – before going on to ask how such knowledge is possible. Barth denies that he is committing himself to any particular theory of knowledge; he is not offering an epistemology. God *gives* himself to be known by us. The account he offers does, however, require that a strong 'realistic' distinction be made between the knower and the known. Thus Barth finds problematic Augustine's account of the soul's mystical ascent in *Confessions* IX, beautiful as it surely is, in so far as it elides this difference

(II/1, 10–12). A relation of covenant fellowship requires otherness as well as intimacy, and God never ceases to stand over against creatures as a specific person. Such affirmations are required if we are to maintain the Bible's powerful sense of God as a historical agent who speaks, claims, promises, chastises, and shows mercy (II/1, 13).

The problem that confronts Barth as he reflects on the knowledge of God is this: how can we affirm the reality of such knowledge, while still ensuring that God remains the acting subject, always free in the relation he establishes with us? As a means of answering this question, Barth introduces the important distinction between God's primary and secondary objectivity. Primary objectivity means that God is first of all an object to himself: already in eternity, the Father knows himself as he turns to another – the Son. But this 'other' already contains a reference to humanity, given the Son's assumption of human nature as Christ. Since God graciously consents to recognize himself in this particular creature, we too are given permission to find God there. Hence to know the man Jesus is to know God – a knowledge possible only by grace, to be sure, but in grace truly so. Moreover, God's setting-apart of Jesus attaches a promise to other creaturely realities, which may likewise become means for the knowledge of God. The word 'become' is important here. For Barth, the knowledge of God is always an event, never something we can securely claim as our own possession. But when this event occurs, God becomes available to us analogically, through the words and events of creaturely reality. This is God's secondary objectivity. It is worth noting that the distinction between primary and secondary objectivity derives to a great extent from Barth's Reformed sensibilities. Distinguishing the two kinds of objectivity insures that God's presence in worldly things will always be indirect; by contrast, Catholics and Lutherans are less averse to positing a 'real presence' of God in creation – though not necessarily a saving presence, as Luther himself constantly insists. For Barth, the idea that creatures are *merely* forms of God's secondary objectivity – and even that only by God's gracious decision – is an important means of safeguarding the distinction between Creator and creature.

The concept of secondary objectivity is closely related to what was said in I/1 concerning the divine hiddenness. Even when we come to know God through human language or gesture, the creaturely medium itself always remains ambiguous; it is possible that the event of revelation will not take place, that we will simply be left with the empty image. Nonetheless, it would be wrong to think of Barth's attitude toward knowledge of God as mainly skeptical. In the church, God is known: in the man Jesus, in Israel, and the Church, indeed in any created reality that may serve as a sign of God's action. And where the word 'sign' is employed, we are not far from the notion of sacrament:

That the eternal Word as such became flesh is a unique occurrence. It happened only once. It is not therefore the starting-point for a general concept of incarnation. But its attestation through the existence of the man Jesus is a beginning of which there are continuations; a sacramental continuity stretches backwards into the existence of the people Israel, whose Messiah He is, and forward into the existence of the apostolate and the Church founded on the apostolate. The humanity of Jesus Christ as such is the first sacrament, the foundation of everything that God instituted and used in his revelation as a secondary objectivity both before and after the epiphany of Jesus Christ. (II/1, 54)

Later in life Barth would retract what he says here, arguing that the humanity of Jesus is the only 'sacrament' properly so called (see chapter 6 below). But here in II/1 he is willing to speak of Jesus as the first sacrament, the foundation of a 'sacramental continuity' reaching back into Israel and forward into the church. His locating of sacraments in the general class known as 'signs' places him squarely in the Western tradition of thinking on sacraments, initiated by Augustine and further developed by medieval and Reformation theologians. It suggests the direction in which his thought might have developed, even if he failed to follow his own lead.

We know God, then, only as he gives himself to be known: in Jesus Christ and in the sacramental attestations that point to him. And the knowledge so given is a personal knowledge: we know God as the One 'whom we must fear above all things because we may love him above all things'. The language is borrowed from Luther's *Small Catechism*, whose exposition of the ten commandments is punctuated by the refrain *Wir sollen Gott fürchten und lieben* – 'we must fear and love God'. It is important to note that for Barth, the fear of God is both real – it is an appropriate response to the one who is Lord of our life and death – and governed by a liberating permission. We *must* fear God because we *may* love him. Clearly 'fear' in this context is something quite different from an abstract religious awe or terror. What we fear is what has a final claim on us, but in faith we discover that the only final claim on us is the God who loves us, and who calls us to love him in return. If nothing else, this discussion shows the extent to which Barth's discussion of the knowledge of God is no mere epistemology!

If paragraph 25 explores the conviction that God is known, paragraph 26 addresses the question 'How is such knowledge possible?' Much of this paragraph is taken up with a sustained assault on natural theology – arguments purporting to show that there is at least some knowledge of God outside the sphere of revelation. Barth examines a number of reasons that have been given for engaging in natural theology. Some have argued that the enterprise is self-evident, or that it is a necessary tool for mission and apologetics. An argument he takes more seriously is the claim that natural theology is warranted by Scripture itself: the Psalms and Wisdom literature both suggest that the creation bears witness to its Creator, a view Paul seems to endorse in the first chapter of Romans (Romans 1:19 ff.). Nonetheless, Barth argues that even with the best of motivations, natural theology always involves a fatal concession to unbelief. To seek a neutral 'common ground' between believer and unbeliever is already to abandon the church's faith in the gospel. The reason for this is not that the believer has the knowledge of God, whereas the unbeliever does not. No one *has* the knowledge of God. Rather, the impossibility of natural theology reflects human beings' radical dependence on God's grace – a condition in which both believers and unbelievers find themselves. Thus, Barth argues that we betray our responsibilities to the unbeliever if we fail to be clear about this. Natural theology is precisely an exercise in 'bad faith', in so far as it suggests a neutral meeting ground for faith and unbelief; the actuality of God's revelation in Christ makes such a neutral meeting impossible. We cannot argue someone else into the faith. All we can do is bear witness, speaking the things of God in a language appropriate to the situation.

Readers who find themselves dissenting from this outlook are in good company. Barth's position was a minority view at the time he was writing, and it is a minority view today. Probably most Christian theologians continue to endorse some form of natural theological argumentation, if only to defeat the claims of those who say faith in God is unreasonable. Yet to speak of Barth's 'position' may be to misrepresent what he is trying to accomplish here. He is nothing if not consistent: having defined natural theology as unbelief, his analysis does not (strictly speaking) take the form of an argument against it. Ironically, mounting arguments *against* natural theology turns out to be just as much a form of natural theology as making a case on its behalf! The debate itself diverts attention from God's revelation to questions of human knowing. Thus Barth situates his engagement with natural theology entirely within a constructive account of God's gracious action. He wants to remind the reader that he is not proposing a correct method for knowing God, as an alternative to the incorrect method proposed by natural theology. There is no such method; all human discourse about God is just that – human, all too human. This limitation applies as much to the theologian who (like Barth) self-consciously begins with revelation, as to those who offer arguments for God's existence.

Barth concludes this long discussion by asking why natural theology is so persistent, why it occurs again and again in the life of the church despite the clarity of God's self-disclosure in revelation. His answer: natural theology turns out to be simply 'the vitality of man as such', asserting himself in defiance of God (II/1, 165). We can no more defeat natural theology than we can defeat our own unbelief. The answer to the problem of natural theology does not, therefore, consist in finding a method superior to it, but in acknowledging that our human unbelief is scattered and undone by God's action. Positively speaking, there exists the human being who is ready and eager to know God – Jesus Christ himself, in whom our own destiny as knowers of God is already a reality.

Barth's argument in paragraph 26 is structurally similar to other places in the *Dogmatics* where he discusses 'unreal' qualities like sin and evil – in the present context, sin in its form as unbelief. He is not saying that unbelief exists; the experience is endemic of doubt. What he is saying is that unbelief must not be systematized, assumed as a fixed principle, and so made the focus of apologetic arguments. The danger in such systematization is a double one. On the one hand, it means an effective denial of God's grace and of our own share in that grace; natural theology means taking our unbelief far too seriously. On the other hand, the attempt to undergird faith by means of arguments involves a normalizing of the gospel, as we tailor the message to meet our supposed needs. 'Viewed as the absorbing and domesticating of revelation, the triumph of natural theology in the church is quite simply the process of rendering the gospel *bourgeois*.'[4] Conversely, the subversiveness of the gospel goes hand in hand with affirming our total dependence on God's grace. If we turn to God *sola gratia* and *sola fide*, we will see that our unbelief has already been overcome in Jesus Christ, and that our calling is not to recommend ourselves to the world but to bear witness.

As I have said, Barth's principled rejection of natural theology is highly controversial. Some might argue that he has skewed the argument by the way he defines his terms. Perhaps natural theology is not a form of unbelief, a rejection of revelation, but a procedure aimed at showing how the world (even in the midst of and despite its unbelief) cannot help testifying to its Creator?[5] Moreover, it should be pointed out that even on Barth's own terms, his critique of natural theology does not entail a rejection of all apologetics. Within the *Church Dogmatics*, Barth himself is quite capable of offering *ad hoc* apologetic arguments of various sorts, sometimes historical, sometimes of a broadly cultural or experiential character. The denial of natural theology is not meant to foreclose conversation between believer and unbeliever, but to exclude the kind of conversation in which the believer has already ceded far too much in advance.

Barth's larger goal in this discussion is to reverse our persistent habit of beginning with ourselves. Focused on the question of what it means to know God, we discover in the course of reading that our own epistemic stance is of secondary importance. Knowing God makes sense only as a 'being known' (cf. Gal. 4:9; 1 Cor. 13:12). And in Jesus Christ, this 'being known' is a reality. The first thing to be learned in this doctrine is that we are insiders and not outsiders to the knowledge of God.

The One Who Loves in Freedom

As complex and engaging as it may be, Barth's inquiry into the knowledge of God is really only a ground-clearing exercise. Natural theology has been dismissed from the field. The only possible basis for our doctrine of God is the witness of Holy Scripture. But what is it that we find there? What description of God actually emerges from our reading of the biblical text?

The most drastically compressed answer to this question is to be found in the title of paragraph 28: 'The Being of God as the One Who Loves in

Freedom'. This is elucidated by the thesis statement immediately following:

> God is who he is in the act of his revelation. God seeks and creates fellowship between himself and us, and therefore he loves us. But he is this loving God without us as Father, Son, and Holy Spirit, in the freedom of the Lord, who has his life from himself. (II/1, 257)

Indeed, Barth suggests that all of dogmatics can be seen as an extended inquiry into the assertion that 'God is'. But that statement itself must not be understood in static or essentialist terms. For Barth, 'God is' means 'God acts.' His fundamental category for understanding the divine being is that of agency – the self-enactment of a person, as he or she realizes a series of intentions across time. God is personal being. But this means that God has a visible, public character; God can be described.

Here Barth rules out two tempting theological options. On the one hand, he rejects the approach that stresses soteriology – the believer's experience of the 'benefits' of salvation – at the expense of talk about the being of God. Theologians who make this move often invoke the name of Melanchthon (see II/1, 259–60), though it would seem that Kant is the more decisive figure; his restriction of reason to this-worldly matters haunts much of modern Christian thought. On the other hand, Barth insists that our account of God's being must not arise from abstract speculation, but must be grounded in the biblical witness. In particular, it must pay close attention to the decisive event in which God *enacts* his being: the life, death, and resurrection of Jesus Christ. It is important to remember that Barth sees Jesus Christ as the organizing centre of the Bible's 'God-talk', even when Jesus is not explicitly at the centre of discussion.

After our discussion of the Trinity in chapter 2, this assertion will perhaps not seem so strange. Barth does not see the meaning of the term 'God' as self-evident. The God attested in the Bible is not some vague transcendence, but the One who comes to us as judgment and salvation in the events concerning Jesus. To tell his story as God's story also requires, of course, talk about the Father as the 'whence' of his life and about the Spirit as the power of his life among us. This triune activity is what we mean when we speak of the being of God. Jesus Christ does not simply show us 'what God is like', a mere parable or symbol of the divine character. He is the very self-enactment of the divine being, God, so to speak, doing his God thing.

But if divine being consists in divine agency, what is it that God actually does? To put it differently, what is Barth's sense of the biblical narrative as a grand, Christologically-centred whole? In an initial and highly suggestive move, he argues that what God centrally does is to establish communion or fellowship (*Gemeinschaft*). This is true not only in God's saving work, but also in creation; creation 'is already a seeking and creating of fellowship' (II/1, 274). The theme of fellowship will emerge again in a powerful way when we examine the doctrine of electing grace.

But there is an even more familiar biblical term for this seeking and creating of fellowship – the word 'love'. God, Barth writes,

> does not exist in solitude but in fellowship. Therefore what he seeks and creates between himself and us is in fact nothing else but what he wills and completes and therefore is in himself ... [I]n giving us himself, he has given us every blessing. We recognize and appreciate this blessing when we describe God's being more specifically in the statement that he is the One who loves. That he is God – the Godhead of God – consists in the fact that he loves, and it is the expression of his loving that he seeks and creates fellowship with us. (II/1, 275)

'God is love', runs the familiar Johannine verse (1 John 4:8, 16). It can fairly be said that Barth seeks to instil this affirmation into the heart and marrow of his theology. The *Church Dogmatics* can be heard as one long series of riffs on the theme 'God is love'. Nonetheless, Barth is alert to the ways in which this claim has been used to underwrite the most sentimentalized and unbiblical forms of language about God. God is love, but love is not God; we must be wary of projecting our own views of love onto the divine being. To describe God as *der Liebende*, 'the One who loves', is to point to an action of which God is the subject. To understand what the phrase intends, we are forced to go back to the biblical story and see just what this agent does. This is but an application of a rule Barth laid down just a few pages earlier: that God's being subsists in God's utterly unique and underivable action; we may not derive our thinking about God from any other source (II/1, 272).

Barth begins with an idea we have already mentioned: that the specific form God's love takes is the establishing of communion between himself and creatures. God 'seeks and creates fellowship between himself and us, and in this way he loves us' (thesis for paragraph 28, rev.). This fellowship is marked by a radical inequality. God not only shares his life with those who are not God, but with those who are radically needy and unworthy. God loves human beings despite their sinful opposition to his love; it is characteristic of God to love his enemies. (The implications of this point for Christian ethics are not mentioned here, but are spelled out clearly elsewhere in the *Dogmatics*.) God's love is also not a means serving some higher goal or purpose, but is an end in itself. Finally, Barth stresses that God has no need of any external object in order to be the One who loves. In the triune life of Father, Son, and Holy Spirit, God is already love, already self-giving communion. Yet in actual fact, the world God has chosen is one in which he lavishly and prodigally pours out his love upon us in Jesus Christ.

Yet as we have already suggested, by itself the assertion that 'God is love' would be highly misleading. We must qualify (not weaken!) the claim by expanding it: God is not simply 'the One who loves' but 'the One who loves in freedom' (*der in der Freiheit liebende*). The qualification is crucial. To say that God is 'the One who loves' is to answer the question as to the 'who' of God, the question of the divine identity. To say that God is the One who loves *in freedom* is to answer the question as to the 'what' of God, the question of the divine essence or of divinity itself (II/1, 300). We recall the important role that the notion of lordship plays in Barth's doctrine of the Trinity. The concept of freedom in the doctrine of God does the same work here as that of lordship. It means that when God loves us, he is not divesting himself of his divinity, becoming as it were safer and more manageable. The divine loving is far more the ultimate exercise in lordship. Here God fulfils his transcendent power and majesty. Here God is indeed wholly other than mortal and sinful human beings. These are themes one instinctively and rightly associates with Barth's thought, and here they are on display in full force. The qualification 'in freedom' means, among many other things, that God loves us in the way that God wills – for example, by executing his judgment upon us as sinners.

Nevertheless, it is important to recognize that when Barth says 'freedom' he does not mean an abstract sovereignty, God's power to do whatever he likes. God is, of course, utterly sovereign. But what finally matters is not God's absolute power to choose, but the actual content of the divine choice. And what God chooses is to love us. The concrete being of God, in other words, consists in the lordly exercise of God's freedom to love – transcendent lordship taking the form of a gift. Both love and freedom finally make sense only as a commentary on Jesus' story:

> Therefore we must not think away the love or the person of God for a single moment if we wish to think rightly and truly of God's divinity. God is free. Because this is the case, we must say expressly in conclusion that the freedom of God is the freedom which consists and fulfils itself in his Son Jesus Christ. In him God has loved himself for all eternity. He has done so in him, in the freedom which renders his life divine, and therefore glorious, triumphant, and strong to save. (II/1, 321)

The dialectic of love and freedom described in paragraph 28 is thus Barth's way of specifying the 'who' and the 'what' of God's being. But the doctrine of God is by no means complete, for precisely *as* the One who loves in freedom God's life is infinitely rich, differentiated, and complex. It is a glorious life, lived out in a multitude of perfections (a word Barth prefers to the more usual term 'attributes'). Paragraphs 29–31 are devoted to an exploration of these perfections. It is important to note that this shift in focus does not mean a change in subject matter. In an echo of the scholastic teaching, according to which God's essence and attributes are one, Barth writes:

> Each posing of the question: In what way is God?, can be understood only as a repetition of the question: Who is God? and any attempt to answer the first question can be only a repetition of the answer God himself has given to the

second .... In describing God as almighty, eternal, wise, or merciful, we are only repeating this answer; we are only naming him again and yet again as the One who loves in freedom. But by reason of the fact that it comes from the living One who loves in freedom this answer is so framed that we must continually repeat it, not speaking of any other but God's one being, but in continual recognition and confirmation of the plenitude and richness of this one being of God. God is in essence all that he is. But he is in essence not only one, but multiple, individual, and diverse. And these are his perfections. (II/1, 331, rev.)

Not surprisingly, Barth groups these perfections in two sets:

§ 30 The Perfections of the Divine Loving

1. The Grace and Holiness of God
2. The Mercy and Righteousness of God
3. The Patience and Wisdom of God

§ 31 The Perfections of the Divine Freedom

1. The Unity and Omnipresence of God
2. The Constancy and Omnipotence of God
3. The Eternity and Glory of God

Leafing through the pages of II/1 will yield a surprising discovery: almost all the small-print biblical excursus are to be found in these concluding two paragraphs, making up some 350 pages of text. Everything in the doctrine of God up till now has been aiming at this point. Having spoken at length about who and what God is, Barth now seeks to describe how God is – and such description can only take the form of lengthy, patient exegesis. Barth's exploration of the divine perfections offers a rich field of inquiry for those interested in his use of Scripture.

While I will leave it to the reader to explore these discussions in detail, a few general comments may be in order. First, the pairing of perfections (grace with holiness, mercy with righteousness, and so forth) is intended as a constant reminder that God's love and freedom may not be separated. Both patience and wisdom, for example, are perfections of that witness to the divine loving. But within this pair, it is patience that displays this loving in a more particular way – as a making of time and space for the other – while wisdom shows how loving patience is in fact strength, an exercise of freedom. It is these paired perfections that together specify the divine loving. This procedure is integral to the nature of the account Barth wishes to offer here. The danger in any discussion of God's being is that we will become so enchanted with our categories that we begin to mistake them for the reality itself. The dialectical pairing of concepts is meant to defeat this temptation.

Second, these paragraphs offer an excellent example of the fitting relation between form and content in Barth's writing. As we noted earlier, Barth thinks God is beautiful; the beauty of theology itself bears testimony to this fact. The point emerges in various places in the *Church Dogmatics*. It is especially evident here, at the conclusion of the first part of the doctrine of God. It is no accident that the catalogue of perfections culminates with discussion of the glory of God, a trait Barth specifically connects with the divine beauty (cf. II/1, 650). To say that God is glorious, and therefore beautiful, is a reminder that God is finally not useful to anyone, but is purely an End in himself. It is a notion that both Augustine of Hippo and Jonathan Edwards would have found congenial.

The Best of all Words

Church Dogmatics II/2 takes up a central theme of the Reformed tradition, and one that has been important for Western Christianity as a whole: the doctrine of election or of predestining grace. For the Reformers, the doctrine became important as an essential corollary to the doctrine of justification by faith. How can I be confident of my own salvation? How can I know that God looks on me as a beloved child, and not as an object of his wrath? Not, the Reformers argued, on the basis of any merit or virtue I look for in myself; Luther's experience had taught him that introspection simply made matters worse. Rather, my confidence is based solely on the graciousness of God as it is revealed in the person of Jesus Christ. What the doctrine of election does is to insist that this divine grace is not some chance occurrence, but rather the outcome of God's eternal decision to be gracious. God is not unreliable or fickle. From all eternity, he has sovereignly chosen to show mercy to whom he wills and to condemn whom he wills. Faith means living in the humble confidence (never the presumptuous certainty) that I myself am among the elect, not because I am better than others, but because God's ways are mysterious, and he knows best how to organize the world. Contrary to what many people think, Calvin did not treat predestination as the central Christian doctrine in his *Institutes*. He assigned it a largely pastoral function; it was intended to offer comfort and encouragement to believers, especially as they experienced suffering or even persecution for their faith.[6]

The problem with the doctrine is that it often failed to provide the very comfort it promised. 'Am I really among the elect? How can I know that I am saved?' Questions like these could not be dispelled, in large part because the divine decree was thought of as hidden. That the biblical God is sovereign seemed difficult to dispute. But *who* is this sovereign God? What sort of God is it who arbitrarily sorts humanity into two piles, the saved and the damned? It is easy to see how this line of thinking might lead to skepticism and atheism at the time of the Enlightenment. If we can know nothing of God's ways, then perhaps there is no God after all. And perhaps this is a better state of affairs in the end than having a God who is a tyrant or a devil.

Barth felt the force of questions like these. As a Reformed theologian, he had a deep investment in recovering the doctrine of election. But he knew that the doctrine needed to be set on a firmer footing than appeal to a mysterious decree, a *decretum absolutum*. Election needed to be brought out into the open. If God is truly revealed to us, then not only the content of the divine election, but the identity of the God who elects can no longer be left hanging – as tended to be the case even in thinkers like Calvin. Not an abstract providence or all-powerful Will, Barth argued, but the *triune* God is the God who elects. The doctrine of election must be materially determined by (not just brought into some kind of relation to) God's self-revelation in Jesus Christ. If we let our thinking be shaped by Scripture, then not only can we speak openly about election, but we can joyfully proclaim it as gospel – the best of all possible words:

> The doctrine of election is the sum of the Gospel because of all words that can be said or heard it is the best: that God elects the human being; that God is for the human being too the One who loves in freedom. It is grounded in the knowledge of Jesus Christ because he is both the electing God and the elect human being in One. (II/1, 3, rev.)

The fact that election is firmly grounded in the knowledge of Jesus Christ means that the 'who' question has been addressed from the very outset. The electing God is none other than the God of Jesus Christ; even more strongly, it is Christ himself who elects! As for the question 'Am I, too, among the elect?', Barth does not so much forbid it as subject it to a kind of therapy. The whole train of reflection that extends over the 800 or so pages of II/2 is intended to help us change the subject. Instead of asking about ourselves – one of Barth's deepest criticisms of the traditional doctrine is that it assumes that 'election' primarily concerns the individual – we find ourselves asking about God. As we learn more about the God of grace, we will find that the question of our own place in relation to God tends to answer itself. Indeed, one can argue that this is what the older doctrine at its best tried to do.

The crucial phrase in the thesis above is that in which Barth speaks of Jesus as 'both the electing God and the elect human being in One'. It is not simply that Christ is the source of knowledge of election, although that is true as well; Christ is here depicted both as the agent of election (in his identity as God) and as the concrete object of election (in his identity as God's human covenant partner). The radicality of this move cannot be overestimated. Barth pictures election as an eternal divine decision, an event that qualifies and disrupts every moment in time. True enough; one might say that election is Barth's mature way of talking about the 'infinite qualitative distinction between time and eternity', which played such an important role in his *Romans*. But now note: the subject-cum-object of election is neither God the Father in the abstract, nor even the Son considered apart from the incarnation, but *Jesus Christ*, the historical person crucified outside the walls of Jerusalem. 'Jesus Christ' in this sense can only mean a history involving what is other than God. The history in question is that of God's triumph over sin and evil at the cross, his rescue of the creature from the abyss of Nothingness. Yet it is not that these events simply take place outside God, in the realm of creation and history. Barth argues that by virtue of God's eternal act of election this history is made internal to the very being of God; not that time and eternity are confused, but that the eternal God 'makes room' in himself for the cross, uttering an eternal Yes to sinners (and at the same time a sovereign 'No' to the evil that threatens his creation). To put it in briefest form, election means God's forging of a covenant of grace, a covenant in which God chooses to die so that sinners might live.

Not only is this not what most people think of when they hear the word 'predestination', it is also deeply counterintuitive. It is so because it violates many of our commonsense notions about what the word 'God' means. 'God' here is an agent characterized as utter freedom (as the first part of the doctrine of God has already established). But precisely God's freedom is a concrete freedom: the freedom to be for us in Jesus. As Barth reads the biblical witness, there is no abstract 'God' who subsequently becomes incarnate in Christ. Rather, the Subject of the incarnation is already the Son identified by reference to his historical work of defeating sin and death, even though from the perspective of eternity this event has 'not yet' taken place. Christ, writes Barth, is 'the Lamb slain, and the Lamb slain from the foundation of the world. For this reason, the *crucified* Jesus is the "image of the invisible God"' (II/2, 123). Not only is God eternally triune, but his triunity is specified by reference to the cross.

Barth's insistence on the concreteness and sovereignty of the divine election tends to unsettle many traditional notions. For example, he has very little room for talk of a *logos asarkos*, a Word without flesh preceding Christ's historical appearance. In an important exegesis of the Johannine prologue (II/2, 95–9), he argues that *houtos* ('this one', the Word existing in the beginning with God) refers not to an abstract divine being, but to the Jesus of the narrative that follows. The author of the gospel 'did not wish to do Jesus the honor of clothing him with the title of "Logos", but rather he did this concept the honor of using it, a few lines later, as a predicate for Jesus'.[7] But again, this does not mean a collapsing of time and eternity. *That* the covenant of grace exists is always sheer grace, sheer self-actualizing gift; Barth carefully safeguards God's precedence in the divine–human relationship. It is simply that the content of God's eternal choice is identical with the historical life and activity of Jesus. In the actuality of grace, there is no *logos asarkos*; the second person of the Trinity and the incarnate Jesus are simply one.[8]

The doctrine of election thus serves to tell us *who* the God of election is. The one true God is the One who has freely bound himself in a covenant with human beings, and will never take back that choice. The covenant of grace enters into God's 'self-definition'. This is why the doctrine of election belongs in the doctrine of God: 'It is part of the doctrine of God because primordially God's election of the human being is a predestination not merely of the human but of himself. Its function is to bear testimony to eternal, free, and unchanging grace as the beginning of all the ways and works of God (II/2, 3, rev.).

What does it mean to say that God predestines himself? Barth actually says that God is the subject of a double predestination (*praedestinatio gemina*), invoking a phrase often used to describe the more severe kind of Reformed thinking. In Calvin, God does not simply decide who will be saved, passing over the less fortunate group; God actively sends some people to hell. Barth certainly does not mean that when he says 'double predestination'. He does agree with the tradition in this respect: election makes no sense at all without some element of rejection. In election God says 'Yes' to something and 'No' to something else. The God depicted in the Bible is a God who makes concrete choices, judgments, discernments; he does not operate in an already 'given' reality prior to himself, but *makes* reality. At this point, we might worry that Barth has slipped back into a picture of God as arbitrary tyrant; but now recall that the subject of this double predestination is *Jesus Christ*. Because the divine Yes and No are in his hands, we can affirm 'eternal, free, and unchanging grace as the beginning of all the ways and works of God'. Election is good news because it is concretely realized in the person of Jesus.

Barth's specific version of double predestination is this: in Christ, God chooses death for himself and life for us. God loses in order that we might win. 'The elect' and 'the rejected' are not two groups of people. Rather, Barth refers all such language primarily to Jesus himself. He is the elect, the beloved chosen by God from all eternity. But for what was he chosen? He was chosen to die. As the elect, he is precisely the rejected one – the 'Lamb of God, who takes away the sins of the world'. Jesus Christ takes the place of sinners – not only in his historical passion and death, as we might expect, but already here in God's eternal act of self-predestination. God rejects or negates Christ. But this means that God himself assumes the burdens of rejection for our sake. God's bearing of our rejection is the negative form that election takes. We will not understand it if we fail to see that this negative aspect serves a positive end. God's will is to give life, to affirm his creatures joyfully in the person of the Son. For Barth, the proper response to election is not tears (at least not tragic tears), but rather awe, wonder, and gratitude. God's No is but the instrument of his Yes. Barth always has ringing in his ears Paul's words in 2 Corinthians, that in Christ 'it is always Yes. For all the promises of God find their Yes in him' (2 Cor. 1:19–20).

It is clear, then, that Barth intends the doctrine of election to speak gospel. It tells us to put away from our minds any picture of God as tyrant or terror, and to look only to Jesus Christ for our understanding of who God is. God is *eternally* bound to us in a covenant of love. But now the question intrudes itself: why should there be the No at all? Why must God's love for his creatures take this terrible, costly form? Paraphrasing Barth's thinking on these matters is especially perilous, especially since we have not yet examined his doctrine of evil (which we will do in the chapter on creation). But a foolishly brief answer might go like this: the negation stems from the fact that God, from all eternity, has chosen to enter into fellowship with sinners. This statement must not be blunted by glossing it as, 'God chose to enter fellowship with human beings, who, in his perfect foreknowledge, he knew would become sinners.' For Barth, that would sell far too short the sovereignty and actuality of God's choices. No, the eternal covenant of grace consists in God's decision to relate to creatures (prior even to their creation) concretely, as the God-who-is-merciful. One can hardly be merciful unless there is someone to show mercy towards. Sinners are those who have surrendered themselves to the power of evil, and it enters into God's eternal identity that he will rescue them from this bondage. This is simply another way of saying that, for Barth, there is no 'second person of the Trinity' in the abstract. There is rather the divine decision to be God in Jesus, to be God at the cross, exposing himself to evil and judgment for the creature's sake.

At this point, we should make explicit something that the reader may have noticed already: that, for Barth, the doctrine of election is intimately related to the doctrine of reconciliation or atonement. He does, to be sure, distinguish the two. The first describes the eternal covenant of grace, while the second describes what God undertakes in history to rescue that covenant in the face of human sin. Yet Barth distinguishes here only to unite. What unites election and reconciliation is that the same subject stands at the centre of both doctrines: Jesus Christ, the same Jesus Christ who was 'crucified under Pontius Pilate'. The eternity in which election takes place is not a second world, a Platonic realm where the Logos 'waits around' until the time of the incarnation. Barth's whole theology leads away from this kind of dualism. Rather, God's eternity has (to be very imprecise) a qualitative reference. It describes God's otherness and unconstrained creativity as God intrudes *into* time, both disrupting and redeeming the latter. There is only one world and one history – the history of God's acts as he engages creation as its Lord and Saviour. Thus when Barth speaks of God's 'eternal election', he does not mean something that simply took place long ago and far away. Election is indeed before all things, but it is also with all things; it is God's sovereign will actualizing itself in our midst. And the content of that activity is simply Jesus Christ, the electing God and the elect human being in one.

All this raises a tantalizing and troubling question: if God eternally chooses fellowship with sinners, does God then choose sin? A fuller answer to this question must await our discussion of evil in chapter 4; however, the short answer is 'No'. Evil and sin are what God utterly rejects. God permits them only in so far as they serve God's own purpose of defeating them and making the covenant a reality: 'I will be your God, and you will be my people.' God wills not evil, but the overcoming of evil for his creature's sake (again, we will explore this dialectic more fully in the next chapter). In the present context, the important point to make is that at the beginning of God's works and ways is a twofold act. God says Yes to himself and to his creature; God says No to what has become of the creature in its lost condition, as willing slave of evil. But the No would destroy the creature unless God intervened. This sounds harsh, but in a way it reflects Barth's understanding of the extraordinary intimacy between God and human beings. God does not deal with us impersonally, issuing a pardon for sin from a safe distance; God enters our condition so as to remake us, fashioning us into the covenant partners we were intended to be. 'Jesus Christ' is the name for this gracious remaking; he is the very reality of the covenant, the embodied communion between God and humankind. He fulfils the covenant in his historical life and suffering. But he *is* the covenant 'already' in eternity. As God chooses to be God-in-Jesus, the destiny of every human being is determined. A key reason that Barth spends so much time on the doctrine of election is so that we will not think meanly of the cross, but learn to see it as God's unconditional act of mercy embracing all people. To affirm election is to affirm 'eternal, free, and unchanging grace as the beginning of all the ways and works of God'.

The vast scope of this claim is easy to miss, especially on an initial reading of the doctrine of election. The assertion that all human beings are elect in Christ is not just a rhetorical flourish; Barth means all members of the species *homo sapiens*, i.e. anyone who shares in the flesh that Christ indwelled – from the first tool-makers on the plains of Africa to the colonizers of space. The covenant God decided for in Jesus Christ embraces all of history, both before and after the incarnation. The vertical determination of humanity in Christ is far more decisive than one's horizontal placement on a time line. The incarnation itself, of course, is a historically particular event. Barth's point is simply that human beings do not first have to do with Christ in his incarnate life. If he is the eternal Son, then he is not simply the fulfilment of creation but its presupposition; he is the Alpha and *therefore* the Omega.[9]

Judgment and Mercy

One of the most extraordinary aspects of the doctrine of election is the way it brings us into the very heart of the Old Testament. This is signalled initially by the prominence of the notion 'covenant fellowship'. Working from the assumption that the central theme of the Bible is redemption from sin, much classical Christian theology has treated the account of 'the Fall' in Genesis 1–3 as if it were the only really crucial part of the Old Testament. God's covenant with Israel then becomes a mere transitory episode, a shadow destined to fade when the reality comes.

Barth's way of reading the Bible defeats such moves. Because he reads God's purposes primarily in terms of covenant, community, and blessing (recall the key role that 'fellowship' has already played in his account of the divine loving), he is able to accord a far more positive role to the central strands of Old Testament narrative. The election of Jesus Christ does not supersede or negate the election of Israel. On the contrary, Israel is elect precisely in and for the sake of Jesus, whose Jewishness is an integral feature of his identity as God's elect.

From this follows one of the more remarkable features of Barth's doctrine of election: its character as a political theology – the politics in question being the historical existence of Israel and the church. This theme is developed in paragraph 34, titled 'The Election of the Community', whose thesis statement begins:

> The election of grace, as the election of Jesus Christ, is simultaneously the eternal election of the one community of God by which the existence of Jesus Christ is to be attested to the whole world and the whole world summoned to faith in Jesus Christ. This one community of God in its form as Israel has to serve the representation of the divine judgment, in its form as the Church the representation of the divine mercy ... (II/2, 195)

In the Old Testament 'election' means 'Israel', since God does not exist without his people. In the New Testament this same language is applied to the church, the *ekklesia* chosen 'in him [Christ] before the foundation of the world' (Eph. 1:4). God's election takes up space in the world through the existence of these peoples. Or should we say, this people: in a decisive stroke, Barth construes Israel and the church as but two forms of a single community, centred in Jesus Christ.

This Christological point of reference needs to be kept constantly in view when considering Barth's thinking about Israel/the church. On the one hand, it points to a certain relativizing of the community. The community is not an end in itself. It exists solely in order to bear witness to the world. On the other hand, God clearly wills to bring people to faith in Christ only through the mediation of the community, and therefore the latter has an extraordinarily dignified role to play in the divine drama. *Extra ecclesiam nulla salus*, Barth writes echoing Cyprian; 'Outside the church there is no salvation.' 'This proposition has its place already in the doctrine of predestination, in the doctrine of God' (II/1, 197).

Hans Frei has observed that beginning with II/2 and throughout subsequent volumes of the *Dogmatics*, Barth's vision became 'increasingly and self-consciously temporal rather than cognitivist. It was a world in which time elapsed, and that was of its very essence'.[10] To a great extent, this attention to temporality reflects the new demands of the subject matter. Election in Scripture is profoundly communal, temporal, and historical; thus when Barth takes up this theme he seems almost instinctively to have adopted a narrative mode of thinking. As Frei notes, II/2 is the volume in which the great sprawling biblical excursus begin to appear, detailing God's active engagement with peoples and individuals in the history he elects to share with them. All this makes for fascinating and demanding reading, and justifies the qualified description of Barth as a 'narrative theologian'.[11]

The narrative quality of II/2 should also serve as an important reminder to the student that, at least in principle, Barth does not consider God's election to be completed. It is true that election in Jesus Christ is eternal, therefore once-for-all. But since the Jesus Christ in whom this election occurs is himself historical, 'eternal' election realizes itself in a series of contingent historical events and encounters. To say 'God elects me from all eternity in Jesus Christ' and to say 'God elects me here and now to a life of witness in this particular congregation' are not, for Barth, mutually exclusive propositions. Predestination 'does not antedate time ... in the form of a letter which, limited in this way, can mean only a dead letter. Predestination precedes time as a living act in the Spirit, similar to the cloud which went before Israel in the wilderness' (II/2, 191). The excursus from which this quotation is drawn develops the idea that election must be developed in dynamic and historical terms – all the more so if it takes Jesus Christ to be the content of election.

We have seen that for Barth, God's election has two sides. It involves both a No and a Yes, a death-dealing rejection of sin and evil and a lifegiving affirmation of covenant love, the first always for the sake of the second. In reading II/2, one should be constantly attentive to the ways in which Barth weaves this pattern of life and death into the text. This is nowhere more evident than in paragraph 34 on Israel and the church. As the community that has heard God's Word and disobeyed it, thereby earning God's condemnation, Israel witnesses to the divine No; as the community called both to hear and to obey, the church witnesses to the divine Yes. Whatever one makes of these claims, it is very important that one attend carefully to what Barth is and is not saying. He is not saying that the people Israel – a term that for him includes not just biblical 'Israelites', but Jews from the fall of Jerusalem to Hitler's Germany – are the rejected of God. On the contrary, God's unchanging love for his people is what makes their repeated unfaithfulness such a terrible act of ingratitude. Nor is he saying that the church is the people that 'gets it right' and thereby displaces Israel from its elect status. Precisely as the community elect to represent the divine mercy, the church is a sinful and undeserving people, no less than Israel itself. Indeed, apart from God's mercy the church would not be a people at all, but simply a ragtag collection of Gentile sinners. Neither community *deserves* the divine love shown to it. Both live by God's mercy alone. But each does so in the shape of its particular, peculiar history in the world, the Jews in the shadow-existence occasioned by their rejection of the Messiah, the church in its imperfect yet grace-sustained life in Christ. Barth is clearly trying to do justice in his own way to Paul's dialectic in Romans 9–11, a running exegesis of which accompanies the entire discussion.

The same pattern of life-in-death can be seen in the section that culminates in the doctrine of election, paragraph 35 on 'The Election of the Individual'. Having shown us across 300 pages that election is not about a heavenly bean-counter, grimly sorting humanity into two piles, but about God's mercy in Jesus Christ, Barth turns at last to the individual elect person. As I said above, this arrangement is designed to defeat the anxious question about one's eternal destiny, 'Am I among the saved?' If the reader has responded well to Barth's treatment, he or she will be less inclined to pursue that question, trusting that one's destiny is in God's good hands. Yet Barth does not intend that Christians simply revel in their elect status; election has a *telos* and bears fruit in action. Freed from anxieties concerning the self, the Christian is liberated for the joyful activity of bearing witness to others. The non-believer is the believer's intense concern – precisely by virtue of Jesus Christ, who died for those whom Paul called 'the ungodly', believer and non-believer alike. Witness is thus the destiny of every Christian, opening onto a far more mysterious and satisfying life than the question 'Am I saved?' could ever provide.

To a great extent Barth works out these dialectics in the small-print passages woven into paragraph 35, which rank among the most brilliant in the entire *Church Dogmatics*. Barth devotes an initial excursus to individual election in Calvin and the Reformers, especially with respect to the 'perseverance of the saints' (II/2, 325–40); this continues the critical dialogue with earlier Protestant theology developed in paragraphs 32 and 33. But far more important and compelling are the excursus devoted to biblical themes. The excursus on the witness to Christ in the Old Testament (354–409) traces the biblical pattern of election and rejection as it appears in three key passages: the instructions concerning sacrifice in Leviticus 14 and 16, the story of David and Saul, and the story of the man of God and the prophet of Bethel in 1 Kings 13. Anyone interested in Barth's use of Scripture will want to read this material with special care; in particular, his reading of the texts from Leviticus offers an intriguing instance of what 'post-critical' exegesis might look like. The excursus on the New Testament picture of Jesus as elect (II/2, 419–49) focuses especially on the apostles, whose unfaithfulness cannot negate Jesus' appointment of them as his witnesses. Finally, Barth explores the theme of 'the rejected' in a fascinating excursus on Judas Iscariot (458–506). He argues that in the figure of Judas we see more clearly than anywhere else the face of the rejected, lost, and godless human being – but even more clearly the grace of God, since it is precisely for this human being that Christ died. Jesus Christ on the cross *is* the rejected of God, the elect One bearing all our rejection. And in light of that fact, we should not give up hope for anyone, not even for Judas – or shall we say especially not for Judas, since Jesus Christ dies precisely for the rejected?

No paraphrase can possibly do justice to these imaginative and powerful readings of Scripture. This is not to say Barth's interpretations are immune from critical questioning. Has Barth simply imposed a Christological grid on the Old Testament, forcing it to say what he likes? Has he run roughshod over the findings of historical criticism? Especially in his treatment of Judas, has he succumbed to a rationalizing optimism, saying far more than Scripture really lets us say about the eschatological future?

However one comes down on these questions, one should take careful note of Barth's desire to treat election as covenant history, lived out in a series of real encounters between God and human beings. That history has Jesus Christ as its ground, centre, and *telos*. Yet it is for all that a real history – one in which my faithful or unfaithful response to the fact of my election makes a real difference. Judas is not the same as Paul; the unbeliever is not the same as the believer; the goal of the covenant of grace is my active, obedient response to grace, precisely so that I may become a witness to others. God's electing grace is not a substitute for the living of my unique life, but rather the ground and presupposition of the latter.

Barth in Dialogue: Michael Wyschogrod on Election

To read the second volume of the *Church Dogmatics* is to feel on every page the presence of an astonishing Person, the God of the Bible, the God who elects and redeems. One of Barth's major goals in *CD* II is that we should apprehend this God as the gracious God. The theme of grace is sounded already in the discussion of the knowledge of God (II/1, paragraphs 25–7) and the reality of God (II/1, paragraphs 28–31); climactically, the doctrine of election speaks of 'eternal, free, and unchanging grace as the beginning of all the ways and works of God'. It is thus tempting to see grace as the key to Barth's theological 'system'.[12]

This temptation is to be resisted, however. God is grace, but grace is not God. To erect grace into a system is to lose sight of the majestic strangeness and otherness of the One who – precisely as gracious! – meets us in Jesus Christ. The picture that emerges from *CD* II is of a God who is utterly free and sovereign, making the 'condescension inconceivably tender' of his grace all the more striking.

But this same God of grace, Barth tells us, is none other than the God of Israel. The history of Christian theology is replete with thinkers (Marcion was the first) who draw a sharp contrast between the loving God of Jesus Christ and the Creator God of the Old Testament, full of wrath and condemnation. Yet Barth will have none of it. Following Calvin, he insists on the unity of God's action across the old and new covenants. The God of the Law and the Prophets is already the God of grace, just as Jesus Christ is unintelligible apart from the promises given to Israel. As he reads the Bible, Barth simply finds it impossible to narrate God's identity apart from that of

Israel. It is no accident that the exegetical heart of *CD* II/2 consists in an exposition of Romans 9–11, where Paul himself struggles to make sense of Israel's destiny in light of God's electing purpose. Barth's theological rediscovery of Israel is among his greatest legacies to the church; as many have argued, it is also a deeply ambiguous legacy.[13] It seems appropriate, then, to conclude this chapter by examining the response of an important Jewish thinker to Barth's thought.

The thinker I have chosen is Michael Wyschogrod, formerly professor of philosophy at Baruch College in New York City. Born of an Orthodox Jewish family in Berlin in 1928, Wyschogrod emigrated with his parents to the United States in 1939. He was educated at an Orthodox school before going on to study Talmud at Yeshiva University. A youthful interest in philosophy led him first to City University of New York and then to Columbia University, where he completed his doctoral degree in 1952. His dissertation explored the question of ontology in the thought of Kierkegaard and Heidegger.

Wyschogrod reports that he was drawn to Christian theology because it offered resources for an enterprise that, with a few notable exceptions, has never commanded much attention in Judaism: the dialogue between religion and philosophy. At first strongly influenced by Kierkegaard, Wyschogrod found himself increasingly attracted to Barth's thought.[14] Why Barth? The short answer seems to be the radicality of Barth's orientation toward the Bible. Rather than getting lost in historical questions, or dissolving God into vague generalities like the 'ground of being', Barth yields himself to the authority of Scripture. Wyschogrod's own intellectual project can be seen as an attempt to do for Jewish thought what Barth did for Christian theology: to foster a kind of scriptural reasoning in which modern questions are, indeed, taken seriously, but not permitted to dictate the theological agenda. It seems a fitting enterprise for a Jewish thinker who seeks to be orthodox and modern at the same time.

Yet it is not simply Barth's scripturalism that Wyschogrod finds so compelling. Precisely because Barth takes revelation so seriously, he has no choice but to take up the question of Israel:

> Karl Barth is the Christian theologian of our time who is oriented toward Scripture, who does not substitute the Word of Man for that of God.... And because Barth is Scriptural, his attention turns to Israel in a rather unique way which the Jewish theologian reads with avid interest if for no other reason than the feeling that it was not written to be read by a Jew, to be commented on by a Jew, to be challenged by a Jew. ('Why is Barth of Interest', 98)

The Jew does not expect much of a Christian theologian like Bultmann, who, Wyschogrod argues, seems embarrassed by the frankly Jewish character of the Word of God (and employs Heidegerrian strategies for evading it). But 'Barth is different. Because he is so biblical he is, in some sense, a member of the family whom Israel cannot ignore' (ibid.).

Barth's bias toward the concrete, the particular, and the historical is evident in Wyschogrod's own thinking. His book *The Body of Faith: Judaism as Corporeal Election* is an attempt to get Jews to take more seriously their own status as God's elect. Much as Barth criticized the rational and ethical reductions of liberal Protestantism, so Wyschogrod takes aim at similar tendencies in modern Judaism. He argues that the great temptation for Jews is to take refuge in the ethical – as if Jewish existence might be vindicated by the supposedly 'universal' claims of morality. While he gives a large place to ethics, Wyschogrod insists that Judaism is ultimately neither a set of ideas nor a moral code. What God elects is a *people*, a natural family marked by biological inheritance, history, and culture. This means that Wyschogrod by no means scorns the mere 'cultural Judaism' of bagels, lox, cream cheese, and gefilte fish. 'Those who think of such things with derision do not understand Jewish existence as embodied existence' (*Body of Faith*, 26). Whether observant or not, no Jew can escape the fact of his or her election. By contrast, Jewish philosophies of assimilation are fatally compromised by a 'spiritualizing heresy for which the body of Israel is of very little significance' (*Body of Faith*, xvi). Such spiritualizing amounts to a Gnostic denial of a basic fact: that being Jewish is not a matter of choice, but a matter of being chosen. The Jew may deny, but cannot ultimately resign his or her election. Hence Jewish identity always precedes the religious and ethical responsibilities that come with being God's elect.

A Jew who writes a book titled *The Body of Faith* might be expected to have some interesting things to say about incarnation. As one would expect, Wyschogrod thinks the Christian teaching that God became flesh in Jesus to be a mistake. He argues that it compromises the biblical sense of divine transcendence: even in Barth's theology, the Christian notion of reconciliation between God and man finally trumps the distinction between the two ('Why Is Barth of Interest', 104). Nonetheless, Wyschogrod does not treat the Christian mistake about incarnation as an ultimate barrier between Christians and Jews. Judaism knows no incarnation, but it does know an indwelling of God in the tabernacle, the temple – and, most important, in the Jewish people themselves.[15] The danger for Jews is not that they will have too great a faith in God's embodiment, but that they will end up denying it altogether.

At the heart of Wyschogrod's lover's quarrel with Karl Barth is not the theme of incarnation, however, but that of election. Barth knows that the Jews are God's elect. Moreover, he knows that – God being both sovereign and faithful – they remain God's elect, despite their overwhelming rejection of Jesus as Messiah. Wyschogrod quotes with approval the following passage from the doctrine of election:

> For it is incontestable that this people as such is the holy people of God: the people with whom God has dealt … His grace and in His wrath; in the midst of whom He has blessed and judged, enlightened and hardened, accepted and

rejected; whose cause either way He has made His own, and has not ceased to make His own, and will not cease to make His own. They are all of them by nature sanctified by Him, sanctified as ancestors and kinsmen of the Holy One in Israel, in a sense that Gentiles are not by nature, not even the best of Gentiles, not even the Gentile Christians, not even the best of Gentile Christians, in spite of their membership of the Church, – in spite of the fact that they too are now sanctified by the Holy One of Israel and have become Israel. (II/2, 287)

Yet alongside statements like these are more disturbing passages, in which Barth seems to succumb to the long tradition of Christian anti-Judaism. The Jews are indeed elect. But they are elect precisely in their disobedience, their lack of faith, their stubborn clinging to the outward forms of their religion. The dark side of this account is that while Barth does affirm God's mercy toward his sinful people, the doctrine has no place for historical, post-biblical Judaism. This community, which Barth usually refers to as 'the Synagogue', is a historical relic; something which ought not to be in the time after Christ's coming, but which somehow strangely persists.

Wyschogrod himself offers no detailed analysis of Barth's anti-Judaism. But the reasons for it are fairly clear. For Barth, the election of Israel is but a transitory form of a far more basic reality: God's eternal act of election in Jesus Christ.[16] God elects Israel 'to serve the representation of the divine judgment', i.e. to show forth the sinful humanity whom God rejects. When the Son of God himself appears in history, this community loses its reason for being. Why? Because the 'passing man' whom Israel represents *has* in fact passed away, has been judged and annihilated at the cross. In its place is the new, obedient humanity in Jesus Christ. The task of bearing witness to this new humanity has been entrusted to the Church, the community called from among both Jews and Gentiles for the hearing of the divine promise.

The nuances of Barth's position must be appreciated before one proceeds to criticize it. To begin with, nowhere does he say that God elects the Church and rejects Israel, or that Jews have forfeited their election through their unbelief – standard claims of Christian supersessionism. All people are elected in the Elect One of God, Jesus Christ. As the Elect, he alone is capable of bearing all our rejection – and he does bear it, in an inconceivable act of mercy. The line between Israel and the Church falls not between the lost and the saved, but between two kinds of witness. To Israel was given the terrible task of bearing witness to God's No, the judgment that serves the Yes of his grace. To the Church is given the joyful task of bearing witness to the Yes itself. The latter witness displaces the former, as the history of Israel gives way to what Barth calls 'the time of the Church'. Israel no longer has a future – or rather, its future is its destiny of being taken up into the *Church's* witness, the Church called from among Jews and Gentiles. Jews who do not accept the gospel, and who persist in treating Judaism as a way of pleasing God, are tragically mistaken. Yet their unbelief certainly does not invalidate their election. Indeed, Barth has such a powerful sense of this election that he rejects the idea of a specific Christian mission to the Jews. Gentile Christianity of all times and places is but 'a guest in the house of Israel'; Jews being the original recipients of the gospel, how can Christians seek to evangelize them? The most the church can do is to seek to make the synagogue 'jealous', as Paul says in Romans 11 (IV/3, 876–8).

Is Barth, then, a supersessionist? It depends on what one means by the term. If we define supersessionism as the teaching that the church has replaced Israel as God's elect people, then Barth is clearly not a supersessionist. The election of Abraham's seed does not cease with the coming of Christ; if this were true, why would Paul be so exercised about Israel's unbelief in Romans 9–11? As Barth writes:

> Without any doubt the Jews are to this very day the chosen people of God in the same sense as they have been so from the beginning, according to the Old and New Testaments. They have the promise of God; and if we Christians from among the Gentiles have it too, then it is only as those chosen with them; as guests in their house, as new wood grafted onto their old tree.[17]

True enough; but in another sense Barth is a supersessionist in a fairly drastic sense. While the Jews are still God's elect, Jewish institutions – the synagogue, Torah study, kosher observance, the rich material texture of historical Judaism – have for Barth no status whatsoever in the present age. They are a puzzling remnant, a holdover from an era that ended with Christ's death and resurrection. Barth was indeed a supporter of the State of Israel, no doubt a response to what he had seen happen to the Jews under Nazism. He can also speak of the amazing resilience of the Jews throughout history as an attesting sign of God's providence. He liked to quote the answer Frederick the Great received when he asked Zimmermann, his personal physician, for a proof of God's existence: 'Your majesty, the Jews!'[18] Yet aside from this, material Jewish existence has no positive significance in Barth's thought. The reason for this is clear: he thinks of the election of Israel as completely dissolved (*aufgehoben*) in the election of Jesus Christ. God's decision in all eternity to be in covenant relation with humans includes within it his choice of Israel from among the nations. This same decision, however, sets a limit on Israel's witness. For Barth, the particularity and concreteness of election is finally localized in Jesus alone; covenant history 'seems to collapse and disappear into the figure of Jesus Christ'.[19]

This is not the place to try to resolve the complex issues raised by Barth's doctrine of Israel. Instead, I propose to reflect on the possibilities of interaction between two strong voices – Barth and Wyschogrod – and the traditions they represent. To begin with, it should be clear that neither theologian has the slightest interest in a cheap or falsely ironic approach to religious dialogue. Wyschogrod is committed to reading the Jewish Bible from within 'the body of faith', historic Judaism. Barth is committed to reading Christian Scripture as the church's testimony to Jesus Christ.

Indeed, it is precisely Barth's commitment to his Bible that Wyschogrod so deeply respects! Both authors are 'traditioned' in a way that excludes the seeking of a neutral ground where all claims are true, because in the end no one's particular beliefs matter all that much. Neither Barth nor Wyschogrod could accept such an illusory convergence.

Indeed, it is Barth's and Wyschogrod's very particularism that makes the conversation interesting. The divergences are obvious. For Wyschogrod the Elect of God is the Jewish people, for Barth the Elect of God is Jesus Christ (making Jews elect only in a derivative sense). A different story about God is being told in each case. But to acknowledge that Jews and Christians tell different stories doesn't mean there are no convergences between them. Being good readers of a common text (Israel's Scriptures, the Christian Old Testament), both men are drawn to the majestic figure of the Electing God. While the Jew finds the Christian's claims about Jesus strange, he does not see in them a complete misreading of this God's identity. Thus Wyschogrod acknowledges a certain 'Jewishness' in Barth's Christocentrism, in that it captures something of the biblical God's movement into covenant fellowship with human beings. Even Barth's claims about incarnation must command a certain respect from the Jew:

> If Judaism cannot accept incarnation it is because it does not hear this story, because the Word of God as it hears it does not tell it and because Jewish faith does not testify to it. And if the church does accept incarnation, it is not because it somehow discovered that such an event had to occur given the nature of God, or of being, reality, or anything else, but because it hears that this was God's free and gracious decision, a decision not predictable by man. Strangely enough, the disagreement between Judaism and Christianity, when understood in this light, while not reconcilable, can be brought into the context [of] a difference of faith regarding the free and sovereign act of the God of Israel. ('Why Is Barth of Interest', 99–100)

What is envisioned here, clearly, is that Jews and Christians worship the same God, the God of Israel, even as they disagree about the nature of this God's actions.[20]

A genuine encounter of two traditions must also entail the possibility of one tradition's learning from another. In his reflections on Barth, Wyschogrod is quite explicit about this. He says that it was through reading Barth and the apostle Paul that he learned about the sinfulness of Israel, a people that repeatedly returns evil for God's good. In a telling aside, he concedes that it 'might be surprising that this should require a reading of Barth when this point is so clear in the Bible' ('Why Is Barth of Interest', 108). Wyschogrod learns about Israel's sin by reading Barth, but the point is only authorized in so far as it is confirmed in Scripture. In brief, the Christian helps the Jew to a better understanding of the latter's own tradition; nor must the Jew leave his tradition in order to learn from the Christian.

But does the learning move in only one direction? Wyschogrod reports that when he met Barth in 1966, the two became embroiled in a debate about promise and fulfillment – an ancient theme in Jewish–Christian relations. Wyschogrod's account of the meeting is worth quoting in full:

> On a sunny morning in August 1966 I visited Barth in his modest home in the Bruderholzallee in Basel. He had been told that I was a 'Jewish Barthian', and this amused him no end. We spoke about various things and at one point he said: 'You Jews have the promise but not the fulfilment; we Christians have both promise and fulfilment.' Influenced by the banking atmosphere in Basel, I replied, With human promises, one can have the promise but not the fulfilment. The one who promises can die, or change his mind, or not fulfill his promise for any number of reasons. But a promise of God is like money in the bank. If we have the promise, we have its fulfilment and if we do not have the fulfilment we do not have the promise.' There was a period of silence and then he said: 'You know, I never thought of it that way.' I will never forget that meeting. ('A Jewish Perspective', 161)

It is a compelling story, though perhaps one that should not quite be taken at face value. As Eberhard Busch notes, Barth's answer is surprising in light of utterances he makes at many points in his writings, to the effect that the fulfilment is always implicit in God's promises.[21] One's precise location on a time-line is ultimately less important for Barth than the reality of the God in whom promise and fulfilment are one. Barth's comment may have been more a gracious concession to his guest than a sign of new insight; or perhaps the surprise was that a Jew could see things in the same way.

Nonetheless, Barth's gesture to Wyschogrod raises the question whether he might have been open to other challenges to his doctrine of Israel. As we have seen, he seems to reduce Israel's role in covenant history to a mere precursor of Christ; Israel's witness is suspended when Messiah comes. But what if we take seriously Wyschogrod's claim that Israel's election is corporeal? That Israelite–Jewish existence cannot help taking the form of a people, such that a private Judaism is even more unthinkable than a private Christianity? If so, then the wedge Barth seeks to drive between Israel's irrevocable election and its historical existence after 70 C.E. seems highly problematic. If the Jews are elect, then somehow they are elect in their Jewishness, the customs and forms and institutions that have developed in nearly two thousand years of rabbinic Judaism. In short, Jewish life did not come to an end with the death and resurrection of Jesus the Jew.

To be convinced of this, Barth would want to see the biblical evidence, just as Wyschogrod found the fact of Israel's sinfulness confirmed when he read his Bible. Yet perhaps we can say that Barth himself has already provided all the evidence he needs. In his own treatment of Romans 9–11, the fact of Israel's unbelief by no means frustrates God's purposes in election. Paul's intention in these chapters is not so much to find fault with Israel – that, indeed, would be to read Romans anthropocentrically – as to glorify the God who elects.[22] It is not too much to think that God may glorify himself by making space for the body of Israel, the synagogue, as well as by making space for the body of Christ, the church. In the face of this mystery, we will avoid the facile solutions that present themselves: Christian supersessionism, which refuses to acknowledge the permanency of Israel's election, and two-covenant theories, which substitute modern religious pluralism for convictions deeply held by Jews and Christians alike. We simply do not know how church and synagogue make one people of God. We do know that one Lord sovereignly disposes over both communities, leading them toward whatever destiny he has in store.

Barth's doctrine of election raises other large questions about the overall structure of his thought. In particular, it presses the issue whether God's eternal act of election does not finally end up absorbing creation and history, or negating the role of creaturely freedom. Is God's human covenant partner really a partner, or simply a spectator of a drama played out by God alone? We will keep these issues in mind as we turn to our next chapter, dealing with Barth's doctrine of creation.

Notes

1 Katherine Sonderegger, *That Jesus Christ Was Born a Jew: Karl Barth's 'Doctrine of Israel'* (University Park: Pennsylvania State University Press, 1992).
2 Dietrich Bonhoeffer, *Letters and Papers From Prison*, ed. Eberhard Bethge (London: SCM Press, 1971), 171.
3 Thomas Aquinas, *Summa Theologiae*, I.13.11.
4 *KD* II/1, 157, present author's translation, Barth's emphasis; cf. *CD* II/1, 141.
5 This is roughly the argument of Eugene F. Rogers, Jr., in his *Thomas Aquinas and Karl Barth: Sacred Doctrine and the Natural Knowledge of God* (Notre Dame: University of Notre Dame Press, 1995). See also Stanley Hauerwas, *With the Grain of the Universe: The Church's Witness and Natural Theology* (Grand Rapids: Brazos Press, 2001).
6 See William Placher, 'Calvin's Rhetoric of Faith', in Placher, *The Domestication of Transcendence: How Modern Thinking About God Went Wrong* (Louisville: Westminster/John Knox Press, 1996).
7 *KD* II/2, S. 104, present author's translation; cf. *CD* II/2, 97.
8 Taking up this point again in IV/1, Barth notes that the concept of a *logos asarkos* refers not to anything revealed – hence we can have nothing to say about it – but simply reminds us that God's grace towards us has its 'free basis in the inner being and essence of God' (IV/1, 52). Theology knows Jesus Christ only by virtue of his coming in the flesh.
9 Robert Jenson's *Alpha and Omega: A Study in the Theology of Karl Barth* (New York: Thomas Nelson, 1963) is still an invaluable resource for understanding Barth's way of relating covenant, creation, and reconciliation.
10 Hans Frei, *Types of Christian Theology* (New Haven: Yale University Press, 1992), 160.
11 See David Ford, *Barth and God's Story: Biblical Narrative and the Theological Method of Karl Barth in the 'Church Dogmatics'* (Frankfurt: Peter Lang, 1981).
12 This is the thesis of G. C. Berkouwer, *The Triumph of Grace in the Theology of Karl Barth* (Grand Rapids: Eerdmans, 1956). Barth's response to Berkouwer can be found in IV/3, 173 ff.
13 Barth's 'doctrine of Israel' has generated an enormous literature, both in German and in English. See Sonderegger's *That Jesus Christ Was Born a Jew* (cited in note 1, above)

for a sure-handed guide to this material.

14   Wyschogrod has written about Barth on several occasions. See his 'Why Was and Is the Theology of Karl Barth of Interest to a Jewish Theologian?', in *Footnotes to a Theology: the Karl Barth Colloquium of 1972*, ed. Martin Rumscheidt (Waterloo, Ontario: Studies in Religion/Sciences Religieuses, 1974); idem, 'A Jewish Perspective on Karl Barth', in *How Karl Barth Changed My Mind*, ed. Donald McKim (Grand Rapids: Eerdmans, 1986); idem, *The Body of Faith: Judaism as Corporeal Election* (Minneapolis: Seabury Press, 1983), especially chapter 2. References to these works will be cited parenthetically in the text. A helpful collection of Wyschogrod's shorter writings now exists in his *Abraham's Promise: Judaism and Jewish–Christian Relations*, ed. R. Kendall Soulen (Grand Rapids: Eerdmans, 2004).

15   See Wyschogrod, 'A Jewish Perspective on Incarnation', *Modern Theology* April 1996, 195–209.

16   I here follow the analysis of Kendall Soulen in his *The God of Israel and Christian Theology* (Minneapolis: Fortress Press, 1996), 85–94.

17   Barth, 'The Jewish Problem and the Christian Answer', in *Against the Stream: Shorter Postwar Writings* (London: SCM Press, 1954), 200.

18   Barth, *Dogmatics in Outline*, 75.

19   Soulen, *The God of Israel and Christian Theology*, 94.

20   'Jews and Christians worship the same God' – the opening thesis of 'A Jewish Statement on Christians and Christianity', in *Christianity in Jewish Terms*, ed. Tikva Frymer-Kensky *et al.* (Boulder: Westview Press, 2000). The 'Jewish Statement' would have been unthinkable apart from Wyschogrod's pioneering work.

21   See Eberhard Busch's account of the meeting in Barth, *Gespräche 1964–68* (Zürich: Theologischer Verlag, 1997), 309.

22   For this argument, see Douglas Harink, *Paul Among the Postliberals: Pauline Theology Beyond Christendom and Modernity* (Grand Rapids: Brazos Press, 2002), chapter 4.

Chapter 4

Heaven and Earth: Creation

> Heaven is the creation inconceivable to the human being, earth the creation
> conceivable to him. He himself is the creature on the boundary between heaven
> and earth. The covenant between God and man is the meaning and the glory, the
> ground and the goal of heaven and earth and the whole creation.
> – Barth, *Dogmatics in Outline*[1]

Why God Created the World

Barth's theology of creation is not what made him famous. For a long time
it was thought that, indeed, he could have very little to say about creation at
all, given his rejection of natural theology and his (supposedly)
overwhelmingly negative view of human nature. Yet in fact something very
much like the opposite is true. Barth does not treat creation as the central
'fact' in the divine–human relationship. Just so, he is free to treat creation as
a peculiar gift in its own right, with its own unique place in the economy of
grace. Stretching a point, I would even say that Barth enjoys himself in this
volume as nowhere else in the *Dogmatics*: seriousness in approaching
creation is not incompatible with delight in the subject matter. Not for
nothing does *CD* III offer us Barth's reflections on such matters as erotic
love, angels, prayer, and the nature of Christian joy, besides the topics one
would normally expect to be treated in this doctrine.

Reflection on our basic move in this chapter can begin with a familiar
claim of theological anthropology: that human beings are created in the
imago dei, the image of God (Genesis 1:26). What is meant by this assertion?
In the history of theology all manner of things have been put forward as
candidates for the *imago dei*. Humans are said to be in God's image because
they (in contrast to the other creatures) have an immortal soul, or because
they are possessed of reason, or because they have the moral law inscribed
in their hearts, or because they imitate God by sharing his dominion over the
earth. Without denying any of this, Barth fastens onto an aspect of the
biblical witness that has been curiously underweighted, if not ignored
entirely. The most illuminating text is perhaps Colossians 1:15: 'He [Jesus]
is the image of the invisible God, the first-born of all creation; for in him all
things in heaven and on earth were created … all things have been created
through him and for him.' The image of God, in other words, is not a
capacity that human beings possess, whether reason or morality or self-
shaping agency. The image of God is this man as the destiny in which all of
creation will be fulfilled. Rather than the image being an attribute, it is the

relation believers bear to the true man, Jesus Christ.

We may put it another way: why did God create the world?[2] The Christian tradition has been surprisingly reticent about addressing this question. When theologians have raised it at all, they have either said the answers lie shrouded in mystery, or have pointed to God's desire to be glorified in and through the creation. Barth thinks the first answer too agnostic, the second correct but still lacking in concreteness. For the Bible itself tells us why God made the world: so that God can shower grace upon his creature in the person of his Son. Creation, while a gift of God in its own right, never exists except as ordered toward its consummation in Christ. Our 'basic move' is thus the dependence of creation on the specific reality of Jesus Christ, who is the Alpha as well as the Omega.

Barth has a technical formula for expressing all this that has become famous: 'Creation is the external basis of the covenant, and the covenant is the internal basis of creation.' We saw what the term 'covenant' means in the previous chapter: God's self-giving commitment in Christ to be our God, binding himself in an eternal fellowship with humankind. If this covenant defines God's own identity, then it makes no sense to speak of creation in an abstract sense. Just as the Old Testament knows that the Creator is YHWH, the One who led Israel out of Egypt, so the New Testament knows that creation takes place in and for Jesus Christ (and is therefore also connected with God's love for Israel). Or to put it still another way, the agent of creation is not the god of the philosophers, but the triune God; hence our knowledge of it is intimately tied up with its destiny in Christ and the Spirit.

Barth argues this point at length in paragraph 40, which opens his account of creation in III/1. The claim that 'God created the world' is not an obvious fact that can be read from our experience: knowledge of creation is no less a confession of faith than the belief that Jesus rose from the dead. Creation can only be properly discerned and celebrated when we discern its destiny in Christ. This is no merely theoretical assertion, but one with enormous practical consequences. It implies the fundamentally positive Christian attitude toward the world, not just as a spiritual reality, but in its social and material dimensions as well. Precisely because knowledge of creation is a matter of faith, it is a fully self-involving form of knowledge. To know God as Creator is to be called to a life of joy, gratitude, and active engagement with the world; it means receiving and affirming one's own life as a gift.

As in every part of Christian doctrine, the affirmations made here – and others that flow from them – also entail some serious denials. We will examine these as we review specific issues in *CD* III. First, however, we need to say something about the language we use for talking about creation.

Imagining Genesis

What was God doing before he created the universe? As a traditional answer runs, 'creating hell, for people who ask such questions'. Augustine found this response frivolous, while Calvin saw it as a proper rebuke of human curiosity.[3] Nonetheless, both thinkers would have agreed that the question prompting it makes no sense: since time itself is part of what God creates, there is no 'before' or 'when' to creation. God stands outside of time (that is what it means to be eternal) in order to create a temporal universe. If this is true, it has important implications for how we read the biblical creation accounts. It means we should look on stories like Genesis 1–2 as naïve, narrative depictions of a truth essentially untouched by time. The world itself has a first moment, of course – the first point on its temporal axis; but God's relation to it is strictly atemporal.

Barth is not satisfied with this traditional way of stating the matter. To be sure, he agrees that God's act of creation eludes any attempt at straightforward description: we cannot capture the origin of history in historiographical terms. But that does not mean God's action is itself timeless. If creation has Christ as its basis and goal, then the beginning cannot be thought of as essentially different from this end. As Barth writes:

> According to Scripture there are no timeless truths, but all truths according to Scripture are specific acts of God in which he unveils himself; acts which as such have an eternal character embracing all times, but also a concretely temporal character. As Jesus Christ himself is eternal as God and stands as Lord above all times, but is also concretely temporal and in this way the real Lord of the world and his community, so it is with creation. (III/1, 60)

Creation is indeed a specific act, taking place 'in the beginning'. But as is often the case in Barth, this particular reaches beyond itself to embrace all things: from the farthest galaxy to the seed growing in my garden. Moreover, this first gift shares in the concretely temporal character of the covenant fulfilled in Jesus Christ. If this were not the case, then God's grace in Christ would be operating in a foreign realm; nature and grace would confront each other as strangers, and God could have no genuine fellowship with his world.

These affirmations rule out two possibilities for our talk about creation. On the one hand, we may not describe creation using the language of myth, in so far as myth pertains to those timeless truths about the cosmos of which pagan religion speaks. Creation is an event proceeding from God's free act, not a cycle of eternal return. On the other hand, since only faith grasps the world as created, we cannot understand creation by employing the tools of secular science, whether history, cosmology, or evolutionary biology. Such disciplines speak of creatures in abstraction from their destiny in Christ, and so never manage to speak of them as *creatures* at all. Add to this the simple fact that we cannot step outside our creatureliness so as to observe our creaturely coming-to-be.

Faith excludes the spectator's stance; this is as true for creation as it is for every other Christian doctrine. This raises the question of whether Barth follows Kant in drawing a sharp line between matters of fact and matters of value, or between science and religion/ethics. A sign that he worried about this issue appears in the preface to III/1, where he acknowledges that he has not tackled the scientific issues posed by creation, but has limited himself to exegesis of the Genesis accounts. Nonetheless, he does not close the door to other forms of inquiry: 'I am of the opinion ... that future workers in the field of Christian doctrine of creation will find many problems worth pondering in defining the point and manner of this twofold boundary [between theology and science]' (III/1, x).[4]

Beyond the alternatives of myth or history lies a third category, which Barth calls 'saga'.[5] We might refer to it simply as 'story'. As sagas, the stories in the opening chapters of Genesis differ not only from modern history-writing, but even from the histories recounted in other parts of the Bible. By contrast with the more or less 'realistic' storytelling in the books of Samuel and Kings, for example, the stories in Genesis 1–2 do not make the same sort of claim for factual veracity. They have the character of poetic legend more than of historic chronicle. But for all that, they are not timeless myths. The events they narrate do not 'stand for' ideas or principles, but command our attention as things that have actually happened:

> The biblical creation saga speaks ... without any nods or winks, without irony, without condescension, without accommodation. Its divination and poetry are intended to say exactly what it says in itself and in this connection. It does not merely use narrative as an accepted form. It is itself a narrative through and through. It has no philosophical system as an accompanying *alter ego* whose language can express abstractly what it says concretely. What it says can be said only in the form of its own narrative and what follows. (III/1, 87)

That the Genesis stories are clearly works of a master poet should not count against them. Such literal-mindedness would, Barth writes, reflect merely 'a ridiculous and middle-class habit of the modern Western mind which is supremely fantastic in its chronic lack of imagination ...' (III/1, 81). It should be noted that Barth thinks *all* of Scripture is shot through with this imaginative element, albeit in varying degrees. It is clearly in evidence, for example, in the New Testament accounts of the resurrection. How else can we speak of miracle other than by using our imaginations? (III/1, 78). In this way the first creation and the new creation are linked: both must be described using language that stretches our ordinary, earthbound habits of thought and speech.[6]

Creation and Covenant

All this sets an agenda for the first instalment of Barth's doctrine of creation, most of which consists of an extended exegesis of Genesis 1 and 2.

Famously, critical scholars in the nineteenth and early twentieth centuries saw two different hands at work here. They argued that Genesis 1 goes back to a 'Priestly' source (P), written after the Babylonian exile, and attributed Genesis 2 to an author known as the 'Jahvist' (J). Barth's use of this insight typifies his overall approach to historical criticism: while he does not think that theology must follow the lead of the historians, it may do so where this holds promise of illuminating the text. But this is precisely the case with respect to the first two chapters of Genesis. Distinguishing two creation stories helps us see the outer and inner dimensions of creation, its status both as a preparation for the covenant (the witness of the Priestly account) but also as a participation in the covenant (the witness of the J writer). We may note in passing that the source-critical picture has become much more complicated and contested since Barth's day; he would no doubt take this as vindication of his refusal to tie himself to particular critical theories. What matters in the end is not sources, but the witness that emerges from the text as it stands.

To say that 'creation is the external basis of the covenant' is to say that creation is an appropriate setting for the divine acts of mercy that will follow. Barth writes that creation in Genesis 1 is 'comparable to the building of a temple, the arrangement and construction of which is determined both in detail and as a whole by the liturgy which it is to serve' (III/1, 98). The temple is not an end in itself, but exists for the sake of the liturgy that takes place within it: thus he reads the whole of the first creation story as moving toward this liturgical consummation: God's 'Sabbath freedom, Sabbath rest and Sabbath joy, in which man, too, is summoned to participate' (III/1, 98). Here at the very beginning of his account, Barth offers a crucial hermeneutical clue for understanding his entire doctrine of creation. Creation is in no sense *necessary*; it exists *only* for the sake of God's overflowing grace. Conversely, because creation has this basis we can be completely and utterly confident in it, not worrying that God was compelled to create – perhaps as a means of working out some inner conflict? – or that creation lacks a perfection we have somehow to provide ourselves.

A single example may serve to illustrate Barth's exegetical development of these themes. Genesis 1:2 reads 'And the earth was formless and empty, and darkness was upon the face of the deep.' It is a classic textual crux. The passage can be read in Gnostic fashion, as referring to some pre-existing matter God struggled to work into shape. This mythic picture raises troubling theological questions. How can creation be solely and entirely God's good gift if there is this prior reality? Must we posit a rival deity to account for the formless void? No wonder the early church firmly rejected this view, insisting that God's creative act is absolute; God created the 'world from nothing' (*ex nihilo*), with no external constraints upon his action. On the other hand, even orthodox exegetes have suggested that perhaps God created chaos first and subsequently fashioned it into the world as we know it. Not only does this reading seem to follow the natural sense of the text, but it may be especially attractive in an age that thinks in terms of evolutionary change.

And yet Barth rejects the second alternative as firmly as he does the first. In a detailed excursus, he argues that the biblical writer could not possibly have meant that God created a world *tohu v'bohu*, 'waste and void'. Nor is the spirit depicted as brooding over the waters to be seen as the 'real' Spirit of God. Rather, Barth argues that the phrase evokes the world that *might* have been had God not uttered his life-giving Word. Verse 2 thus offers 'a portrait, deliberately taken from myth, of the world which according to his revelation was negated, rejected, ignored and left behind in his actual creation' (III/1, 108). This is admittedly a very strange (and strangely powerful) way of reading the text. It nicely underscores Barth's insistence on seeing creation as already an action of divine grace. For the pattern we see here is one we have already encountered: it is the logic of election, God's triumphant Yes that includes his No pronounced upon evil. Creation is not, of course, the decisive locus of this triumph. That honour belongs to Christ's victory on the cross. But it anticipates and bears witness to that victory, as God decides in favour of his good world and against the horrors of chaos. As Kathryn Tanner writes of Barth's doctrine, 'What God rejects in Christ is not a mere neutral non-being, and therefore creation too suggests deliverance.'[7]

This passage helps to focus the larger logic of Barth's account of creation. On the one hand, creation points ahead to that which fulfils it; it is the 'external basis of the covenant'. On the other hand, precisely this relationship secures creation's status as a divine gift, with an integrity all its own. Viewing creation in the context of the covenant, we cannot treat it as a mere world of facts in which we must create our own meanings. The world is inherently meaningful because God loves it, affirming it as an 'other' and as the recipient of his gifts: 'And God saw everything he had made, and behold, it was very good.' Barth underscores this point through a rich exegesis of the work of the six days in Genesis 1:1–31.

Corresponding to 'creation as the external basis of the covenant' is 'the covenant as the internal basis of creation', which forms the peculiar theme of Genesis 2. Here creation not only bears testimony to the covenant, but in some mysterious sense actually participates in it. Barth can even speak of a 'sacramental' view of creation at work in this second narrative (III/1, 233). The focus of the J account, of course, is God's creation of Adam and Eve and his placing them in the garden. If this story has a sacramental character, it is because it shows God not just making creatures but engaging them, sharing life with them in their own world. Barth thus stresses that Eden is not so much a perfect place, a utopian Paradise, as simply a good place: the place where God and human beings live together in covenant fellowship. Here God cares for his creatures, and creatures live by God's gracious provision. Indeed, God's command to Adam and Eve not to eat the fruit of one particular tree is simply one of many signs of God's care for them. Yet Barth does not want us to dwell too much even on this good place. Rather than evoking nostalgia for a lost past, the creation sagas tell us something important about the grace and constancy that God shows for his creatures. This constancy will not be revoked even when the covenant between them is troubled by sin – a disturbance that the narrative immediately following (Genesis 3) does no more than foreshadow.

After hundreds of pages of exegesis, Barth devotes the concluding section of III/1 (paragraph 42, 'The Yes of God the Creator') to drawing out the practical consequences of faith in creation. Here one is reminded of Wittgenstein's famous assertion that 'the world of the happy man is a different one from that of the unhappy man'.[8] I take the point of this saying to be not that the world fluctuates with our beliefs about it, but that apprehending truth cannot be separated from the shaping of the will and the affections; the latter are integral to our attempts to speak of 'reality'. While Barth cautions against identifying faith in creation with the adoption of any particular philosophical stance (cf. III/1, 340 ff.), I suspect he would have had no little sympathy for Wittgenstein's dictum. For when the Christian speaks of creation, she refers not to some neutral reality, but rather to the world God has radically affirmed in Jesus Christ. In Barth's language, creation is 'benefit', a gift that demands to be received as such. To miss its character as benefit is to miss the thing itself. The key here lies in acknowledgment of creation's sheerly gratuitous character, which can only be received in faith. To speak of creation as benefit is to place the emphasis on God's action, and not on myself as recipient. Thus Barth contrasts faith in creation with the characteristically modern attitude in which my own existence forms the necessary point of departure – the Cartesian 'I think, therefore I am'. In the sphere of Christian faith, the locus of certainty resides elsewhere: God creates me, therefore I am. The excursus on Descartes that follows is a good instance of Barth writing in an *ad hoc* apologetic mode, as he criticizes the idea that certainty about ourselves as creatures can be derived from introspection (III/1, 350 ff.). Even our *self*-knowledge as creatures can come only as God's gift.

The gift-character of creation applies no less to the concrete texture of human experience, to the fact that life is marked by both vitality and weakness, joy and sorrow, gain and loss. What are we to make of these antitheses? We can become invincible optimists, living in denial of the shadow-side of life; we can become world-weary pessimists, denying all the reasons there are to be glad; worst of all is the moderating skeptic who 'no longer cares either to laugh or weep', the only person who truly deserves to be called 'godless' (III/1, 78). All of these are forms of denial. The Christian, however, can both laugh and weep, enduring life's contradictions in the knowledge that the Creator has himself willed to be subject to them in the person of the Son. Moreover, we must not think of creation as an equal balance of light and shadow, *yin* and *yang*. In God's action at the cross, the Yes has already triumphed. Death and sorrow are destined to pass away, even if they are all too much a feature of our present experience:

Not, then, a static perfection of God beyond and above creaturely imperfection, but the contesting and overcoming of the imperfection of the creature by God's own intervention on its behalf. In the interests of this divine conflict and victory, it [the creature] may be imperfect, and even in its imperfection it already shares in God's own perfection. It does so in God's living action in Jesus Christ. It is the divine conflict and victory which forms the climax of the covenant and therefore the meaning and end of creation. And in him the created world is already perfect in spite of its imperfections, for the Creator is himself a creature, both sharing its creaturely peril, and guaranteeing and already actualizing its hope. If the created world is understood in the light of the divine mercy revealed in Jesus Christ ... its justification and perfection will infallibly be perceived and it will be seen to be the best of all possible worlds. (III/1, 385)

'The best of all possible worlds': the phrase alludes to Leibniz, whose Enlightenment optimism forms the subject of the final excursus of III/1. We must simply note the enormous risks Barth takes at this point. God justifies, says *yes* to his creation despite its present imperfections – an echo, clearly, of the doctrine of justification by faith. This opens the way for the fundamentally world-affirming attitude of the Christian, which, to be sure, is not quite the same as optimism. But such world-affirmation comes at a price. Unlike Leibniz, Barth has no rational theodicy to offer; the only justification for the horrors of existence is God's bearing the contradictions of creation in his own body. Christians have no answer to the 'problem' of evil, in so far as this 'problem' reflects a peculiarly modern construction in which the human being stands at the centre of theological concern. In comparison with this construct, Christian vision of life can be seen to be both more affirming (creation is gift, despite the shadows that attend it) and more hopeful (God has triumphed over evil and death, and calls us to joyful participation in that victory).

The Human Creature

Much modern thought about human nature begins by noting its essentially unfinished quality. Whereas the animal simply is, human beings become: they transcend themselves, projecting themselves in freedom into an uncertain future. Moreover, for this tradition – we can think of it as 'existentialist' in the broadest sense – the fact of death lends a peculiar urgency to human existence. Knowing that I will die, I make my decisions in the awareness that I am called to enact *this* life, *this* identity, in the time and circumstances given to me. In short, the 'I' emerges in the unique story I manage to tell between birth and death.

At a sheerly descriptive or phenomenological level, Barth stands firmly within this tradition of thought. He is in his own way an existentialist; thus, themes such as freedom, agency, finitude, and death play a prominent role in his theological anthropology. Nonetheless, Barth does not view human beings as constituted *by* their freedom in any immanent sense. What makes us human is nothing intrinsic to ourselves, but rather the fact of our standing in covenant relation to God. Moreover, we know that when Barth says 'grace' or 'covenant', he always means the concrete person of Jesus Christ. And so we come back to Barth's basic move in the doctrine of creation: the *one human being Jesus of Nazareth* is the image of God. That Jesus is the grace of God for us, that he names us his brothers and sisters – that is what constitutes our own lives as distinctively human.

It is worth pausing a moment to acknowledge this challenge to the modern, immanent construction of human identity. According to Barth, my identity derives not from my rational autonomy, my capacity for self-making, but rather from the fact that I am claimed by the first-century Jew, Jesus of Nazareth. But this move must result in a radical redefinition of concepts like 'human identity' and 'personhood'. For 'being claimed by Jesus' is a condition I share with the slumdweller, the spina bifida baby, and the terrorist – as also with the investment banker, the professional athlete, and the saint. Weak and strong alike are encompassed within Jesus, the image of God. Personhood turns out not to consist in a quality at all, but in a sheerly gracious and particular relationship God establishes with the individual in Christ. At the very least, this seems a rather eccentric understanding of what it means to be a person.

Precisely so: for ek-centric literally means being off-centre, having one's centre located outside a given boundary. Barth thinks about human identity in ek-centric terms, referring it to the particular life of the man Jesus. To be sure, this does not exclude our saying more general things about human nature: a Christian doctrine of the person must be developed in reflective and rational terms. It does mean that Christian anthropology will make constant reference to Jesus as 'true man', in whom human existence has been faithfully actualized once for all. Barth reasons from this concrete particular to the universally human.

Church Dogmatics III/2 is one of the most carefully and beautifully structured volumes of the entire work. In his introductory discussion, Barth makes his case for grounding anthropology in the knowledge of Jesus Christ: 'As the man Jesus is himself the revealing Word of God, he is the source of our knowledge of the nature of man as created by God' (III/2, 3). Each of the four paragraphs that follow examines a dimension of this human nature. Paragraph 44, 'Man as the Creature of God', explores humanity's unique vocation as the creature made for fellowship with God, in light of Jesus' identity as the 'man for God'. This vocation is a task, though the task is but a response to God's prior gift: 'As the history of the divine deliverance for each and every human being is wholly exclusively [Jesus Christ], so he himself is wholly and exclusively the history of the divine deliverance for each and every human being' (III/2, 70). Paragraph 45, 'Man in His Determination as the Covenant Partner of God', describes the relational character of human existence in light of Jesus as 'the man for others'. Jesus' whole life was characterized by his existence as one who serves, a point Barth backs up with a wealth of exegesis. In short, all humanity is 'co-humanity' (*Mitmenschlichkeit*); I contradict my humanity every time I try to live as though my neighbour did not exist.

The theme of co-humanity deserves further comment, given the central role it plays in Barth's theology and especially his ethics. The language of 'I and Thou' obviously echoes that of Jewish philosopher Martin Buber, and behind him Ludwig Feuerbach, who likewise emphasized the essentially social character of the human being. What is interesting is not that Barth employs personalist themes, which had become part of the common coinage of mid-twentieth-century philosophy and theology, but rather the way he employs them. Thus, he does not depict Jesus Christ simply as a model of availability to the other; he is the incarnation of God's availability to us. But God's actions toward creatures always point back to the mystery of his inner life. For Barth, the ultimate pattern of I–Thou encounter is that of the Trinity, in the mutual self-giving of Father and Son in the unity of the Spirit. It is thus that Barth seeks to ground talk of co-humanity not just in Christology, but in the eternal life of the Godhead.

Barth's talk of co-humanity is as much a political statement as it is a claim about interpersonal relations. Recall that his larger concern here is with the covenant of grace, a covenant that has an essentially social character: it consists in God's binding himself to a people (and through that people to all of humankind). Moreover, Jesus focused his attention not on Israel in general, but on the sick and the weak, tax collectors and sinners. Although Barth does not draw explicit political conclusions from this, his other writings make clear what these are: Jesus as the 'man for others' implies a 'church for others', whose witness consists largely in its life of service to the world. The theme plays a major role in the doctrine of reconciliation, especially in the ecclesiology set forth in IV/3.

But we do not have to look to the church to find a sign of our created co-humanity. Rather, God has inscribed one deep within human flesh itself: the sheer fact of sexual differentiation. Already in III/1, Barth pointed out that the most obvious interpretation of the words 'in the image of God he created them' is the immediately succeeding phrase, 'male and female he created them' (Genesis 1:27). This differentiation of humankind into two sexes serves to ground our co-humanity in the very structure of embodied life. Note that Barth is not speaking in the first instance about marriage, but about the distinction of male and female as such. Man and woman exist to help and serve each other; no person is sovereignly autonomous in the way that modern culture tends to celebrate; in their fundamental dependence on each other, human beings live out their vocation to be an image of the Trinity.

It would be easier for us if Barth developed his view of male–female relations in terms of sheer egalitarian reciprocity, but he does not. On his reading, the Bible clearly speaks in terms of precedence and subordination; man comes first, and woman follows; man is superior, woman inferior. To be sure, this claim must immediately be qualified. Thus Barth emphasizes that man's superior role consists in his vocation to serve, and is not a warrant for exploitation. Likewise, woman's inferior role does not make her a slave: she, too, is possessed of an autonomy and dignity that man must honour. It is only in their *co*-humanity that they constitute the creaturely image of God. The fact remains that Barth's understanding of the sexes is frankly hierarchical – as, indeed, is his doctrine of the Trinity itself.[9] Three things can be said to this. First, even if one is unhappy with the conclusions Barth draws, one can at least acknowledge that he has not taken the easy way out. Texts like Colossians 3:18–19 and Ephesians 5:22–33 are there in the pages of Scripture, and they cannot be erased simply by repeated quotations of Galatians 3:28. Second, a good deal of contemporary feminist thought, both inside and outside the church, also seeks to move beyond the liberal rhetoric of equality, which in its own way tends to obscure women's irreducible otherness. And third, one might ask whether Barth's teaching at this point is not shaped too much by nineteenth-century images of romantic love, rather than by the biblical witness. The Bible portrays men and women as engaged in a mysterious dance, a living sacrament of Christ's relation to the church, and for which 'equality' is indeed a woefully inadequate characterization. Whether this mystery translates into Barth's own rather narrow picture of sexual roles is another question.

Barth, as I said, affirms in modified form the existentialist picture of the human being as self-transcending subject. This can be clearly seen in a thesis that appears not in *CD* III but in *Dogmatics in Outline*: 'Heaven is the creation inconceivable to man, earth the creation conceivable to him. He himself is the creature on the boundary between heaven and earth.'[10]

That human beings exist in a relation to 'heaven' – the created world that lies beyond all human reckoning – is a way of denoting our transcendent nature, our being drawn out of the mere givenness of life into relation with God. Human existence has a restless, dynamic quality; note that Barth consistently speaks of it as a 'history'. Yet no matter how high we ascend, we will always be children of earth, the creation that is conceivable to us. Humans are precisely those who inhabit the boundary between heaven and earth, spirit and nature, the infinite and the finite. Note, however, how easy it would be for this picture to be split up into mutually excluding alternatives. We are beings bound for heaven – who must then leave our earthly identities behind. We are children of earth – and remaining loyal to earth, have no choice but to forfeit heaven. *Bleib der Erde treu*, wrote Nietzsche; 'Stay true to the earth', a sentiment echoed by that most anti-gnostic of modern Christian writers, Dietrich Bonhoeffer.

Barth's picture of human existence, however, does not force us to make these choices. We return to our basic move: Jesus Christ is the human being made in the image of God. *He* inhabits the boundary between heaven and earth. Human transcendence, therefore, lies not in the embrace of some alienating spirituality, but in accepting the promise of his risen and glorified body. As Fergus Kerr has argued, Barth's anthropology allows us to think of a 'beyond' to life without having to despise our finitude. We can feel at home inside our own skins, precisely because Jesus has affirmed our embodied existence by taking up space inside it.[11] The ultimate warrant for Barth's view of humanity is thus John 3:14: 'The Word became flesh, and lived among us.'

These remarks may be helpful to keep in mind as one reads the final two sections of *CD* III/2: paragraph 46, 'Man as Soul and Body', and paragraph 47, 'Man in His Time'. In both instances, Barth acknowledges a certain duality to life. We are embodied beings, yet with the capacity to discipline and direct our bodies to attain certain ends. We are also radically temporal beings, who live with the awareness that we must die. Yet death is not the final word about us; we can accept death without fear, in the knowledge that God has both conquered death and, in Jesus, the Lord of time, taken our time into his eternity:

> Man lives in the allotted span of his present, past and future life. The One who was before him and will be after him, and who therefore fixes the boundaries of his being, is the eternal God, his Creator and Covenant-partner. He is the hope in which man may live in his time. (III/2, 437)

The exegetical excursus in paragraph 47 are especially rich. While Barth would disapprove of the phrase 'theology of death' – theology has to do with life, not death! – these passages say much about his approach to human finitude. It might be worth comparing 'Man in His Time' with modern theological works that address similar themes, such as Karl Rahner's *Theology of Death* or Eberhard Jüngel's *Death: the Riddle and the Mystery*.

Angels, Evil and God's Care for Creation

Church Dogmatics III/1 and III/2 set forth the main, positive content of the doctrine of creation: the ordering of creation to covenant, and the specific character of the human creature as God's covenant partner. Yet several issues still remain unaddressed. The world proceeds perfect from God's hand, yet it is also sustained by him across time; creation is utterly good, yet it is threatened by evil at every moment; human beings occupy the boundary between heaven and earth, yet according to the biblical witness heaven has some mysterious inhabitants of its own. This unfinished business sets the triple agenda of III/3: divine providence, the Nihil, and the angels.

Christian faith confesses God as Creator, the One who brings all things in heaven and on earth into being. To confess providence is to say that this same God does not abandon the world, but lovingly directs it toward a goal. Barth writes:

The doctrine of providence deals with the history of created being as such, in the sense that in every respect and in its whole span this proceeds under the fatherly care of God the Creator, whose will is done and is to be seen in his election of grace, and therefore in the history of the covenant between himself and man, and therefore in Jesus Christ. (Thesis to paragraph 48, III/3, 3)

As this thesis statement suggests, Barth does not think of providence first of all in terms of some general oversight of creation. Instead, God's universal rule is a function of a more particular lordship: his eternal determination to be God for us in Jesus Christ. As Tanner puts it, providence '*is* simply that determination in its implications for the history of the world as a whole'; it is election 'unrolled in time'.[12] This connection between predestination and providence obtains down to the smallest details of finite existence. As God involves himself intimately in the creature's welfare in election, so he involves himself intimately in its earthly life; God actively 'preserves, accompanies, and rules' the creation. God is the Lord, and his will will be done – infallibly so.

This view needs to be carefully distinguished, however, from the belief that God 'makes' everything happen. A careful reading of paragraphs 48 and 49 will show that Barth takes great pains to guard against all merely mechanical or deterministic understandings of God's rule. God neither coerces creatures, nor lives their lives for them, nor cuts them loose to find their own way; that would suggest a zero-sum game, in which God and creatures are forced to compete for scant resources of agency or power. That is scarcely the picture of God's care for the world seen in the Bible. It is no accident that the thesis statement cited above echoes the language of the Lord's Prayer. The Lord of creation is not a tyrant, but the Father in heaven. God's will is done, but not without the urgent prayers of his children. Indeed, Barth conceives of Christian prayer as a kind of paradigm instance of Christian action (see III/3, 264) and therefore of human freedom itself. Men and women are most free precisely at the point where they are most dependent on God; far from destroying human spontaneity, grace unleashes it.[13] The link between prayer and freedom reoccurs at many places in the *Dogmatics*, most notably in the ethics of reconciliation.

Thus Barth offers no theoretical resolution of the problem of divine and human freedom. Nor does he simply affirm both, resorting to easy talk about 'paradox' (a category he almost never invokes; it goes against the grain of his rationalism). What he gives us instead is a series of ordered descriptions of divine and human agency, imitating the pattern found in the Bible. The divine agency always takes priority; the human response is real only as it is shaped and conditioned by grace – freedom in the modern sense of pure, self-actualizing autonomy is a fiction – but the response is nonetheless fully free. This procedure seeks to honour the rational coherence of Christian beliefs about divine power and human freedom, while avoiding a closure that would threaten the integrity of either. We cannot offer explanations as to *how* divine and human agency cohere; but our affirming both is by no means inconsistent. Here, if anywhere, we encounter that 'high tolerance for mystery' that George Hunsinger names as one of the features of Barth's theology. As Flannery O'Connor said concerning a character in one of her works: 'Freedom cannot be conceived simply. It is a mystery and one which a novel ... can only be asked to deepen'.[14] Barth would certainly have agreed, though with the caveat that the novelist and the theologian seek to deepen the mystery in quite different ways.

Before God accompanies or rules creation, however, he 'preserves' it. Preserves it from what? Already in Barth's exegesis of Genesis 1, we saw him depicting God's creative work as an act of rescue; the Yes to creation involves a No to the chaos, evil, and destruction that would mark a world without grace. God thus preserves creation from something far worse than mere neutral non-existence. That 'something' is Nothing, or what Barth calls *das Nichtige*. The term is famously untranslatable. The least inadequate rendering I know of is 'the Nihil', with its useful echoes of 'nihilism' and 'annihilation', and it is the word I will employ here. Barth takes up this theme in paragraph 50, under the heading 'God and the Nihil'.[15]

Does the Nihil exist, or doesn't it? It is very difficult to give a straightforward answer to this question. Indeed, one suspects Barth employs the concept as a way of subverting straightforward answers in this area. Even more so than creaturely freedom, evil defies systematic treatment (III/3, 293–4) . But we can say this much: the Nihil is not real in the way that God and creatures are real. God says yes to his own life and yes to the creature's life, but to chaos and destruction, sin and death he has only no to say. God says no to Auschwitz, and no to the most trivial and commonplace sins of the individual. For the Christian there is really only one definition of evil, and that is 'whatever God does not want'.

To say no more than this might suggest a view of evil as mere appearance or illusion – not at all what Barth intends here. For 'what God does not want' after all happens. Wars are fought, murders committed, injustices done. One can hardly doubt the existential reality of evil as a factor in our experience. It is then tempting to seek to account for evil by describing it as the result of bad choices: God made human beings free, and they misused their freedom by sinfully turning away from God. Evil is the price God paid for a free world – the familiar free will defense, reconciling the divine justice with the divine love. Barth does not resort to this apologetic strategy. It would empty the notion of freedom of all content, suggesting that God offers evil as one option among others; good and evil would then stand equally balanced. But the whole force of Barth's doctrine of election is to say that God rejects evil, wills to exclude it from his creation. This also means that we cannot make sense of evil by tracing it to some flaw in creation itself. We saw earlier that creation has a shadow side, a dimension of loss and sadness that makes our lives bittersweet. Barth is emphatic, however, that this feature of creation is not what we mean by evil (and cites the music of Mozart to prove it; III/3,

297–9). Indeed, there is no *accounting* for evil at all; Barth resolutely refuses to satisfy our demand for a theodicy.

At this point we need to remind ourselves once again of Barth's basic move in the doctrine of creation. God made the world so that, in Jesus, he could 'so love' it (John 3:16). And this provides us with the clue we need. In deciding for Jesus and his cross, God triumphs over the powers of darkness at a single stroke; thus creation comes into being with this victory behind it. But what God does all at once and eternally, the creature can only experience in time. That, in effect, is what history is: God's tolerating evil just long enough so that the creature can witness God's victory, and just so participate in it. Death, evil, and the Nihil hold no terrors for us, because God has dealt decisively with these powers once and for all. The creature therefore has no other destiny than a life of joyful gratitude for what God has done.

If there is a constant in Christian theologies of evil, it is no doubt the idea that God permits – but does not directly cause – evil to occur. The idea of God's permission or toleration of evil occurs, indeed, in Scripture itself, and it reappears in all the great Christian thinkers. Broadly speaking, this is Barth's answer as well. But he gives the notion a uniquely Christological twist. To put it in as compressed form as possible, Barth concentrates God's permission of evil at creation and his triumph over it into a single event, and in such a way that the triumph precedes the permission. That is, evil has no other 'reality' than that which derives from its pre-emptive negation. It 'is' not, because God rejects it. And God rejects it so radically that he allows it to exist only as that which has already been annihilated – that is, as the Nihil. Yet to the extent that human beings fail to trust in God's grace, they surrender to the power of this unreal thing; this is precisely what we mean by 'sin'. Indeed, human beings of themselves completely lack the resources that would allow them to deal with the Nihil. They can only pray that God will deliver them from evil, confident in the victory that Jesus Christ has already won over the Nihil. As always, the overall force of Barth's account is to underscore the utter faithfulness and reliability of God, such that the encounter with evil need never generate any ultimate anxiety: 'If God is for us, who is against us?' (Romans 8:32).

Barth's teaching about the Nihil has attracted two sorts of criticism, each the reverse of the other. One school says that in thinking about evil only from the perspective of its defeat – a defeat insured from all eternity through God's electing decree – Barth renders history and spiritual struggle meaningless. Why should I pray, go to church, do battle on behalf of justice if everything has already been accomplished in advance? The devil is not given his due because there is no devil, no real 'opposition' to God. Another school worries that by making God's triumph over evil the ground of creation, Barth makes evil necessary – for what is a victory without an opponent? In this account, does not God's permission of evil amount to a tacit approval? These two criticisms finally amount to different forms of the same charge, namely that Barth teaches the doctrine of *apokatastasis* – the inevitable restitution of all things.

While Barth's specific concept of the Nihil has found few followers, his approach to the question of evil raises issues any theology must confront. Should one attempt to offer a theodicy, as many theologians and philosophers do even today? What assumptions about God, the world, and human suffering underlie such efforts? Is there something fundamentally askew when we make 'evil', in the abstract, a focus of Christian reflection? Or are we not rather called to proclaim Christ's victory over evil, and join in the ongoing struggle against the principalities and powers of this world? Whether one follows Barth in this area or not, one can at least acknowledge his unwillingness to give the devil more than his due.[16] We will return to this set of questions in the discussion at the end of the chapter.

Having left the depths of hell behind, Barth concludes III/3 on a far more cheerful note: with a glance toward the arching vaults of heaven. Paragraph 51 contains Barth's angelology, under the title 'The Ambassadors of God and Their Opponents'. Perhaps nowhere else in the doctrine of creation does Barth write so strongly against the grain of modern, secular sensibilities. For his rival Rudolf Bultmann, heaven and angels belong to those parts of the Bible that need to be demythologized, along with demons, virginal conceptions, and empty tombs. For Barth, however, angels are crucial actors in the biblical narrative. That we cannot literally picture what they are like is a trivial objection. After all, we also cannot picture the act of creation, yet we trust the stories in Genesis 1–2 to be an adequate witness to God's creative work. Just so, the Old and New Testament witness to angels comes to us in imaginative form – which is exactly as it should be, given the wondrous character of the angels themselves.

Indeed, the word 'witness' is peculiarly apt here. For Barth interprets angelic nature purely in terms of angelic function; the angels who appear in the pages of Scripture are witnesses, messengers, as the Greek word *angelos* itself suggests:

> God's action in Jesus Christ, and therefore his lordship over his creature, is called the 'kingdom of heaven' because first and supremely it claims for itself the upper world. From this God selects and sends his messengers, the angels, who precede the revelation and doing of his will on earth as objective and authentic witnesses, who accompany it as faithful servants of God and man, and who victoriously ward off the opposing forms and forces of chaos. (Thesis to paragraph 51, III/3, 369)

Barth opens his account with a discussion of 'The Limits of Angelology', in which he criticizes various patristic, medieval, and modern approaches to the topic. His worries are clear enough: the subject of angels invites speculation, and the history of Christian reflection on angels (for example, Pseudo-Dionysius on the angelic hierarchies) has often seemed to have little to do with the creatures depicted in the Bible. Yet as is so often the case, Barth begins with critical delimitations so that he can say what he wants to say with greater confidence. Talk about angels must be disciplined by the witness of Scripture; but what does Scripture itself have to say?

The interpretive move Barth makes at this point is crucial. For angels belong to the gospel in so far as *heaven* belongs to the gospel, or more precisely: as the kingdom of heaven does (the phrase comes from Matthew's gospel, but reflects wider scriptural usage; see the excursus on 433–41). God does not exercise his rule over creation in a vacuum. According to the Bible, God carves out a distinctive place for himself *within* creation, and it is from here that his kingly reign proceeds: 'Thy kingdom come, thy will be done, on earth as it is in heaven'. Thus Barth writes that 'God rules in heaven as in a creaturely sphere' (III/3, 447). I would suggest that this insight is pathsetting, quite beyond the specific strengths and weaknesses of Barth's angelology. It is an implicit rebuke to the modern de-spatialization of God – to the notion that if God is transcendent, the beyond of the finite cosmos, he cannot also take up space within it.

But if heaven is a creaturely realm, it must be populated by creatures; these are the angels. Who are they and what do they do? They are not free agents, but agents of God's will and work. They serve, bear witness, and offer assistance. The angels are 'God's pure witnesses, beside whom there is none to compare on earth, who are therefore needed on earth, and who by the goodness of God are given to us in their reality' (III/3, 483–4). This witness is utterly indispensable:

> Without the angels God himself would not be revealed and perceptible. Without them he would be hopelessly confused with some earthly circumstance, whether in the form of a sublime idea or a golden calf. But by means of his holy angels he sees to it that this dimension is always open and perceptible. (III/3, 485)

It is not, of course, that angels take the place of Christ or the Holy Spirit; they do not 'mediate' revelation in that sense (as the letter to the Hebrews makes clear). God's action in the world is not limited to the angelic witness (III/3, 493). On the other hand, there is nothing superfluous in the divine economy. If the biblical narrative is filled with angels, this is but an indication that God chooses to glorify himself in a creaturely garb. What the doctrine has to do with, in the end, is the concrete means God chooses to be transcendent ('heavenly') in the midst of the cosmos known to us (the 'earthly'), in such a way as to enhance rather than dissolve mystery. Angels, in effect, mark the trans-empirical presence and agency of God among us, disrupting reality in ways that bear witness to the kingdom.

Barth's angelology is a fascinating example of the way in which tradition and modernity mingle in his thought. On the side of tradition is simply the fact that he includes this topic in his *Dogmatics*. The entire discussion is an implicit rebuke of Bultmann, who would exclude angels from his account of existence because it reflects a mythical, pre-modern consciousness. Humanity has grown up, and while there was a time for belief in angels that day is long past. For Barth, not only are such bold assertions only hopelessly anthropocentric, but even fail to embody the true spirit of the Enlightenment. To find out what is real we do not make *a priori* assumptions about what can and cannot be true; we engage in inquiry – in this case, inquiry into the angelic agency that accompanies and serves the kingdom. If the biblical witness points us in this direction, then we are not engaged in myth-mongering, but describing reality; 'our only concern is with what is' (III/3, 517). At the same time, it cannot be denied that Barth engages in a kind of demythologizing of his own. His angels are not free-floating, supernatural presences inviting all sorts of speculation about their nature, names, and hierarchies (and they are certainly not the sentimentalized angels of contemporary pop culture). While we must say angels are real, their reality is exhausted by the service they render to the kingdom of God. Barth subjects talk about angels to rational discipline, but it is a discipline that springs from the *ratio fidei*, not from the limits set by the (severely impoverished) modern imagination.

Much briefer than Barth's discussion of the angels is his account of their opponents, the demons (III/3, 519–31). He goes out of his way to insist that angels and demons are not two species within a common genus. *Pace* much of the tradition, devils are not fallen angels; they are, rather, manifestations of the chaos and nothingness which constantly threaten creation, but which (as we have already seen) are powerless against God's No. Like evil itself, demons must be reckoned with: 'They are' (523). But they intrude in the world only as that which we must radically oppose, in whom we cannot 'believe' even for a moment. Indeed, demons are in some sense '*the* myth, the myth of all mythologies' (521). As in his overall account of evil, Barth warns us that there is danger in not taking demons and the devil seriously at all, and an even greater danger in taking them too seriously. The challenge of the demonic is to refuse to let it grasp our imagination, but rather to let ourselves be summoned (by our fellow-creatures the angels) to faith in Christ's triumph over evil, and hence to a serious engagement with evil in our own world:

> It is Jesus Christ, God in his person, who as the Lord and Victor overthrows nothingness and its lying powers. It is in the history of his conflict, of the kingdom of God dawning in him … that it is not merely true, but at the cost of the sacrifice of the Son of God and therefore in glory it becomes true, that nothingness and demons have nothing to declare … In Jesus Christ himself this triumph is won only in the history of that conflict. And our celebration of it, our liberation from demons, can take place only as we participate in this history. (III/3, 530)

The fourth part of *CD* III deals with the ethics of creation. Having situated human beings in relation to God as their Creator, Barth asks what this relatedness means for the moral act: 'to what extent the one command of the one God who is gracious to human beings in Jesus Christ is also the command of their Creator' (III/4, 3). Organized around the theme of freedom, this part-volume not only addresses a standard raft of 'moral' issues – war, contraception, abortion, homosexuality, and the like – but also such matters as keeping the Sabbath and the role of honour in personal identity. To a great extent, the concreteness of these discussions makes up for the relative abstractness of the treatment of God's command in *CD* II/2. We will discuss the ethics of creation in greater detail in chapter 7.

Barth in Dialogue: Stanley Hauerwas on Suffering

The overall thrust of Barth's doctrine of creation is to allow human beings boldly to affirm their finitude. The world, our bodies, our limited span of existence are not aspects of a curse to be overcome or 'transcended'. The redemption God offers us is not redemption from this world and this life, but redemption of this world and this life. This deeply anti-Gnostic point lies behind Barth's radically Christological interpretation of creation. Precisely because creation has its destiny in Jesus – the concrete realization of God's gracious covenant with humankind – we can be confident that the world truly is, and is to be celebrated. Faith in creation is simply equivalent to praise of the triune Creator, who pronounces his blessing on all things as the climax of his work: 'God saw everything that he had made, and indeed, it was very good' (Genesis 1:31).

Very good; but the world often does not *seem* good, especially when we are threatened with illness or other forms of unexplained suffering. The existence of evil in a world supposedly created by God seems, to many, to pose one of the major challenges to Christian faith. What would a theological textbook be without a discussion of 'the problem of evil'? Yet as we have seen, Barth strongly denies that Christian dogmatics has any place for a theodicy. He argues that the project assumes a neutral standpoint from which we can comprehend both God and evil, and from which we can then try to work out the relation between the two. For Barth, however, no such standpoint exists. The believer knows about evil only from within the drama of creation and covenant; she is not a spectator, but a participant. And from within the drama, one can only confess God's victory over evil (the Nihil) that occurred with his initial decision for covenant fellowship. One reason Barth approaches the issues this way is precisely so that Christian faith in creation's goodness remains uncompromised. The believer indeed 'has to do' with evil – as that which God has overcome for our sake, as that from which we must continually pray to be delivered. Where we do not have to do with evil, however, is in the context of creation. Suffering and decay, disappointment and death; all belong to the twilight that is part of our experience of this world. Yet they are not *per se* evil. They are but manifestations of creation's 'shadow side', serving as a testimony to our utter dependence upon God for our life and salvation.

In the remainder of this chapter, I propose to bring Barth's thinking about finitude and the shadow side of creation into dialogue with the work of Stanley Hauerwas. To be sure, Hauerwas is more commonly associated with topics such as the church and the shaping of moral character than with the theology of creation. Yet while he may lack a developed doctrine of creation, his writings on medical ethics constitute a powerful engagement with the theme of finitude – what it means to be God's embodied creatures. Like all Hauerwas's work, his essays on medicine are an inquiry into the coherence of Christian convictions with Christian practice. Just as 'beliefs' for Hauerwas are not simply mental events, so 'actions' are more than just our choices; both proceed from something more basic – a way of life or *ethos* that determines who we are. To describe this way of life we must attend to such matters as the stories we tell, the practices we engage in, and the communities of which we are a part. Thus an essay titled 'Practicing Patience: How Christians Should Be Sick' is not simply an exploration of a particular virtue; it opens up into theological reflection on the God who calls us to be patient, and who is himself patient with us. If one can speak of Hauerwas's method, one might describe it as a complex mediation between ordinary life – the experience of being sick, cultural attitudes toward death, the institutions of modern medicine – and the particular story told by the Christian community.[17] The result is what might be called an *ad hoc* apologetics of creation, aimed at helping the reader see how her own life and even suffering might make sense as the gift of a good Creator. This form of inquiry provides an illuminating contrast with Barth, who, at least on the surface, approaches finitude and suffering solely from within the confines of the biblical narrative. In what follows, I will focus on two particular works of Hauerwas: the essay titled 'Should Suffering Be Eliminated? What the Retarded Have to Teach Us', and the short book titled *Naming the Silences: God, Medicine, and Suffering*.[18]

'Should Suffering Be Eliminated' opens with a simple question: should society set as a goal the preventing of retardation? At a utilitarian level, the answer seems simple; if retardation were eliminated (for example, through better prenatal care), resources now devoted to care of the retarded might be freed up for other purposes. Moreover, why not seek to prevent a condition that subjects children to often painful and difficult lives? Yet there is something that bothers us about such answers, Hauerwas suggests. Besides the particular moral issues involved in care of the retarded – matters such as discrimination, equal rights, and the risk of paternalism – retardation raises basic questions concerning what it means to be human. In particular, it poses the question of suffering:

> I suspect that at least part of the reason it seems so obvious that we ought to prevent retardation is the conviction that we ought to prevent suffering. No one

should will that an animal should suffer gratuitously. No one should will that a child should endure an illness. No one should will that another person be born retarded. That suffering should be avoided is a belief as deep as any we have. That someone born retarded suffers is obvious. Therefore, if we believe we ought to prevent suffering, it seems we ought to prevent retardation. (561)

But while this assumption 'draws upon some of our most profound moral convictions', it simplifies matters grossly. Much of Hauerwas's essay is devoted to exploring the complexities involved in the notion of suffering. *Contra* the modern ideal of total self-possession, he argues that being limited, subject to forces beyond one's control, is in fact basic to the human condition. None of us 'has' our identity as something we own. All of us are in the position of having to integrate pain, frustration, and incompleteness into the overall fabric of our life's story. Moreover, we also 'suffer' the actions of others upon us; while we like to pretend that we are strong, the fact is that we depend on others for our existence. The retarded bring this uncomfortable fact to our awareness. The question that finally confronts us is not what we should 'do about' retardation, or even what we should 'do for' the retarded. The question is whether we are open to sharing our lives with (and receiving from) these people who are profoundly different from ourselves, hence being freed from 'the false and vicious circle of having to appear strong before others' weakness' (573).

This is an all-too-hasty summary of a complex essay, but it allows us to see certain themes emerge that are typical of Hauerwas's work. There is the critique of modern individualist notions of the self. If the retarded are genuinely members of the human community, then can we sustain the notion that my identity, my 'I', finally consists in what I think or accomplish on my own?[19] There is the appreciation of finitude. For moderns, the notion that there are limitations on my project (including the limitations imposed by my body) is finally intolerable. Such Gnosticism stands in sharp contrast to the Christian acceptance of embodied life, with its inexplicable sorrows and disappointments. To avoid all suffering would mean avoiding the particular, contingent goodness of this world. Finally, there is the pervasive Hauerwasian theme of community: the essay characteristically concludes with thoughts on sharing our joys and sorrows with those who differ from us. The theme is obviously indebted to Barth's notion of created co-humanity. It also hints at Hauerwas's thinking on the church, explicitly spelled out in works like *A Community of Character* and *The Peaceable Kingdom*.

The goal of this essay might fairly be described as 'locating' the notion of suffering in human existence, drawing on the particular example of the retarded. What Hauerwas does not do, however, is seek to *explain* suffering. Indeed, he worries that his reflections on the role suffering plays in our lives might be interpreted as a generalized approval of suffering as, say, an opportunity for growth: 'I am not suggesting that every form of pain or suffering can or should be seen as some good or challenge. Extreme suffering can as easily destroy as enhance. Nor do I suggest that we should be the kind of people who can transform any suffering into benefit' (564). To do so would come perilously close to providing a theodicy – a project Hauerwas joins Barth in explicitly rejecting.

His most extensive thoughts on this topic occur in the book *Naming the Silences*. In this haunting, evocative meditation on the relation of God to suffering, Hauerwas focuses on an especially 'hard case': the suffering of children. Much of the book consists of commentary on stories (novels as well as non-fiction accounts) intended to bring such suffering before our eyes. Indeed, the story form is integral to the book's argument: part of Hauerwas's point is that any attempt to theorize suffering is badly mistaken. He rejects such theories for two reasons. First, writers in this area tend to assume that they are addressing 'the' problem of God and suffering, whereas in fact theodicies are always historically located; they presuppose a particular god and a particular experience of human suffering. For Hauerwas, a Christian account of suffering can only proceed from faith in the triune God, the God of the cross. This is not at all clear in many contemporary discussions of theodicy.

Hauerwas's second reason for rejecting theodicy is that, however well-intentioned, it tends to domesticate the anger we rightly feel in the face of suffering. *Naming the Silences* begins with an extended paraphrase of Peter DeVries' extraordinary novel, *The Blood of the Lamb*, which has as its central event a child's death by cancer. Central to Hauerwas's argument is the refusal of the book's protagonist, Don Wanderhope, to be consoled in the face of his daughter Carol's death. Wanderhope is a second-generation Dutch-American who has indeed wandered far from his family's Calvinist faith. He would seem to be the prototypical modern atheist: he rejects God so as to remain loyal to suffering humanity, embodied in his own beloved Carol. Yet rather like Job, Wanderhope's rage at God comes closer to genuine faith than do the neat answers of conventional religion. Here in a nutshell is Hauerwas's apologetic strategy: to show that faith in the triune God does not require us to surrender our human rage, but invites us into a strange communion with One who will not abandon us.

> There is no hope for us if our only hope in the face of suffering is that we can 'learn from it', or that we can use what we learn from the treatment of that suffering to overcome eventually what has caused it ... or that we can use suffering to organize our energies to mount effective protests against oppression. Rather, our only hope lies in whether we can place alongside the story of the pointless suffering of a child like Carol a story of suffering that helps us know we are not thereby abandoned. This, I think, is to get the question of 'theodicy' right. (34)

The question, in short, is not whether, but at whom, we hurl our angry imprecations at heaven.

Every theodicy presupposes a particular god. In *Naming the Silences* – and indeed, in many of his other writings on medical ethics – Hauerwas takes aim at a theodicy and a god that pervades contemporary life: the god of medicine. It is important to note that Hauerwas does not make doctors or medicine out to be the villains in his story, although there are aspects of modern medical practice he sharply calls into question.[20] Rather, the problem is the unrealistic expectations we place on medicine. Modern technocratic medicine raises the hope that we may overcome all suffering, pain, and even death itself – in effect, a denial of our existence as creatures. Such hope flourishes, Hauerwas argues, in a world that lacks any unifying story, and in which each must therefore confront his or her death alone. We look to science and medicine for an answer to the absurdity of our pain, and they respond in the only way they know how: by trying to 'fix' it, assuring us that everything will come out all right. Unlike the Christian God, the god of modern liberal societies is a sentimentalist, whose main function is to do everything he can to rescue the individual from the pain of embodied life. This faith sets up a very particular, historically situated theodicy. Its central puzzle is this: why a deity who *can* do everything and *wants* to do everything to relieve my finitude, fails in this effort. And if 'god cannot eliminate suffering, even though god may have the power to do so, then we will have to do god's task to insure that god can remain god' (48).

At this point, we can pause to compare Hauerwas's critique of theodicy with Barth's thoughts on creation's 'shadow side' in *CD* III/3. Barth ranges his reflections under the title 'The Misconception of Nothingness'. A certain apologetic intent is implied by the title itself. As we have seen, Barth resolutely rejects the idea that the shadows and disappointments of creaturely life are themselves evil, i.e. manifestations of the Nihil. The identification of finitude with real evil is inherently Gnostic, a 'slander on creation' and on the Creator (III/3, 299). Moreover, such an identification also allows us to naturalize evil to a certain extent. Modern theodicy begins with outrage against evil, but the very explanations it offers point at a kind of acceptance, as if knowing why evil is permitted allows us to make our peace with it. For Barth as for Hauerwas, evil constitutes a practical challenge rather than a theoretical puzzle. There are other similarities as well. Chief among them is the fact that neither Barth nor Hauerwas treats suffering or the fact of physical death as the most important threat from which humanity must be delivered. For the Christian, there are far worse things than dying.

Yet the differences between Barth and Hauerwas are also apparent. For Barth, the context in which we even come to talk about a shadow side of creation is directly Christological. How do we know that life's sorrows as well as joys, ends as well as beginnings, failures as well as successes, are all gifts of a good Creator? Because in Jesus Christ, the good Creator has declared that it is so:

For in him [Jesus Christ] God has made himself the Subject of both aspects of creaturely existence. And having made it his own in Jesus Christ, he has affirmed it in its totality, reconciling its inner antithesis in his own person. The creature does not have the character of nothingness as and because it is a creature and partakes in this antithesis. On the contrary, this is its perfection and the proof of its creation in and for Jesus Christ. In this it is determined for its place in the covenant of God. In this it is energized and equipped for life in fellowship with its Creator, for work in his service, for faith, obedience and prayer ... *For God himself has revealed and shown that this is the determination of his will by himself becoming a creature under this determination.* (III/3, 296; emphasis added)

Note that this is not a case of God simply meeting the cries of the sufferer with a sheer assertion of divine power (the reason so many readers find themselves dissatisfied with God's answer to Job). Barth makes clear that God's blessing on creation is spoken from *within* his primal decision to live as a creature, and hence to endure the tensions of both aspects of created existence. Creation exists for the sake of the covenant – that is, for the sake of God's faithfulness to creatures in Jesus Christ. It is in light of this revealed constancy that the sorrows and contradictions of life are endurable for the Christian. They are endurable not because 'God suffers with us', but because the yes and no of creation are gathered within the victorious Yes that is Jesus himself.

By contrast to Barth's Christological handling of these issues, Hauerwas addresses suffering in a quasi-apologetic way. Thus, in *Naming the Silences*, the question of suffering bears the closest possible connection to questions of human loneliness and solidarity. Through his loss of Carol, Don Wanderhope comes to discover 'how long, how long is the mourners' bench upon which we sit, arms linked in undeluded friendship, all of us, brief links, ourselves, in the eternal pity'.[21] Wanderhope pictures a solidarity in suffering among those who have finally learned to be rid of God. Rather than seeking to refute Wanderhope's atheism, Hauerwas takes it as a prophetic challenge to the church. The church is not called on to offer easy solutions to people's suffering. It is called to be a community where believers simply, in quiet ways, bear with each other in their pain.

Hauerwas underscores this point in the final story of the book, rehearsing Myra Bluebond-Langner's remarkable chronicle of her work among children dying of leukemia.[22] In her account, neither the children nor their caregivers are depicted as perfect; she does not sentimentalize her subjects. However, what she describes (and embodies) is a kind of care in which fellow sufferers help each other to 'name the silences'. Hauerwas comments:

We have no theodicy that can soften the pain of our death and the death of our children, but we believe that we share a common story which makes it possible for us to be with one another especially as we die. There can be no way to remove the loneliness of the death of leukemic children unless they see witnesses in the lives of those who care for them a confidence rooted in friendship with God and with one another. That, finally, is the only response we have to the 'problem' of the death of our children. (148)

Hauerwas, then, approaches creaturely suffering to a certain extent 'from below'. While he certainly writes from the perspective of Christian faith, he is wary of writing about suffering in a way that would take him too far from the mourners' bench that, ultimately, all of us share with Don Wanderhope. The descriptive power of his account is undeniable. Moreover, who would not want the church to be the kind of community Hauerwas describes, a suffering presence in the midst of so much human pain?

The risk of any apologetics – even, or rather especially an apologetics highly critical of modernity – is that theology will orient itself to a story other than the gospel. Hauerwas is well aware of this danger. He acknowledges that by emphasizing compassion for each other's hurt, he may simply end up underwriting 'an extremely attractive and humane form of unbelief' – namely, that 'in the absence of God the best we can do is comfort one another in the loneliness and the silences created by our suffering' (148). Still, he is willing to take this risk. His conviction seems to be that if one is to offer Christianity as an alternative to such humanism, one needs to take the latter seriously – even to the extent of finding it 'extremely attractive'. Hauerwas does not want to say that the Don Wanderhopes of this world are simply wrong. Rather, he wants to invite them into a community that lives by the story of the cross, and that is encompassing enough to honour all human grief. No knock-down demonstrations are possible in this area; all believer and unbeliever can do is share the mourners' bench, comparing their ways of life and the stories that sustain them.

But has Hauerwas got the Christian story right? Barth's main objection to this approach 'from below' might be that, despite the rejection of theodicy, it still results in a systemic distortion of Christian teaching. In the *Church Dogmatics*, after all, Barth's account of creation's shadow side comes only after an extended treatment of the gift of creaturely life – and before that, of the Creator's eternal constancy toward all he has made. In this world light and shadow, joy and sadness are intermingled. Because God's Yes to his creation is so final and ultimate, our attitude toward the world can encompass loss without being overcome by it. Barth's favourite parable for this conviction is, of course, the music of Mozart, of whom he writes:

[Mozart] had heard, and causes those who have ears to hear, even today, what we shall not see until the end of time – the whole context of providence. As though in the light of this end, he heard the harmony of creation to which the shadow belongs but in which the shadow is not darkness, deficiency is not defeat, sadness cannot become despair, trouble cannot degenerate into tragedy and infinite melancholy is not ultimately forced to claim undisputed sway. Thus the cheerfulness in this harmony is not without its limits. But the light shines all the more brightly because it breaks forth from the shadow.... Mozart saw this light no more than we do, but he heard the whole world of creation enveloped by this light. (III/3, 298)

With Mozart in mind, Barth might fairly ask Hauerwas if he does not sometimes treat the darker aspects of existence as if the light of Christ has not already shined upon them.[23] Moreover, if the light does shine, then there is more to say about the church than its undeniable vocation to help people name the silences. Such ministry will be persuasive only to the extent that the church also worships and praises the good Creator, answering God's Yes with an Amen of its own. Only so can theology avoid falling prey to the lures of false optimism and false pessimism alike.

Hauerwas would surely not disagree with these points, though he might answer that his work has its own ways of addressing them. But I imagine him posing a counter-question to Barth. Given that the light does shine, and that we can rejoice wholeheartedly in creation; the fact remains that children die of leukaemia. As Barth himself admits, we shall not see 'the whole context of providence' until the end of time. But if so, is it right to suggest that the ways of God have been justified to us in advance? That God's triumph over the Nihil from all eternity is what allows us to celebrate this world as total, unreserved gift? The danger in Barth's approach to suffering may be that it moves too quickly into the mode of affirmation. Mozart's music is beautiful, but our lives very often are not. As long as this is true, then the church cannot afford to be less than a place where people take the time to be with each other in the midst of great grief. Indeed, such presence is itself a powerful witness to the goodness of the God who made us.

Notes

1   Barth, *Dogmatics in Outline* (London: SCM Press, 1949), 59, rev.
2   For this way of putting the matter I am indebted to Robert Jenson, *Alpha and Omega: A Study in the Theology of Karl Barth* (New York: Thomas Nelson, 1963), 21 ff.
3   See Augustine, *Confessions*, 11.12; Calvin, *Institutes*, Book I, 14.1.
4   Of Barth's students it is Thomas Torrance who has done the most toward filling this lacuna. See his *Transformation and Convergence in the Frame of Knowledge: Explorations in the Interrelations of Scientific and Theological Enterprise* (Grand Rapids: Eerdmans, 1984).
5   No doubt Barth has in mind the Icelandic sagas, which are both historical – they are not myths, in so far as they refer to real characters and events in the early settlement of Iceland – and clearly overlaid with legendary elements.
6   For a positive account of imagination in theology that has affinities to Barth's views, though expressed in a philosophical idiom, see Garrett Green, *Imagining God: Theology and the Religious Imagination* (Grand Rapids: Eerdmans, 1998).
7   Kathryn Tanner, 'Creation and Providence', in *The Cambridge Companion to Karl Barth*, ed. John Webster (Cambridge: Cambridge University Press, 2000), 119.
8   Ludwig Wittgenstein, *Tractatus Logico-Philosophicus*, 6.43.
9   Barth thinks that Jesus' historical obedience to the Father mirrors something eternally present in God's own life; there is something like humility and obedience in God. See

IV/1, 192 ff.

10 Barth, *Dogmatics in Outline*, 59.

11 Fergus Kerr, *Immortal Longings: Versions of Transcending Humanity* (Notre Dame, Indiana: University of Notre Dame Press, 1997).

12 Tanner, 'Creation and Providence', 121, emphasis in original.

13 As Tanner points out, the person of Jesus furnishes the paradigm here: 'If God is who God is in Jesus, God should be at work everywhere in much the same way: directing, in an irresistible but non-coercive fashion, a history between God and creatures whereby the two are one in act yet remain completely themselves.' Tanner, 'Creation and Providence', 125.

14 Flannery O'Connor, 'Author's Note to the Second Edition' [of *Wise Blood*], in idem, *Collected Works* (New York: Library of America, 1988), 1265.

15 It seems to have been Arthur C. Cochrane of Dubuque Seminary who first rendered *das Nichtige* using the Latin word 'Nihil'. See his translation of Otto Weber's *Karl Barth's Church Dogmatics: An Introductory Report* (Philadelphia: Westminster Press, 1953), 187. The translators of *CD* use 'Nothingness', which connotes mere absence and fails to capture Barth's sense of evil's agressive character.

16 On the topic of the devil, see Barth's response to Gustav Wingren in *CD* III/3, 260–61.

17 Samuel Wells has described these two strands of Hauerwas' thought as 'narrative from above' and 'narrative from below'. See Wells, *Transforming Fate Into Destiny: The Theological Ethics of Stanley Hauerwas* (Carlisle: Paternoster Press, 1998), chapter 3.

18 Stanley Hauerwas, 'Should Suffering Be Eliminated? What the Retarded Have to Teach Us', in *The Hauerwas Reader*, ed. John Berkman and Michael Cartwright (Durham, NC: Duke University Press, 2001); *Naming the Silences: God, Medicine, and the Problem of Suffering* (Grand Rapids: Eerdmans, 1990). Both these works will be cited parenthetically in the text. *Naming the Silences* was reissued by Eerdmans in 1994 as *God, Medicine, and Suffering* – an unfortunate weakening of an evocative title.

19 Hauerwas frequently criticizes the modern 'onion peel view of the self', in which a person's true identity is thought to lie hidden behind the concrete relationships and entailments of one's life. A similar concern can be found in the work of Charles Taylor; see his *Sources of the Self: the Making of Modern Identity* (Cambridge, MA: Harvard University Press, 1989). Explicitly behind Taylor, implicitly behind Hauerwas, is a certain 'Hegelian' critique of the Enlightenment de-historicizing of the self, which deprives a person of precisely those things that, in actual living, he or she cares about most deeply.

20 Indeed, physicians often come off looking quite good in his work. See especially the essay 'Salvation and Health: Why Medicine Needs the Church', in *The Hauerwas Reader*, 539–55.

21 DeVries, *The Blood of the Lamb*; cited in Hauerwas, *Naming the Silences*, 29.

22 Myra Bluebond-Langner, *The Private Worlds of Dying Children* (Princeton: Princeton University Press, 1978).

23 This discussion may have left the unfortunate and misleading impression that Hauerwas focuses only on the 'tragic' aspects of creaturely life. This is by no means the case. His reflections on the moral significance of ordinary behaviour (friendship, the family, bearing children) as well as on the temporal character of human life (which he often unfolds in terms of the virtue of patience) can be read as 'notes toward a theology of creation'. See, for example, his 'Taking Time for Peace: The Ethical Significance of the Trivial', in *Christian Existence Today* (Durham, NC: Labyrinth Press, 1988).

Chapter 5

Into the Far Country: Reconciliation

[T]he death of Jesus is in its final ground occasioned not by the will of man but by the love of God. He gave His only begotten Son ... The divine purpose of the mission of Jesus is, therefore, salvation and not judgement, eternal life and not destruction or corruption.
– Sir Edwyn Hoskyns[1]

Jesus is Victor!
– J. C. Blumhardt[2]

The Victory of the Crucified

Historically, theological reflection on Jesus Christ has centred on two major sets of concerns. The first asks 'What does it mean to say that the divine Logos and the human Jesus of Nazareth are "the same one", a single undivided person?' – the question that dominated the Christological controversies of the fifth century. The second asks 'Why did Jesus have to die? In what sense was his death on the cross part of the divine plan and purpose?' – the question classically addressed by St Anselm in his treatise *Cur Deus Homo*. We thus tend to distinguish between incarnation and atonement, or between the person and the work of Jesus Christ. While some such division of the terrain seems inevitable, modern theologians – perhaps reacting to one-sided Protestant theologies of atonement – have tended to stress the unity between person and work. This is already true in Schleiermacher's *The Christian Faith*, where Jesus' unique self-consciousness, his awareness of God, is simply identical with the salvation he mediates.

Barth, likewise, seeks to integrate talk about person and work within a comprehensive account of 'reconciliation' – his word for the complex event that happened in Jesus. The doctrine of reconciliation is more than just a theology of the cross, although the cross remains utterly central. The event it deals with embraces incarnation, crucifixion, and resurrection; the Spirit, the church, and Christian ethics; the individual life of faith, love, and hope. The entire work can be seen as an extended commentary on Paul's words: 'So if anyone is in Christ, there is a new creation: everything old has passed away; see, everything has become new! All this is from God, who reconciled us to himself through Christ, and has given us the ministry of reconciliation; that is, in Christ God was reconciling the world to himself ... (2 Cor. 5:17–19).

By way of introduction, we need to make four preliminary comments about this doctrine: (1) God's work of reconciliation describes a history, happening, or event; (2) This history is the fulfilment of the divine covenant of grace; (3) It encompasses the dual moments of cross and resurrection; (4) It is a history with eschatological force.

1. We begin with Barth's claim that 'Reconciliation is history' (IV/1, 57). To some extent, this conviction is simply an expression of Barth's Christological particularism and realism. When the Christian says 'Jesus Christ', he or she does not mean some timeless, mythical saviour, but the first-century Jew of Nazareth. Barth makes this anti-Gnostic point in a particular context: his opposition to the theology of Bultmann, which was at the height of its influence in the 1950s. Bultmann, too, stressed the historical (*geschichtlich*) character of the gospel, which could not be reduced to some timeless truth. Barth and Bultmann would have agreed that the gospel is news. Yet Barth feared that existentialist theology so stressed the subjective side of the event, its signficance for personal faith, that the content virtually disappears. Only if the gospel is first about Jesus can we rightly say that it is about the faith of the individual.

This Christological point has a hermeneutical corollary: if reconciliation is identical with the particular history that unfolds in Christ, then we come to know about it by reading Scripture as a witness to this history. And within Scripture, Barth lays special emphasis on its narrative portions. It is fair to say that the temporal character of God's world comes to expression in *CD* IV as nowhere else in the *Dogmatics*.[3] Partly this is a function of the subject matter; in discussing Jesus, telling his story would seem to be an inevitable part of the enterprise. Partly, too, it reflects a conviction about God's faithfulness toward and within the world of creation, which becomes an ever more prominent theme in Barth's later work – not a change of conviction, but certainly a shift in emphasis. God never ceases to surprise us; yet even his surprises are consistent with the overall fabric of his grace.

2. Reconciliation is the fulfilment of the divine covenant. It is virtually impossible to overstate the importance of this idea in Barth's thinking on reconciliation. Why is it important? Because when we explore New Testament statements like 'God so loved the world, that he gave his only Son', or 'God was in Christ, reconciling the world to himself', everything depends on who we think to be the subject of those sentences. As we have seen, the doctrine of election tells of God's free and eternal self-determination to be the God of covenant love. But if this is so, it decisively shapes how we will approach the question of Christ's reconciling work. Whatever reconciliation means, it cannot mean that God has somehow changed his mind about us, or that grace comes in only as God's contingent answer to sin. The love demonstrated in the cross of Jesus Christ is no Plan B, no emergency measure implemented only when all else had failed. Rather, the cross was God's eternal intention; it marks nothing less than the content of God's self-determination in election. Reconciliation is thus in Barth's

words a 'necessary happening', an event eternally foreseen before the world was made: the Creator was never other than the One who 'justifies the ungodly' (Romans 4:5).

This conviction, too, has its corollaries. One of these is that Barth does not follow the intuitive pattern of creation–sin–incarnation in thinking about Christ's work. Rather than beginning with the 'problem' of sin, he begins with the divine action of grace and works backward: sin is to be understood only in light of its overcoming. To sin is not simply to break some abstract law, but to refuse to be loved by God in Christ – a love that both humbles us and lifts us up. Thus, each of Barth's three analyses of sin in this doctrine follows an extensive exposition of Christology. Another corollary of linking reconciliation and covenant is the prominent role played by Israel. 'The Word did not simply become any "flesh", any man humbled and suffering. It became Jewish flesh' (IV/1, 166). Among its other virtues, Barth's orientation to the Old Testament insures that his theology of the cross never becomes Marcionite. It is not that 'the law' is displaced by 'the gospel', as Israel is displaced by the church. Rather, Israel and the church alike are grasped by a divine love that seeks to redeem the whole of creation.

Indeed, the larger significance of Barth's beginning with covenant is simply the way it underscores the divine love. To repeat the claim of Edwyn Hoskyns in the epigraph to this chapter, the death of Jesus 'is in its final ground occasioned not by the will of man but by the love of God'. Reconciliation has no other ground or content than the divine love (though, as we saw in chapter 3, Barth always insists on the freedom and majesty of that love). This means, among many other things, that the cross is not to be seen as the *cause* of God's love for sinners, in the sense of a condition that needed to be fulfilled. Rather, the cross is the *outcome* of God's love. To be sure, Barth's doctrine of reconciliation does contain a representative or substitutionary element, as must any theology that takes seriously the New Testament claim that Christ died 'for us'. But his teaching is quite different from what often passed as 'substitutionary atonement' in later theology. To read *Church Dogmatics* IV is to be confronted again and again with the positive, creative intention of the divine loving as it is enacted in Jesus Christ. To cite Hoskyns again: 'The divine purpose of the mission of Jesus is, therefore, salvation and not judgement, eternal life and not destruction or corruption.'

3. Reconciliation encompasses the moments both of Good Friday and of Easter, crucifixion and resurrection. Indeed, one might say that this dialectical pairing is a basic aspect of Barth's theological imagination. Neither moment exists by itself: cross without resurrection would mean an unchristian pessimism, while resurrection without cross would mean triumphalism, the 'theology of glory' against which Luther warned. Nor does Easter emerge from Good Friday by some historical necessity or organic process, like the eternal cycle of the seasons. Rather, cross and resurrection, death and life, are related as two moments within God's free action. The

cross is the sign and enactment of God's judgment, his No to the sinful creature; but the light of resurrection discloses that this No is in fact the most profound Yes, an unsurpassable act of divine love. God judges *so that* he may show mercy, and indeed the judgment is the mercy itself.

Already from this brief description, we can see how the sequence of cross and resurrection is related to other themes in Barth. It is already implicit, for example, in his theology of revelation: God reveals himself to us (Resurrection) in the midst of hiddenness (Good Friday) so that we might become knowers and lovers of God (Pentecost). Or: the Word (the content of revelation) is spoken in the Father's freedom (the subject of revelation), and apprehended in the power of the Spirit (the goal of revelation). This trinitarian pattern is likewise apparent in the doctrine of election, where Good Friday and Easter find their precise analogue in the No and Yes of eternal grace.

All this may seem somewhat strained and artificial, as if Barth were simply playing dialectical games; the hand of Hegel is fairly evident. It is important to bear in mind that these various moments are a tool, intended to describe the actual history that unfolds in Jesus Christ. Stated in other terms: Barth is less interested in 'crucifixion' as a category than he is in the Risen Crucified One, whose death and life together constitute reconciliation. This is why Barth insisted so strongly on the resurrection's historical character, against the tendency in the Bultmann school to deny or at least highly qualify this claim. He did this not for reasons of rationalist apologetics – 'proving' the resurrection was the farthest thing from his mind – but rather to safeguard the centrality of Christ for Christian faith. If resurrection simply names something that happens to me on the basis of Jesus' death, then the gospel becomes one more way of talking about the self; nor does it change matters any if we insist that the new life occurs by grace alone. Barth thus insists that the resurrection is not simply the believer's subjective response *to* Jesus, but an event *in* Jesus' own story and experience. The gospel message is first of all about something that happened with Jesus; but because it is about him, it *also* tells us something important about our own lives.

4. Reconciliation has eschatological force. This is not to say the same as saying that Barth identifies the event of reconciliation with the eschaton or the kingdom of God. The eschaton represents the final unveiling of all things, when the contradictions and ambiguities of our lives will yield to the manifestation of God's glory. This will occur at Christ's final coming or *parousia*. Yet Barth expands the category of *parousia* to include Easter and Pentecost as well; the *parousia* is not limited to his final return (IV/3, 293 ff.) More important than the different forms of this appearing, however, is the identity of the One who appears. Jesus comes as He who promises eternal life to human beings. But since he himself is the very content of what he promises, we cannot say that the promise lies merely in the future. In the Spirit's gift of hope, Christ reaches into present reality and transforms it. And the site of that transformation is the being of the Christian herself:

In the person of the Christian the world of men strives after and seizes the goal and future given to it in Jesus Christ. It waits for it, it hastens towards it, it reaches out for it. In the act of Christian hope that which is promised (as promised and therefore future) is already present. Jesus Christ as the (promised and coming) eternally living One is already present. Not merely virtually and effectively, but actually and actively in the person of the Christian. (IV/1, 119)

These themes come to fruition in IV/3, and even more so in *The Christian Life*, the chapter on ethics that concludes the doctrine of reconciliation. But they are present and hinted at throughout *CD* IV. The eschatological thrust of Christ's work means that reconciliation, for Barth, is never simply a retrospective act of 'balancing the books', as tends to happen in many theologies of atonement.[4] The retrospective aspect is there: reconciliation is an act of judgment that sets things right between God and human beings. But far more than that, it sets men and women free to participate in the 'glorious freedom of the children of God' – a freedom that Barth construes in decidedly active terms, so that Christian ethics becomes almost a sub-department of eschatology.

With these general observations in view, we can now state Barth's basic move in this doctrine. It is simply his equating of reconciliation with the concrete person of Jesus Christ, crucified and risen. 'Jesus Christ is the reconciliation' (IV/1, 34). He is the agent of reconciliation, the action of reconciliation itself, and the one who mediates and guarantees the effects of that action to others. He is the fulfilment of Israel's history, in whom all history reaches its fitting conclusion. He is not simply the condition of possibility for God's bestowing grace. He *is* grace – the triune life pouring itself out one Friday afternoon (but because then, always and everywhere) in the body of a particular Jew (but because in him, for Jew and Gentile alike):

Jesus Christ is reconciliation [*Jesus Christus ist die Versöhnung*].[5] But that means that he is the maintaining and accomplishing and fulfilling of the divine covenant as executed by God himself. He is the eschatological realization of the will of God for Israel and therefore for the whole race ... In his own person he is the eschatological sovereign act of God who renews human beings and summons them to obedience by forgiving their sins. And in that capacity he reveals that the meaning and power of the covenant with Israel for the whole race is that it is a covenant of free and therefore effective grace. (IV/1, 34–5)

It is almost impossible to overstate just how radically and completely Barth seeks to locate the reality of reconciliation in Jesus Christ himself. He seeks every opportunity to subvert the assumption that Christ's work sets up a possibility which humans must now actualize in faith – the basic error he saw at work in Bultmann's theology.[6] To Barth, Bultmann simply seemed to be restating (in sophisticated form, to be sure) the confusion between faith or experience and that which faith perceives. Theological existentialism simply marked one more phase in the Kantian programme of Ritschl and Herrmann, in which Christianity is reinterpreted in terms of the modern quest for personal meaning and dignity. It is not that Barth scorned this quest; he simply did not think it should be confused with the Christian gospel, whose centre is the actions and sufferings of the triune God rather than the human subject.

Where does reconciliation take place? In the particular history of Jesus the Jew who died on a first-century Roman cross. His cross – disclosed in his resurrection from the dead – marks nothing less than God's cosmic, apocalyptic transformation of all reality. Or one might say that, in that the crucified Jesus lives, the whole world is reconciled to God. More simply still, 'Jesus Christ is the reconciliation.'

A Threefold Movement: The Doctrine's Structure

Even more so than in earlier volumes, the very form of the doctrine of reconciliation is intended to display its content. A brief discussion of the – rather involved – structure of the work is therefore in order.

We have seen that the heart of reconciliation is Jesus Christ, crucified and risen. But who is Jesus Christ? Barth offers us three complementary descriptions. Jesus Christ is the Son of God, the second person of the Trinity; he is the Son of Man, the human Jesus of Nazareth; and he is the one in whom God and man co-exist in a common history. Roughly speaking, these three aspects form the basic plan of *CD* IV. Volume IV/1 describes the history of reconciliation as a sheer divine act of grace, focusing on Jesus' identity as God; IV/2 narrates this same history from the perspective of Jesus' humanity; while IV/3 centres on Jesus' identity as Mediator, God and man in perfect union. Three descriptions, but rehearsing a single story centred on a single concrete agent.

When we examined Barth's doctrines of revelation and of God, we saw how much he favours the language of event, action, happening, history – what George Hunsinger calls the motif of 'actualism'.[7] This is no less true in the present doctrine. It is because Barth insists on viewing reconciliation as history that, in his account, the traditional Christological formula 'one person in two natures' does not play a prominent role. Not that Barth thinks he differs materially from what the Church Fathers affirmed at Chalcedon. But to his ear, 'natures' language is inherently static and ahistorical. Worse, it might suggest that we know what a 'divine nature' and a 'human nature' are in advance of consulting the biblical witness (IV/1, 133). By contrast, Barth proposes that Jesus Christ serves as the unique norm for our talk about both God and the human person. It is he alone who shows us what God, the true God, is really like (for he *is* true God), and likewise what it is to be truly human – 'Behold the man!', a moment when Pilate spoke better than he knew.

In his attempt to overcome talk about 'natures', Barth finds help in the teaching of Protestant orthodoxy concerning Christ's successive 'states' of existence.[8] In this schema, the Son of God who abides eternally with the Father freely undergoes humiliation in the flesh (*status exinanitionis*), after which he is exalted to glory at the Father's right hand (*status exaltationis*). Here we see the 'parabola' classically described by Paul in Philippians 2:5–11. Instead of 'states', however, Barth prefers to speak in more dynamic terms of the three ways or directions in which Jesus Christ lives out his unique history. He enacts a movement downward – God's unimaginable, self-humbling passage into the realm of sin and death. Christ also enacts a movement upward, as the lowly human being exalted to a life of active, covenant fellowship with God. We need only add that in contrast to the traditional teaching on the states, Jesus' three ways of existence are simultaneous rather than successive: his whole story is that of God's humility and humanity's exaltation, and the performative force of his story is its manifestation in human existence. What Jesus is in himself, he shares with us – his identity as the Mediator.

One final set of traditional categories deserves mention. In the *Institutes*, Calvin famously speaks of Christ's threefold office as prophet, priest, and king – the classic forms of authority in ancient Israel. Barth likewise works these messianic titles into his presentation, though changing their order. It is as Son of God that Jesus offers his high priestly sacrifice (IV/1), as Son of Man that he rules as Israel's and the world's king (IV/2), and as Mediator that he speaks the final prophetic word (IV/3). As with Calvin, Barth uses these titles to relate Jesus typologically to the Scriptures of Israel.

This brings us to another key aspect of *CD* IV: the fact that it is not simply a Christology, but a comprehensive account of reconciliation, embracing such diverse matters as sin, justification, sanctification, the church and its mission, ethics, and the sacraments. This wide net is Barth's attempt to show that reconciliation involves not just the reality of the Risen Crucified, but the transforming work of the Holy Spirit in the human sphere. *Pace* the neo-Protestant tradition, the performative aspects of Christianity do not have to be undergirded by some independent analysis of human existence. Rather, they are the direct implication of grace itself: God's grace is not content to remain objectively outside us, but constantly moves toward subjective appropriation in us. Indeed, this material on Spirit, the church, and the Christian life that accounts in part for the enormous size of *CD* IV. This is somewhat ironic, considering Barth's reputation for not having much to say about the human being!

In a previous chapter I mentioned that Barth's theology is marked by a complex series of 'correspondences' between the divine and human. While creaturely realities are never strictly identical with God's action, by grace they may (in the analogy of faith) become correspondences or echoes of that action. The reader should be alert to this pattern of thinking in *CD* IV, where the accounts of salvation and the Spirit's work 'echo' the Christology at every turn. Thus, the divine humility that is the *leitmotif* of IV/1 implies the humble character of all things human: justification is by grace alone, the

CHURCH DOGMATICS IV

DOGMATICS	CD IV/1	CD IV/1	CD IV/1
Christology:			
Person	The Lord as Servant: *vere deus* (true God)	The Servant as Lord: *vere homo* (true man)	The true Witness
Office	The Judge judged in our place: The obedience of the Son of God=*munus sacerdotale* (priestly office)	The Royal Man: The exaltation of the Son of Man=*munus regale* (royal office)	Jesus is Victor: The glory of the Mediator=*munus propheticum* (prophetic office)
State/Way	The way of the Son of God into the far country=*status exinanitionis* (state of self-emptying)	The homecoming of the Son of Man=*status exaltationis* (state of exaltation)	The Light of life=the unity of both states
Doctrine of Sin:			
Sin as	Pride and Fall	Sloth and misery	Falsehood and condemnation
Soteriology:	The judgment of God as the justification of humanity	The direction of God as the sanctification of humanity	The promise of God as the vocation of humanity

	Gathering the community	Upbuilding the community	Sending the community
Pneumatology: **The work of the Holy Spirit** in the community in the individual	**Faith**	**Love**	**Hope**
ETHICS CD IV/4 **The Christian life as an appeal to God**	Baptism – with water – as the foundation of the Christian life in prayer for the Holy Spirit	The Lord's Prayer – Our Father – as (instruction in) the fulfilment of the Christian life	(The Lord's Supper – Eucharist – as the renewal of the Christian life in thanksgiving)

Source: Eberhard Jüngel, *Karl Barth: A Theological Legacy,* translated by Garrett E. Paul (Philadelphia: Westminster Press, 1986), 48–9. Used with permission from Westminster John Knox Press.

church a fragile and imperfect community of sinners, faith the humility of obedience that can only approach God with open hands. The complement to this picture is found in IV/2, where the emphasis falls rather on God's exalting of human beings to a life of responsible action. The soteriological accent thus falls on sanctification; the church is described as the community that builds itself up through its worship and polity; and the virtue celebrated is not faith but Christian love. A similar pattern may be observed in IV/3's emphasis on Christ as truth.

The Way of the Son: The Cross as Apocalypse (*CD* IV/1)

The heart of Barth's thinking on reconciliation can be found in *CD* IV/1, which treats Christ's death and resurrection in their character as divine action. It is a compelling work, and offers one of the best points of entry into the *Church Dogmatics* as a whole. The account that follows dwells at length on this part-volume, before moving on to a somewhat briefer consideration of IV/2 and IV/3.

The opening paragraph of *CD* IV/1 (§57, 'The Work of God the Reconciler') seeks to establish Jesus himself as the content of reconciliation, and therefore as the heart of the Christian message. This paragraph is reminiscent of liberal Protestant discussions of the 'essence of Christianity'. Instead of essences, however, Barth speaks of an event: Jesus as the event of 'God with us'. This event has no presupposition, no condition of possibility other than God's eternal will for covenant. Extraordinarily, reconciliation does not even presuppose sin, even though Barth consistently defines it as God's grace shown to sinners. As we saw in chapter 4, this is not because he denies that sin and evil are 'real', but because he wants to avoid any static picture in which God simply accepts their existence. The cross of Christ does not so much presuppose sin as attack it.

The force of this discussion is that, when we have to do with the cross, we are never dealing with anything less than God's eternal, unchanging purpose towards his creatures. For Barth, what happens in Jesus is not mainly about the overcoming of sin, although his story cannot be told apart from some reference to sin. Rather, Jesus is about God's sharing his life with us; not a balancing of the books, but the fulfilling of a covenant. In this opening material, one already catches a hint of the affective tone that marks much of *CD* IV: a kind of sombre joy, both celebrating Christ's victory and acknowledging what it cost God to achieve it.

Barth details the event of reconciliation itself in paragraph 59, 'The Obedience of the Son of God'; it is perhaps the most important single paragraph in all of *CD* IV, and among the most powerful in Barth's whole corpus.[9] Its three parts address three interrelated questions. 'The Way of the Son of God Into the Far Country' tells us who is the agent of reconciliation – the identity question; 'The Judge Judged in Our Place' tells us what he accomplished – the action question; while 'The Verdict of the Father' describes the existential relevance of this action for every human life, what we might whimsically call the 'So what?' question. We are immediately reminded of Barth's analysis of the Word of God in terms of subject, action, and effect; speaker, speech, and performance; Father, Son, and Holy Spirit. Now, however, the formal trinitarian categories give way to the telling of a story – the story of Christ crucified and risen.

Barth's narrative approach is clearly signalled in the title of §59.1, 'The Way of the Son of God Into the Far Country', with its powerful allusion to Jesus' parable of the lost son (Luke 15:11–24).[10] While the translator adopts the Lucan phrase 'into a far country', Barth's expression is in fact more forceful than that. The German is *in die Fremde*; we might translate it as 'into an alien land' or even 'into strangeness'. The son in the parable does indeed enter a strange realm, degrading himself in that most Gentile of occupations, the tending of swine. His humiliation serves as a type for Christ's own self-humbling descent into suffering and death. While Barth stresses God's radical assumption of our lost condition, he is careful not to introduce any sort of compulsion or alienation into the divine being. The Son of God undertakes this journey freely. He is able to do so because God has the antecedent capacity to be God for the creature, even in the alien form of creaturely life marked by sin. Thus Barth stresses that atonement does not imply any rift or paradox in the divine being: the incarnation is precisely an act that *affirms* God's triune identity. At the cross God indeed 'gives himself, but he does not give himself away' (IV/1, 185).

Having identified the agent, Barth now turns to the question of the agent's action. 'The Judge Judged in Our Place' (section 59.2) is his account of the work of Christ in the strict sense. It largely consists in a powerful reading of the passion narratives. Indeed, given that reconciliation is history, the narrative form seems especially fitting:

> It came to pass, as we have just said; as we do when we tell the story of something that happened in the world at a definite place and a definite point in time. To think the matter out further and to understand it in detail, all that remains actually for us to do is simply to recount it in the manner of a story which has come to pass (which it is), to bring it before ourselves as something which has objectively happened. There and then, in the existence of the man Jesus of Nazareth, who was the Son of God, this event came to pass … It took place in him, in the one man, and therefore there and then, *illic et tunc*, and in significance *hic et nunc*, also for us in our modern here and now. To be known and explained and proclaimed with this significance it cannot and must not be ignored or dissolved in favour of its significance, so that it disappears into it. (IV/1, 223, rev.)

Barth's insistence on a plain sense, even naive reading of the story ('all that remains actually for us to do is simply to recount it') is in large part a reaction to Bultmann's existentialist hermeneutics. Instead of emphasizing the performative force or 'use' of the story, Barth argues that the story describes something real quite apart from our human response to it. The story is not true because of its meaningfulness for individual faith. Rather, faith finds the story meaningful because it is true.

Barth reads Jesus' story as God's judgment of the world – an emphasis that reflects not only important themes in Paul, but the classic Western view of salvation as righteousness. He speaks of Christ as the Judge, as the judged, as the event of judgment, and as the One who acted justly. While Barth finds this language uniquely fitting, he reminds us that theology should not be a slave to its categories (see the long excursus, IV/1, 273–83). Scripture makes other concepts available for reflecting on Christ's death; thus reconciliation can be understood as a ransom for captives, or as God's victory over the principalities and powers. More central than either of these notions are the cultic and sacrificial categories that pervade both the Old and New Testaments. Indeed, Barth concludes section 59.2 by briefly sketching the outlines of such a cultic reading: we might equally well describe Jesus as 'The High Priest Sacrificed in Our Place'.

Barth offers his detailed reading of the passion narratives in an important excursus (IV/1, 224 ff.). The story he tells reflects the logic of what Luther called the 'miraculous exchange' between God and sinners. This exchange is implied by the very shape of the gospel narrative. At the beginning of the gospels, Jesus is clearly the one in charge of events, the eschatological judge who brings God's rule to bear on corrupt and oppressive human powers. By the end of the story, he has been reduced to a largely passive figure. He who gathered a community of disciples is betrayed by Judas and denied by Peter; he who proclaimed God's righteousness becomes a pawn in the hands of Caiphas and Pilate; he who was adored by the crowds now hears their taunts of 'Crucify him!' Yet while these human actors all have their assigned roles in the drama, they are not ultimately what leads Jesus to his death. Rather, hovering over the entire action is the divine necessity of his passion, marked in the gospels by the 'pitiless' phrase 'it is necessary' (Greek δεῖ; IV/1, 194). In the end, it is not the pathetic representatives of earthly power who wield the cross, but the One to whom Jesus yields himself in total obedience at Gethsemane.[11]

We can no longer evade the question: what actually happened in the death of Christ? Here we must return once again to the identity of the agent. Everything in Barth's analysis turns on the fact that the one who died at Golgotha was not simply a human being, no matter how faithful or obedient. Rather, God is himself the subject of this story, and the human suffering and death of Jesus are God's own suffering and death. That does not, to be sure, detract from their human character; Barth is quite clear that the Son does not die some sort of 'divine death', but the historical death of this one crucified Jew. Yet because this is the death of God's Son, something happens here that could not be accomplished by any human action or suffering.

What happened? *CD* IV/1 employs the specific terminology of judgment – God's negative verdict on what his human creatures have made of themselves. This juridical language is important to Barth, and we will spend more time on it below. But it is also important to set it in a wider frame of reference. When Barth speaks of judgment, he means an apocalyptic event, God's action of restoring and renewing the whole creation (think again of 2 Corinthians 5).[12] At the cross, God does not bring about any possibility immanent in the first creation – although as ordered to the covenant, creation itself remains 'very good'. Human sin is by definition the rejection of grace; how then could it manifest a capacity for receiving grace? Rather, God saves the world at the cross by remaking it. The death of Jesus Christ is God's negation of the world, the end of the world as a sphere shaped by human agency and striving. At the cross, nothing less took place than the end of history: 'Human history was actually terminated at this point' (IV/1, 734). In the terms set by apocalyptic, the new creation can only appear by a radical act of divine remaking: 'everything old has passed away; see, everything has become new!'

Obviously Barth's account of the world ending at the cross depends on an inclusive Christology, in which the Son of God assumes flesh in the widest possible sense: the life story of every person, indeed the entire sweep of human history. In its universalism, and in its sense that all men and women subsist in this one Man, this Christology has often been called 'Platonist'. Yet one might equally think of Paul's reflections on Adam and Christ in Romans 5, where each figure is clearly more than an individual, but a corporate reality, summing up an entire history of human life before God. At any rate, this is how Barth views the matter. The world came to an end at the cross, ending every last possibility of human agency; there are no agents left to act.

'Apocalypse' literally means 'unveiling', the disclosure of a mystery hidden from view. There would be no apocalypse unless God's remaking of the world were disclosed to someone; or to put it differently, unless God's negative action had some positive end in view. Barth associates this moment of disclosure with Jesus' resurrection, which forms the theme of 'The Verdict of the Father' (§59.3) – the first of three long treatises on the resurrection in *CD* IV. He emphasizes that God was under no constraint to raise Jesus from the dead. There is nothing incomplete about the cross, such that it would require a further action by God to make it salutary. God might have turned his face from the dead Jesus (and therefore from creation) and left it at that; 'My God, my God, why have you forsaken me' would then have been the final words of the human story.

Yet conditions contrary to fact run against the grain of Barth's theology. He emphasizes that the resurrection did not 'have' to happen (humanly speaking) because he wants to emphasize the sheer grace and mercy of what did happen (and which was therefore necessary in a far deeper sense). A God who simply turned his face from the world would not in fact be the God of creation and covenant. God 'would not have confirmed his original choice between heaven and earth on the one hand and chaos on the other, his decision for light and his rejection of darkness' (Gen. 1:3; IV/1, 306). But such a God would precisely not be the triune God, the God of the eternal covenant of grace – the only God there is.

'The Verdict of the Father' is therefore his triumphant vindication of the Son's work. In light of the resurrection, we see that the No of the cross is not an end in itself, but exists only in service of God's Yes – a Yes to Jesus that is at the same time a Yes to humankind. Barth warns against any preaching of Good Friday in abstraction from Easter.[13] The cross is teleologically ordered to the resurrection. They constitute irreducible moments within a single divine action. If the cross brings about the end of the old creation, the resurrection marks the birth of the new:

> Thus the death and resurrection of Jesus Christ are together – his death in the power and effectiveness and truth and lasting newness given to it by his resurrection – the basis of the alteration of the situation of the people of all times. In virtue of the divine right established in the death of Jesus Christ, in virtue of the justification which has come to them in his resurrection, they are no longer what they were but they are already what they are to be. They are no longer the enemies of God but his friends, his children. They are no longer turned away from him, but away from their own being in the past, and turned to him. They are no longer sinners, but righteous. They are no longer lost, but saved … The resurrection of Jesus Christ affirms that which is actual in his death, the conversion of all people to God which has taken place in him. (IV/1, 316–17, rev.)

In any theology, the question arises as to how the grace of God is appropriated or applied by the believer. A classic Roman Catholic answer is 'by participating in the sacramental economy of the church'. A classic Protestant answer is 'by hearing the Word and clinging to Christ in faith'. While Barth clearly makes a place for both the church and faith within his doctrine of reconciliation, he refuses to cast either in a mediating role – or if so, only in a very attenuated sense. For Barth, the resurrection is nothing less than God's own mediation to us of the atonement. It is not so much that believers 'apply' Christ's work to themselves, as that God 'applies' it to them. This is why Barth stresses that it is the *Father's* verdict that makes human beings participants in the new creation. Even more radically than Jesus' death – which, after all, involved an element of human doing, in the actions that led him to the cross – the resurrection marks a moment of pure divine intervention. Only God can bring a new world into being, dividing light from darkness as he had at creation. Only the risen Christ can mediate his work to us, not the church or historical tradition or even faith itself – although again, there is a place for these: Christ's presence is 'not without the mediation of recollection, tradition, and proclamation; [he is] the living Word of God, but not without the ministry of the attesting word of man which is proclaimed and heard' (IV/1, 318).

Nonetheless, the Father's verdict does open up a 'space' for the church.

Between the forty days of the resurrection appearances, in which Jesus made himself directly visible to the apostles, and his final *parousia* at the end, comes what Barth calls 'the time of the community'. Here, as in the corresponding treatments of the resurrection in IV/2 and IV/3, faith in the Risen One is tantamount to being his witness. The church's task is simply to proclaim the divine verdict to those who know it not:

> [The community] does not come before the world, therefore, as an accuser, as a prosecutor, as a judge, as an executioner. It comes before it as the herald of this Yes which God has spoken to it. It will be careful not to present God as a jealous competitor, a malevolent opponent, or a dangerous enemy. It will not try to conceal the fact that as the Creator God has loved it from all eternity, and that he has put this love into action in the death of Jesus Christ. The community lives by the fact that the first and final Word of God is this Yes ... It lives by the fact that Jesus lives, and therefore for the task of telling this good news to all people, to a people which is troubled because it has not yet been told to it, or not told in such a way that it has brought about its liberation. (IV/1, 347)

The Royal Man: Incarnation and Agency (*CD* IV/2)

As we have just seen, the cross/resurrection event is a sheer divine act of grace, an act to which the sinful creature contributes nothing at all. Yet this does not exclude there being a human component in the work of salvation. As it lies in the loving freedom of God to work out our salvation through the Son's taking on human flesh, so our own flesh is transformed and renewed by his action. Indeed, the new life in Christ is nothing less than the beginnings of our participation in God's triune life – a patristic theme that Barth makes his own, though he expresses it in a somewhat different idiom than did the Fathers. The focus of *CD* IV/2 is this new humanity, exalted by God in the person of Jesus.

The Christology of this volume follows the same pattern of agent–action–impact that we observed in IV/1. 'The Homecoming of the Son of Man' (§64.1) answers the 'agent' question, taking up the question of incarnation – the second such treatise in the *Dogmatics*, the first occuring in *CD* I/2. As we mentioned when discussing that earlier treatment, Barth sees the Son assuming not some pre-adamic human nature, but precisely 'flesh' in the negative Pauline sense (IV/1, 25). While this had been a distinctly minority view in the tradition, it is necessitated by the pattern of blessed exchange that shapes Barth's treatment of salvation. It is by bearing the reality of the old creature that God brings the new to birth. Jesus Christ is himself the new human being, the apocalyptic new creation realized in cross and resurrection.

Barth deals with the activity of this agent in §64.2, 'The Royal Man', with a dual emphasis on the speech and action of Jesus. By his words, Jesus proclaims the kingdom of God; by his powerful acts of healing the sick and feeding the hungry, he makes the kingdom a present event. But his words are at the same time performative utterances, enacting what they say, while his actions are simply his proclamation made visible. Word and signs together declare that this man is, in Origen's phrase, the *autobasileia* – the personal embodiment of the reign of God (IV/2, 163). The resulting picture of Jesus as the truly free, truly lordly human being is Barth's answer to liberal Protestant portrayals of the 'human Jesus'. It is significant that he honours the intention of these portrayals, even as he rejects the attempt to reconstruct Jesus' humanity 'as it really was' behind the canonical text. He assumes the gospels themselves bear sufficient witness to Jesus' identity.

But what does the new creation, realized in Jesus, have to do with human life as we know it – with ourselves? Just as in IV/1, the question of force or impact is addressed by means of the resurrection. It is because the Crucified has been raised from the dead that he is present to his community in a very specific role: as giver of *Weisung*, 'direction'. What Barth calls 'the direction of the Son' (§65.3) is Jesus' active, admonitory and life-shaping activity toward his people – an eminently practical relation, pointing ahead to Barth's later discussion of sanctification. At the same time, the direction Christ gives by the power of the Spirit is the source of their participation in God's triune life. Again forming a parallel to IV/1, this appeal to the Risen Lord allows Barth to bypass the usual sorts of questions about the relevance, possibility, or truth-value of the new life. Jesus' direction is inherent in his very identity as the Son of Man; his very being is the answer to this question. Because he has been raised from the dead, we too share in the life he lives to God.

If Christ as the royal man is the paradigm of human agency, this offers a clue to another side of sin: sin as sloth, our dull resistance to God's gift of freedom. This theme is taken up in paragraph 65, 'The Sloth and Misery of Man'. Barth notes that ever since Augustine, Western theology has tended to treat pride as the chief of sins – an image that fits well with modernity's notion of the Promethean human being, the person who, like Goethe's Faust, asserts himself over against nature and his fellows. But does not this image itself imply a certain romanticizing of sin? Barth reminds us that sin has another dimension – not prideful self-assertion, but the evasion of responsibility; not the misuse of freedom, but its refusal. In brief, there is an inherently demeaning side to sin, in so far as it implies the failure to realize God's call for human beings actively to respond to his love. This insight must be carefully distinguished from the idea that sin is basically a failure in 'self-realization'. The correct context for thinking about these matters is God's grace, not the human striving for autonomy.[14] Like the parallel treatment of sin in IV/1, this treatment of sloth makes its case by drawing on examples from the Old Testament; it offers indirect testimony to Barth's concern for the Christian moral life.

The analysis of sin as sloth is but the prelude to a rich account of sanctification (paragraph 66, The Sanctification of Man). Here Barth shows his true colours as a Reformed theologian. While he acknowledges that both justification and sanctification are key aspects of the new life in Christ, his interest clearly falls more on the side of sanctification. Justification is not an end in itself, precisely in that God justifies us for a purpose: the love of God and neighbour, addressed in paragraph 68, 'The Holy Spirit and Christian Love'. While Barth draws a sharp distinction between *eros* and *agape*, the first being a self-seeking love, the second love of the other for the other's own sake, he refuses to set this antithesis at the heart of his treatment.[15] Rather, Christian love (*agape*) is grounded in God's love for us – and just so is a human act, a spontaneous movement of the believer in imitation of God (IV/2, 780). Barth notes that modern Protestantism, influenced by Kant, has tended to be suspicious of talk about loving God or loving Jesus: moral action must be kept 'clean' of the self's desire. But such an attitude fails to reflect the outlook of the New Testament. Christian love is the appropriate response to God's love, a free act, an act of self-giving, in which the believer is drawn into an 'eccentric' life – that is, a life with its centre in the beloved. Love is a determination of the whole human being; nor is it without its affective component: 'The genuine, positive, and truly inexpressible joy of the one who loves consists simply in this, that he may love as one loved by God, as God's child ... That means exaltation and gain, peace and joy. It is a reason for laughing, even when our eyes are full of tears.'[16] Indeed, Barth notes that a certain 'cheerfulness' inevitably characterizes the person who loves (IV/2, 789). He then goes on to examine the love of neighbour which imitates the love of God. It is not a love of 'humanity' in the abstract, but a concrete love, directed first of all to the particular sisters and brothers given to us in the community of faith. This does not mean that love is restricted to the Christian neighbour. Rather, the Christian must always be prepared to receive the stranger *as* the neighbour, the person given to us to care for in specific circumstances. It is clear from this discussion that Barth affirms universality, but seeks to ground it in something more substantial than a mere universal benevolence. It is worth noting that the whole drift of this discussion makes 'love' a concern for the whole community, as it seeks to imitate the love of God in Christ. Here again, Barth's concern for sanctification and ethics comes to the fore.

Even the doctrine of the church in IV/2 is marked by a concern for sanctification, treating the 'upbuilding' of the church as an ordered community of worship, mutual care, and witness to the world. We will address this aspect of Barth's ecclesiology in chapter 6.

Jesus is Victor: Prophecy and Promise (*CD* IV/3)

According to Barth, the accounts of Christ's identity as truly God and as truly human exhaust the material content of the doctrine of reconciliation. Jesus Christ *is* the self-humbling of God and God's elevation of the human being, and this just is the atonement. In a very real sense, then, there is nothing more to be said.

But Barth still has a great deal more to say, and this 'more' is contained in *CD* IV/3, titled 'The Glory of the Mediator'. If the description of Jesus' identity is already complete, why this third treatment of reconciliation? Because Barth cannot resist calling attention yet again to the revelatory, self-disclosing, reality-making quality of what took place once for all in the life, death, and resurrection of Jesus. He not only *is* the reconciliation, he effectively *announces* the reconciliation to all human beings. Barth has, of course, already implied as much in his accounts of the resurrection in IV/1 and IV/2. The Verdict of the Father and the Direction of the Son both have to do with the inclusive character of reconciliation; by the sheer grace of God, what Jesus is in himself becomes truly ours as well. But what may not be so clear from those discussions is that the inclusion is not some timeless bracket set around world history; that would, after all, leave Christ still on the outside of our reality looking in. Rather, Jesus Christ as the particular historical person who lived and died in first-century Palestine is also, and as such, the Mediator hiddenly present to all of history. We do not need to worry, with Lessing and Kierkegaard, about how we might achieve contemporaneity with this figure from the past. The reality of reconciliation (IV/1 and IV/2) embraces the event of its presence to any imaginable historical circumstance, from the Roman empire and feudal Europe, to the colonization of the Americas, to the present-day world of cyberspace and bioengineering. Christ's ontological reality embraces all these, and therefore he can be present to all of them. Or to put it in the traditional language, Christ who is King and High Priest is also Christ the Prophet.

We thus see how two of Barth's key claims, 'Jesus Christ is reconciliation' and 'reconciliation is history', come together. On the one hand, Christ's atoning work is final, once and for all, never to be repeated. Reconciliation is historical in the sense that 'it came to pass' in the story that unfolded between Bethlehem's stable and Joseph's tomb. On the other hand, this history is anything but dead history. On the contrary – the Crucified continues to be 'historical'; not that his identity requires any further completion by us, but in the sense that in his completed identity he finds ever new ways of drawing us into participation, communion with himself. There is no contingent event of history – no clash of armies, no personal or social tragedy, no private joy – that lies beyond the reach of the risen Crucified. Reconciliation is history – our history. Indeed, this conviction is utterly central to the confession that 'Jesus Christ is Lord'.

It is precisely because of his confidence in Christ's universal lordship that Barth can, in this volume, take the risk of speaking about secular realities as witnesses to the Word of God. Here we find the famous discussion of 'other lights' (IV/3, 97) or 'parables of the kingdom' (114) that speak from beyond the walls of the church.[17] At first glance, it might seem that Barth is here taking back what he said in earlier volumes in refutation of natural theology. But only a superficial reading would arrive at this conclusion. Barth is as resolute as ever that no creaturely reality possesses the capacity to speak to us of God. Indeed, he carefully delimits the discussion of secular parables in IV/3 by reiterating his previous claims about the utter uniqueness of Jesus Christ. It is no accident that the thesis statement of paragraph 69 is taken from the Barmen Declaration: 'Jesus Christ, as he is attested in all of Scripture, is the one Word of God, whom we must hear, whom we must trust and obey in life and in death.'

The atmosphere in which this whole discussion moves is that of Christ's presence and power as the risen Lord, not just one who lived long ago, but one who lives now. Jesus Christ is 'the light of life', the truth of God in person. But if so, why should he not be free to speak in an extraordinary way in the general sphere of creation? It is precisely because all reality subsists 'in Christ' that any and all created things may (if God so wills) offer testimony to him. Whether the church in fact hears the truth in the secular sphere must, of course, be tested by the Word of God – that is, in light of Scripture. Without trimming his Christocentrism one whit, Barth here seeks to affirm the possibility of the church's learning from the world, which may at times (through no particular virtue of its own) have a better grasp of the biblical message than do Christians. It is always possible that we may overhear the gospel message in unexpected places.

Yet whatever glimpses of God's truth the created world may afford, that truth remains hidden under a veil in the present age. When Barth discusses the resurrection in IV/3, it is under the rubric The Promise of the Spirit (§69.4). That the Christian community has nothing but this promise to go on means that its life can only be one of hope. But since this same Spirit is that of the risen Jesus, there is no place for anxiety or uncertainty in the church's life, much less for a defensive posture vis-à-vis the world. The Spirit is promised to the world too, though for now only the community actively lives by the promise:

> The recipients, bearers and possessors of the promise given by the Holy Spirit are *Christians,* people for whom Jesus Christ not only is who he is, the Son of God and man ... for whom he is present and active not merely in fact and objectively, but who also know him as the One he is, who know his presence and work in subjective correspondence with his objective reality ... and who in knowing him know themselves as people reconciled, justified and sanctified in him, and may thus make use of the freedom indicated to them in him. (IV/3, 352, rev.)

To deny the effective reality of reconciliation is wilfully to resist the grace of Jesus Christ, the true witness – sin in its most acute, subtle, and developed form, as 'the lie' (paragraph 70). But sin in this form too is no match for the truth: 'The light shines in the darkness, and the darkness has never overcome it' (John 1:5). The second half of IV/3 is taken up with the calling of the church and of the individual Christian to be themselves a kind of lesser light,

a humble reflection of the glory of Christ the Mediator. It is no accident that
Barth here takes up the church's specifically missionary task, for it is here
that she lives most plainly not for her own advantage, but for the world
beloved of God.

Barth in Dialogue: Robert Jenson on Crucifixion and Resurrection

Barth sees the doctrine of reconciliation as the heart of the dogmatic
enterprise, mirroring the centrality of Christ himself in the Christian
message.[18] In what follows, I will try to offer a critical perspective on Barth's
account by contrasting it with that of Lutheran theologian Robert Jenson,
writing in the first volume of his *Systematic Theology*.[19] Jenson has been
deeply influenced by Barth, and indeed has published several major
interpretations of his theology – the only one of the interlocutors in this book
to have done so. Jenson creatively appropriates such key Barthian themes as
eschatology, Trinity, the critique of religion, and the ordering of creation to
covenant. One teaching he does not adopt is Barth's identification of
reconciliation with the being of Christ himself; indeed, he sees it as a
theological mistake of the first order. At this point, their imaginations simply
diverge.

Yet perhaps it is better to begin by noting a basic area of agreement. For
Jenson as for Barth, the gospel is the announcement of something that has
happened, with the result that theology must be seen as mainly a descriptive
enterprise: an attempt to come to terms with the event of God with us.
Moreover, such description takes place within the church. Theology is born
in the church's witness to the mystery of God's self-giving to the world. The
theologian's first task is simply to hear the story, and only then try to discern
its rational coherence.

But the climax of the story is the passion and resurrection of Jesus. When
Barth begins his theological analysis of the passion narrative, he pauses to
remind us that, in a sense, all commentary is superfluous: the story interprets
itself. 'We may well ask,' he writes, 'whether the preaching of Good Friday
would not in many cases be better if it took the form, not of all kinds of
inadequate theology, but of a simple repetition … of the evangelical passion
narrative' (IV/1, 290). Jenson has a similar conviction about the primacy of
the story. But in his case, it is a matter not simply of rehearsing the story, but
of enacting it: theological reflection on Jesus' death begins in the liturgy.
Thus he proposes that 'what must fundamentally happen in the church, as
right interpretation of the Crucifixion, is that the traditional Good Friday
Liturgy, with its unique prayers … be celebrated' (190). Indeed, he suggests
that the primary 'explanation' of the atonement consists in the church's
celebration of the *Triduum*, the 'Three Days' stretching from Maundy
Thursday to Easter Sunday. For Jenson, the only way to grasp this drama is
to participate in it.

Systematic theology, then, in the form of liturgics? Barth would surely find the idea very strange. More is at stake here than simply his focus on the Word, as opposed to Jenson's emphasis on liturgy and sacrament. More broadly, what is at stake here are two distinct understandings of the church. For Barth, the church stands before the cross solely in its role as a witness – the prodigious finger of John the Baptist. The church exists 'eccentrically'. For Jenson, the church indeed bears witness; but part of what it bears witness to *is its own participation in the drama*. Thus Jenson can write that 'Crucifixion and Resurrection together are the church's *Pasch*, her passing over from being no people to being God's people, her rescue from alienation to fellowship, her reconciliation. Only as this is enacted in the church is the Crucifixion understood' (190). Be it noted that this move is not intended to elevate the church to a position where she has no need of reconciliation; she is herself a community of sinners, a 'no people' who become 'God's people' only through the new Exodus in Christ. Nonetheless, the church for Jenson has a kind of performative centrality that is lacking in Barth. To account for this difference in ecclesiology, we must sketch, first, the overall shape of Jenson's project, and second his specific account of reconciliation as it appears in *Systematic Theology* I.[20]

If there is any constant in Jenson's thought, it is the idea that the God of the Bible is sheerly different from other candidates for deity. This is one reason the doctrine of the Trinity plays such a central role in his thought: it renders the identity of God. Christians worship no generic deity, but a God known in the contingent form of a story: 'God is whoever raised Jesus from the dead, having before raised Israel from Egypt' (63). The reference to Israel is not accidental: like Barth, Jenson works hard to overcome the ingrained Marcionism of much Christian theology. The cross of Jesus the Jew makes little sense apart from the Exodus, Sinai, and Zion.

But if the triune God is identified by a narrative, then this says something important about God's own life: God's 'hypostatic being, his self-identity, is constituted in *dramatic coherence*' (64; emphasis in original). To put it in simplest form, God is not simply known in a story, God *is* a story. God's very character is to be involved in the changes and chances of life. Jenson relentlessly hammers away at the notion that God stands 'outside' time, manipulating events but himself remaining aloof from them. The biblical God is radically different. Unlike the deity of Aristotle and Plotinus, whose perfection consists in his (its?) immunity to change, the perfection of the biblical God consists in his creative willingness to take risks. God exists not as a guarantor of the status quo, but as the One who promises a future to his people. God is eternal not in the sense that he is unchanging, but in the sense that he is utterly faithful. God is, in short, the God of Exodus and of Resurrection.

Jenson's theology is in many ways representative of the 'theology of hope', with its stress on God's promise-making as that which moves history forward. Whereas human beings inevitably long for stasis, order, predictability, God posits a way of life for Israel that is instead forward-looking, marked by anticipation of a future rather than nostalgia for the past. By themselves, these themes might simply denote a vague 'openness to the future', devoid of particular content. But Jenson's version of the future is quite specific. It is not human experience generally, but Israel's experience with its God that raises the question of the future. Thus Ezekiel's question, 'Shall these bones live?', is the question of whether YHWH will be able to maintain his faithfulness to Israel even beyond death. Moreover, Jensom sees this question as crucial not simply for Israel, but for God himself. If God's identity is narratively constituted, then we must say that God does not 'know in advance' how the covenant will be secured:

> The problematic of Ezekiel is interior to the identity of Israel's God, and drives necessarily forward to some resolution or dissolution ... [T]he Lord's resolve to meet and overcome death and the constitution of his self-identity in dramatic coherence are but one truth about him. For if death-and-resurrection occurs, this is the infinite crisis and resolution, and so God's own. (66)

This line of inquiry suggests just how central the category of 'resurrection' is in Jenson's thought. When he comes to treat of the resurrection of Jesus, it will not simply be as an afterthought to the atonement. Rather, the resurrection is the answer to the central crisis of God's identity: how to be God for *these* creatures, drawing them into intimate communion with himself despite the limitations of this world.

It is fair to say that Jenson's eschatology has a strongly Eastern flavour, in that resurrection appears mainly as the answer to the problem of death and of creation's 'bondage to decay' (Romans 8:21). Nonetheless, he does not slight the problem of sin. For – once again – if God's identity is narratively constituted, then who we are will make a great deal of difference to who God is: 'God's history with us is decisively shaped by our betrayal of the "with us"' (72). Indeed, Jenson sees this notion as so deeply ingrained in Scripture that it makes little sense to ask, 'What would have happened had Adam not sinned? Would the Son of God still have become incarnate?' – a standard puzzle in medieval theology. Following Barth closely at this point, Jenson argues that the Bible offers no speculation on a world in which the Fall never happened, and where sin and evil never intrude. The world as we know it is the world concretely determined by God's reconciling action in Jesus Christ. And that means that sin is in some sense 'presupposed' – not in the sense that God wills it, but in the sense that God wills to overcome it at the cross (73).[21] Jenson has a larger place than Barth for the *O felix culpa*, the 'happy fault' celebrated in medieval liturgies. Whatever else might have been, the biblical narrative tells of a fellowship established between God and sinners.

But what does the cross actually accomplish? Jenson points out that the church's first atonement theory was not a theory at all, but the evangelical passion narratives, which artfully weave the story of Jesus' suffering into that of Israel; the narrative itself does this in subtle ways, quite apart from explicit citations of texts like Isaiah 53 or Psalm 22. Later theology demanded greater clarity. What does it mean when we say that Jesus died 'for us'? Jenson criticizes traditional accounts of the atonement partly for their particular shortcomings – thus, Anselm's satisfaction theory seems to make a resurrection superfluous – but more for an error they share in common: all tend to treat atonement as a transaction between Christ's divine and human natures. Christ, however, is not a composite of substances, but the incarnate Son; atonement must therefore be treated at the level of the one person or agency that he is.

How, then, does Jesus make atonement? Simply by being who he is – the Son of God in human flesh, who lets himself be betrayed to his enemies for their sake ('God in the hands of angry sinners', one might say). Because Jesus is the Son, this act of utter self-giving is itself an inner-triune event, an event in God's life. More precisely, it is 'the event in God that settles what sort of God he is over against the fallen creation'. Jenson elaborates:

> The Crucifixion put it up to the Father: Would he stand to *this* alleged Son? To *this* candidate to be his own self-identifying Word? Would he be a God who, for example, hosts publicans and sinners, who justifies the ungodly? The Resurrection was the Father's Yes. We may say: the Resurrection settled that the Crucifixion's sort of God is indeed the one God; the Crucifixion settled what sort of God it is who established his deity by the Resurrection. Or: the Crucifixion settled *who and what* God is; the Resurrection settled *that* this God is. And just so the Crucifixion settled also who and what we are, if we are anything determinate. (189; emphasis in original)

We might note that the action here described – Jesus' act of total self-identification with sinners, and the Father's 'owning' of this act – occupies the same place as Barth's doctrine of election. Just as with Barth, we are dealing with a divine decision that itself determines the divine character; it is simply that what Barth locates in an 'eternity' complexly related to time, Jenson locates within time itself. God refuses to be God apart from human sin, weakness, and suffering. While the Father could have turned away from those who had killed his Son, he refused to do so. Bound to the Son in the Love that is the Spirit, the Father remains faithful to him even in the midst of suffering and death. The faithfulness of Father, Son, and Spirit to each other is identical with God's faithfulness to sinners; and so it is that God is Love.

Reading even this highly compressed version of Jenson's argument, one can detect themes and motifs obviously indebted to Barth (or to their common heritage in Paul and the Reformation). God as the One who justifies the ungodly; reconciliation as a triune event; the Resurrection as the Father's vindication of the Son – all can be found in the pages of the *Church Dogmatics*. Most basic of all is the notion that God effects atonement by humbly submitting to a shameful human death. For Jenson, too, the Son shows his love for us by undertaking a journey into a far country.

Jenson has clearly learned much from Barth; yet how different is the account of reconciliation he offers! To begin with, there is no talk here of an eternal covenant, broken by human beings but now fulfilled by Christ's death on the cross. Where Barth treats election as the presupposition of reconciliation, Jenson sees no need to press the story back to an eternal covenant of grace. The Crucifixion story as told in the gospels, he writes, '*is* just so the story of God's act to bring us back to himself at his own cost, and of our being brought back. There is no other story behind or beyond it that is the real story of what God does to reconcile us' [emphasis in original]. This could almost be Barth, inveighing against mythic interpretations of the New Testament. Yet the accent in Jenson is very different. His insistence on the sheer primacy of the story means that God's own identity is, in some sense, historically achieved: the gospel 'does not tell of a work done *by* a God antecedently and otherwise determined, but itself determines who and what God is' (165). Barth would clearly find such a claim intolerable. Indeed, one might see Jenson's whole project as an attempt to radicalize Barth's doctrine of the Trinity by rendering it fully historical. For Barth, God is who he is in his act of revelation, in his covenant relation to the world. For Jenson, God becomes who he is *through* this relation. The difference shows up in larger and smaller ways as one reads their respective dogmatics.

Jenson's emphasis on futurity has a major effect on the way he thinks about the cross, for example. Here one finds none of Barth's stress on apocalyptic judgment, no talk about ransom for sin or a judge judged in our place. This is especially striking in a Lutheran theologian, who might have been expected to lay stress on such themes. Indeed, Jenson acknowledges that his theology does 'remove the Crucifixion from a kind of centrality it has sometimes occupied in theology' – a shift in emphasis also shared by other contemporary theologians, such as Walter Kasper and Wolfhart Pannenberg (179). The Crucifixion is God's (Jesus') decision for solidarity with sinners, the event that determines his identity as the God of the ungodly. Yet it saves only by virtue of its dramatic unity with the Resurrection. Why is that?

The reason is clear: because Jesus is risen into God's future, and that future is the actual locus of salvation. The risen Jesus is the reality of the kingdom. When he comes among his disciples, the kingdom comes and salvation occurs. Apart from his suffering and death, he would not be incarnate Love; but apart from his resurrection, that Love would have remained in a garden tomb outside Jerusalem.

Jenson's account of atonement is one that stresses God's faithfulness toward his enemies. At the cross God stares humanity's anger and murderous violence in the face, and does not flinch. It is a biblical theme, and one that has deep resonances with Barth's own retrieval of the notion of 'covenant'. A fair question for Jenson, however, is whether he still doesn't need a more adequate doctrine of what the cross itself actually achieves – a doctrine of atonement. Modern theologies of hope tend to be weak on this score, relocating the conquest of evil to 'the future' or 'the kingdom', and thereby inevitably suggesting that history itself is the apocalypse. Yet for Paul – as in another sense for the author of the fourth gospel – the cross simply is God's invasive apocalyptic action toward creation.[22] The work of Christ must be stated in the perfect tense, even if we must also say that his engagement with the principalities and powers is not yet finished. Thus Paul can describe the gospel simply as 'the word of the cross'.[23]

With Barth, one encounters almost the opposite problem: the victory of God at the cross is so complete that it threatens to obliterate the significance of history – that is, any history other than that of Christ himself. His story is all-encompassing. Everything that happens, from the Red Army defending Stalingrad in 1943 to the sparrow falling in my backyard, occurs within the threefold event that is Jesus Christ. He is the movement of God's self-humbling unto death, he is the exaltation of humanity to fellowship with God, and he is the ever-active and eventful unity between the two. Where Jesus 'happens', reconciliation happens (here a convergence between Jenson and Barth). And there is nowhere in creation where his life and self-witness are absent. In Barth's theology, the event of Jesus Christ is nothing if not capacious.

Too capacious, perhaps? Here we may briefly take note of three standard criticisms of Barth's doctrine of reconciliation. The first is that by making reconciliation internal to the being of Christ, Barth diminishes the significance of other being, and especially that of the human covenant partner. Christ died 'for us', the New Testament states. Does Barth really take this 'us' seriously, granting human beings enough autonomy so that their particular history with God matters? Different theologians will have their own reasons for making this criticism. For Roman Catholics, the issue is the integrity of human nature in relation to grace; for Lutherans, the issue is whether the preaching and hearing of the gospel are determinative of salvation; for evangelicals, the issue is the irreplaceable necessity of personal faith – is the latter swallowed up in some vast universalism? Obviously this clutch of issues is shaped by Barth's view of the priority of election over all other occurrence.

Others have asked not just how real we are in Barth's theology, but how real Jesus is. If the covenant of grace is eternal, for instance, how much do the historical events of cross and resurrection really matter? Any such charge will have to be carefully nuanced, since, as we saw earlier, the content of the eternal covenant is none other than the history of the One who 'suffered under Pontius Pilate'! A more salient criticism may be that Barth is weak on the humanity of the risen Jesus. Thus while he clearly depicts the universal witness of Christ the Prophet as God's activity, does he make equally clear that it is the work of the ascended, human Lord? Does revelation itself tend to make Jesus' humanity redundant? Interestingly, this line of criticism has been especially pressed by Barth's fellow Reformed theologians – the humanity of Christ being a particular concern of the Reformed tradition.[24]

Finally, there is the charge that Barth lacks an adequate theology of the Holy Spirit. Robert Jenson himself has been among the most articulate in developing this line of criticism.[25] We may paraphrase it as follows: if Barth's great strength lies in his powerful unfolding of the drama between Father and Son, his great weakness is that he does not assign the Spirit an equal role in the drama. Barth's theology, in other words, is finally binitarian rather than trinitarian. It is not that Barth fails to speak about the Spirit, but that when he does, the Spirit appears more as Christ's capacity to evoke a subjective response in others than as a 'person' in his own right. In good Augustinian fashion, the Spirit is the bond of love (*vinculum amoris*) linking Father and Son, and who draws human beings into that fellowship. This relatively impersonal doctrine of the Spirit, Jenson argues, comes at the expense of the role the Spirit plays in the New Testament: as the divine Agent who draws us into God's future. For Barth, the Spirit brings into our present life and reality what already is: the fulfilment of the covenant in the Crucified and Risen One. But the Spirit's true role is not just to manifest what is, but to bring about what is still to come: the triune God's drawing of his people into eternal communion with himself, the consummation of his kingdom.

Once again, therefore, the differences between Barth and Jenson turn on questions of eschatology and the church. Because Jenson does not see covenant history as being already completed in Christ, he can assign a more active role to the church in mediating salvation. For Barth, the church bears witness to the Christ who mediates his own presence – the prophetic office. For Jenson, the church is the Spirit's sacramental enactment of communion with Christ. Its Scripture, its liturgy, its historic structures of ministry, are all ingredients in the mystery of the triune God's self-giving to the world. The church's historic identity across time matters, because the church itself is part of the divine drama.

A traditional Easter hymn makes the bold claim: 'The strife is o'er, the battle won.' Barth's doctrine of reconciliation is the theological embodiment of this conviction. Much of it is stated in the perfect tense – the Son *has* triumphed at Calvary, the Father *has* raised him from the dead, the Spirit *has* been poured out in testimony and promise to the world. Barth sees such claims as being fully compatible with present- and future-tense aspects of the gospel. Indeed, Barth would argue that such claims are required precisely by the finality and completeness of Christ's work. The reality of Christ is not a black hole whose gravitational pull is so strong that it prevents even light from escaping. Rather, Christ is the Light itself. He 'funds' other reality, calling each creature to perform its own odd and irreplaceable role in the story. The great Light does not suppress the lesser lights, but empowers them.[26]

Claims like this will not satisfy Barth's critics. Even sympathetic commentators such as Colin Gunton speak of a 'relative underweighting of the pneumatological and ecclesial dimensions of Barth's way of speaking of the appropriation of salvation', concluding that – despite the lengthy treatises on the Spirit's work in *CD* IV – this pneumatology 'cannot say all that a doctrine of the Spirit ought to say'.[27] This seems a fair judgment. Rather than exploring the Spirit's bringing believers to Christ via word, water, wine, and bread, Barth emphasizes the sheer gracious reality of the risen Christ in his self-manifestation to his disciples. The liturgical centre of this account is not so much Pentecost as it is the Forty Days of Easter.

Yet it is not given to every theologian to do everything. What Barth does, and does brilliantly, is to render the identity of the One to whom the Spirit bears witness: the Crucified and Risen Jesus. Sections like 'The Judge Judged in Our Place' and 'The Royal Man' achieve an extraordinary density of description, and must be considered among the true classics of modern Christian thought. The doctrine of reconciliation is Barth's most complete statement about the God who loves in freedom. It is an affirmation that Jesus is victor, and that his victory is the gift he shares with us.

Notes

1 Sir Edwyn Hoskyns, *The Fourth Gospel*, ed. Francis Noel Davey (London: Faber and Faber, 1947), 218–19. Barth cites this passage in IV/1, 72.

2 At the decisive moment in the exorcism of a girl named Gottliebin Dittus, her sister Katherina was heard to cry out: 'Jesus is victor!' The saying became the motto of Blumhardt's healing ministry in southern Germany. See IV/3, 168–71.

3 A pioneering analysis of Barth as narrative theologian can be found in David Ford, *Barth and God's Story* (Frankfurt am Main: Peter Lang, 1981). In the background of Ford's work stands Hans Frei's reading of Barth, seen for example in Frei's essay 'Eberhard Busch's biography of Karl Barth', in Frei, *Types of Christian Theology*, ed. George Hunsinger and William Placher (New Haven: Yale University Press, 1992).

4 On prospective and retrospective dimensions of atonement, see J. MacCleod-Campbell's classic work *The Nature of the Atonement* (Edinburgh: The Handsel Press, 1996), originally published in 1856.

5 *Jesus Christus ist die Versöhnung* might also be translated 'Jesus Christ is *the* reconciliation'. Each translation brings out a different nuance of the German. The first suggests that Jesus defines the concept of reconciliation; the second suggests that he is himself the historical event of reconciliation.

6 'Through Christ ... there was brought no more than the *possibility* of life, which, however, in men of faith becomes certain reality.' Bultmann, *Theology of the New Testament*, vol. I (New York: Charles Scribner's Sons, 1951), 252, emphasis in original; Barth refers to this passage in IV/1, 285.

7 See George Hunsinger, *How to Read Karl Barth: The Shape of His Theology* (New York: Oxford University Press, 1991).

8 See Heinrich Heppe, *Reformed Dogmatics*, ed. Ernst Bizer, trans. G. T. Thomson, foreword by Karl Barth (Grand Rapids: Baker Book House, 1978), chapter 19.

9 I am skipping over paragraph 58, which is Barth's own guide to the structure and organization of the work that follows.

10 The echo is continued in the parallel section in IV/2, titled 'The Homecoming of the Son of Man' (§64.1).

11 See Barth's detailed exegesis of Jesus' prayer to the Father at Gethsemane passage,

which he reads in conjunction with the synoptic temptation narratives; IV/1, 259–73.

12 The apocalyptic dimension of Barth's thought has been powerfully brought out by Douglas Harink, with reference both to *Romans* and to *CD* IV. See Harink, *Paul Among the Postliberals: Pauline Theology Beyond Christendom and Modernity* (Grand Rapids: Brazos Press, 2003), 45–56.

13 Barth even argues that 'there are serious objections to all representations of the crucified Christ as such' (IV/1, 344). This attitude makes his fascination with the Isenheim 'Crucifixion' by Grünewald all the more striking.

14 See Kathryn Greene-McCreight, 'Gender, Sin and Grace: Feminist Theologies Meet Karl Barth's Hamartiology', in *Scottish Journal of Theology* 50/4 (1997), 415–32.

15 Barth singles out Anders Nygren's *Agape and Eros* (London: SPCK, 1954) for especially harsh treatment, at one point calling Nygren's way of contrasting *eros* and *agape* 'Manichean'.

16 *KD* IV/2, 895, present author's translation; cf. *CD* IV/2, 789.

17 See the fine discussion of this material in Hunsinger, *How to Read Karl Barth*, 234 ff.

18 See Barth's comments in I/2, 882; cf. IV1/88: 'All [God's] activity has its heart and end in a single act.'

19 Robert Jenson, *Systematic Theology: Volume I, The Triune God* (New York: Oxford University Press, 1997). References to this work will be given parenthetically in the text.

20 All the basic moves in Jenson's project are on display in the chapter titled 'The Way of God's Identity', chapter 4 in *Systematic Theology* I.

21 Jenson, *Systematic Theology* I, 73; cf. *CD* IV/1, 69. For Jenson's own analysis of Barth on this point, see Jenson, *Alpha and Omega*, 22–64.

22 See Martyn's *Galatians*.

23 Jenson briefly treats the notion of reconciliation as 'sacrifice' (*ST* I, 192). While his account of sacrifice (drawn from ecumenical dialogue on the Eucharist) is insightful, the theme could be developed in a far richer way. One might argue that a cultic account of Jesus' death fits well with Jenson's stress on the Old Testament roots of the passion narratives.

24 A representative comment is that of Thomas Torrance. Commenting on *CD* IV/3, Torrance worries that 'the humanity of the risen Jesus appears to be displaced by "the humanity of God" in his turning toward us'. T. F. Torrance, *Karl Barth: Biblical and Evangelical Theologian* (Edinburgh: T & T Clark, 1990), 134. I am indebted to the late Colin Gunton for this quotation.

25 For what follows see Jenson, *ST* I, 154–5.

26 'The reality of Jesus Christ as the self-positing of God includes within itself all other realities, and it is in him and from him that they have their inalienable substance. Barth's apparent ontological exclusivism is in fact an inclusivism: *solus Christus* embraces and does not suspend or absorb the world of creatures and their actions.' John Webster, *Barth's Ethics of Reconciliation* (Cambridge: Cambridge University Press, 1995), 28–9.

27 Gunton, 'Salvation', in *The Cambridge Companion to Karl Barth*, 152.

Chapter 6

Christian Existence: Church and Ethics

> We are not able to uphold the church, neither could our ancestors do so, nor will our descendants. Rather it is and it was and will be he who said 'I will be with you to the end of the world.' As it stands written in Hebrews 13, 'Jesus Christ, *heri, et hodie, et in secula*. And in the Apocalypse 1, 'he who was and who is and who is to come'. Yes, he is the one, and no other is nor can be.
> – Martin Luther[1]

Freedom for Witness

To ask where 'the' ecclesiology of the *Church Dogmatics* is to be found is, in a sense, to ask a misleading question. Barth has no single treatment of the nature and mission of the church. Rather, reflection on the church arises in a wide variety of contexts: as the community that seeks to be responsible in its speech about God; as a form of the elect community, chosen to testify to God's free grace; as a people gathered, sanctified, and called by the Holy Spirit; as local congregation and as worshipping assembly. The range and complexity of Barth's thinking on the church should caution us against the idea that he identifies the church in only one way, for example, as the 'body of Christ'. His goal is to locate the church within a larger pattern of Trinitarian activity, involving not only the work of Christ and the Father but the Spirit as well.

The present chapter highlights one of these many connections: that which exists between the church and Christian ethics. A grasp of Barth's ethics is crucial for an overall understanding of his theological project. He insisted that ethics be treated not as an afterthought, but within the very fabric of dogmatics. This conviction can be traced to the doctrine of election, where (as we saw in chapter 3) Jesus Christ is described as both the electing God and the elect human being. In Christ, God makes a primal decision for covenant fellowship. This Yes to covenant includes God's Yes to having a free, active, and obedient covenant partner – the man Jesus of Nazareth. But in so far as all human beings are elected in him, they, too, share in his destiny to live by grace, and to bear witness to that grace by their own free action.

But witness to grace is likewise the calling of the church. As in the case of ethics, this is not something the church might or might not choose to do. The church is *essentially* defined by its task of witness. Thus it, too, has its origin in the doctrine of election. God wills eternally that there should be a community (in the twofold form of Israel and the church) that will serve as

t the world that 'does not yet believe'. The character
ely verbal, moreover, but active. The church signifies
e range of activities, including its worship, teaching,
vice to the neighbour – the whole ethos that marks it as
Ecclesiology is 'ethical' in the simple sense that God
n to do something, namely to bear public and embodied
el.

esiology are not identical. No one, not even a fellow
Christian, can ͜ y the divine command in my place; Barth has a profound
sense of the individual's unique calling and responsibility before God.
Likewise, the mystery of the church is more than simply its existence as a
moral community. Nonetheless, there is a profound affinity between the two
themes. As elected in Christ, the human being is always determined *both* for
moral freedom *and* for responsible membership in the Christian community.
At particular points in the *Dogmatics* this connection comes to light in
interesting ways, even if Barth chooses to develop the themes independently.

The basic move in this chapter is a fundamental pattern in Barth's thought,
one that informs everything he has to say about the Christian life. The pattern
goes like this: as a miracle of grace, God's action always precedes that of
human beings; but because grace creates new realities, it also empowers
human beings to be responsible agents. Divine action and human action are
not a zero-sum game. Indeed, free human action is simply the fitting
response to what God has done for us; it is fundamentally a sign of gratitude.
'Grace and gratitude belong together like heaven and earth. Grace evokes
gratitude like the voice of an echo. Gratitude follows grace like thunder
lightning' (IV/1, 41). The paradigm instance of such action is prayer. For in
prayer the human being acts freely, is most truly herself, precisely in
acknowledging her dependence on the grace and mercy of God. This pattern
can be seen in Barth's ethics, where the moral life has less to do with
following certain rules than with discerning the gracious context of one's life
– the activity of the triune God – in particular settings and situations. It can
also be seen in his ecclesiology, where the Christian community, in all its
sinfulness and imperfection, becomes an embodied imitation of Christ
through its activity of witness. Christ's humble descent to a servant existence
(the logic of Philippians 2:5) becomes the church's path as well. As a divine
gift, the church is a miracle; as a human community, the church is constituted
by its human actions and decisions. This pattern of correspondence between
divine and human agency is basic to Barth's theological imagination.

The theme of this chapter, then, is witness to the gospel as it takes shape
in Christian life and Christian community. We will trace it first by examining
Barth's ethics in *CD* II/2 and III/4, dealing respectively with the divine
command and with the ethics of creation. (Although we should constantly
remind ourselves that Barth is 'doing ethics' on every page of the *Dogmatics*
– given the nature of the covenant, to speak of God *is* to engage in moral
reflection.) We will then turn to his treatment of the church in *CD* IV/1–3,

which, especially in IV/2, describes the church in terms of what might be called a 'politics of sanctification'. The chapter concludes with a look at Barth's ethics of reconciliation construed as the invocation of God between baptism and here the themes of ecclesiology and ethics come together with particular force.

Law as Gospel: The Divine Command

Ethics is an extremely popular subject these days, both among academics and in the culture at large. Medical and bioethicists are in especially high demand, given our society's puzzlement about the beginning and end of life and the limits of medical care. Major newspapers run columns with titles like 'The Ethical Advisor', in which moral experts cheerfully answer questions about marital fidelity, plagiarism, and cheating on one's income tax. When corporate executives deceive their shareholders and employees, the cry goes up that the business world has lost all sense of ethics.

In light of this general enthusiasm for ethics, it is sobering to read Barth's famous comment on the moral enterprise: that the 'general conception of ethics coincides exactly with the conception of sin' (II/2, 518). It is important to see that this is a *methodological* remark. Barth is not saying that the world we live in is hopelessly corrupt. Nor is he saying that only Christians are ethical. Rather, he is saying that what modernity calls 'ethics' is governed by assumptions fundamentally at odds with Christian convictions. Modern ethics, in all its many variants – Kantian, Idealist, existentialist, utilitarian – sets the human being at the centre of the cosmos and asks 'What should I do?' Ethics is about the human project, and defines the good in terms of personal autonomy (or, in the form of social ethics, collective wellbeing). For the Christian, this whole enterprise is founded on a misunderstanding. It assumes that the question of the good can be raised in isolation from God who creates and redeems. But God is surely where any genuinely theological ethics must begin. For ethics to be Christian, the theologian must think first of all in terms of what God has done, and only then proceed to consider what that implies about human beings and their moral choices. Rather than beginning with the question 'What should I do?', theological ethics begins by asking 'What is real?'

Barth thus proposes that ethics be treated as part of dogmatics. More precisely, he proposes that reflection on the moral life must take account of the three basic ways in which God engages human beings: as the Creator who made us, as the Reconciler who shares his life with us, and as the Redeemer who destines us for eschatological adoption as his children. While these relations interpenetrate each other – note that the entire Trinity is the subject of all these activities – they are also distinct and relatively independent. The Trinitarian pattern thus shapes the structure of Barth's 'special ethics'. *CD* III/4 sets forth the ethics of creation, while *CD* IV/4 (the fragment on baptism and *The Christian Life*) gives us part of the ethics of reconciliation. Alas, Barth was unable to complete the latter, nor was he able to write the ethics of redemption.

But before special ethics comes general ethics: an account of the basis of human moral obligation. Tellingly, Barth locates general ethics in the doctrine of God ('The Command of God', *CD* II/2, chapter VIII). This decision alone tells us much of what we need to know about his approach to ethics. In sharp contrast to modernity, ethics is not first of all about us; it is about God. The moral law turns out to be but another form of the gospel, grounded in God's electing grace:

> As the doctrine of God's command, ethics interprets the law as the form of the gospel, i.e. as the sanctification which comes to man through the electing God. Because Jesus Christ is the holy God and sanctified man in one, it has its basis in the knowledge of Jesus Christ … Its function is to bear primary witness to the grace of God in so far as this is [God's] salvific binding and obligation of the human being. (II/2, 509, rev.)

The first thing to be said about the moral life, therefore – the answer to the question 'Why be good?' – is that this life unfolds in a context determined by God's gift of himself in Jesus Christ. Before we lift even a finger to act, we have been freed for covenant fellowship with God and our neighbour. Ethics is dispossessed by grace, and grace is a function of God's triune life.

To say that the law is a form of the gospel is a more complex claim than one might suppose. On the one hand, it represents a radical subordination of law to grace. There is no 'natural law', no minimal set of standards that applies to all human beings and that may be known apart from revelation. Barth rejects natural law for the same reason he rejects natural theology: both abstract from the concrete situation of the human being who lives under God's grace. This is not to say that Christian ethics may not learn from other approaches to ethics – a point Barth could perhaps have brought out more clearly than he does. It does say that any ethics calling itself Christian ought to begin with Jesus, and not with some supposedly universal foundation in human experience. Only so can theological ethics be kept truly theological.

On the other hand, to say that the law is a form of the gospel cuts the nerve of all Christian antinomianism – the heresy that says that what grace saves us from is not sin, but the law itself; or (to put it in modern terms) the heresy that says that any form of structured moral obligation is oppressive. Obviously there are passages in St. Paul one might appeal to in support of the view that 'the law' is the enemy. Barth, however, knows that for Paul the Jew, the divine grace includes the sanctification of human life through obedience to God's commandments. It would be fair to say that the overall force of Barth's ethics is just the opposite of antinomianism: the sanctified life is integral to the gift God has bestowed on us in Jesus Christ. Which is but another way of saying that God elects us to live as free witnesses of his grace.

Besides seeking to ground Christian ethics in the gospel, Barth spends a great deal of time in II/2 unpacking the notion of the divine commandment itself. If the general conception of ethics coincides with sin, then Christian ethics coincides with the believer's relation to Jesus Christ; Christ is the content of God's commandment, and knowing what to do in a given situation is a matter of hearing what God, in Christ, has to say. As when he speaks of revelation, Barth consistently highlights the dramatic and startling character of the divine command. Any claim to know in advance what 'the good' consists in is misguided. The human problem is precisely that we *do* construct notions of 'the good', and that they are more often than not corrupted or even demonic. Breaking the closed circle of human certainty requires that we attend to what God is saying, not 'normalizing' the commandment by assimilating it to what we already know, but allowing our moral imaginations to be stretched. The good is never simply 'the natural', but must be *learned*, and that through an encounter with the Word that the Word itself makes possible. Barth also stresses the nexus of divine command and human obedience in order to underscore the personal nature of the Christian moral life. For the Christian, the norm of goodness is not an idea or a principle, but the God who wills us to be his responsible partners under the covenant.

The standard criticism of Barth's notion of the divine commandment is that it is occasionalistic. If the command of God is always so surprising, if we cannot rely on reason or previous experience, is there any room left for reflection and deliberation? Can the Christian offer good reasons for his actions, or is he reduced to saying 'I did it because God commanded me'? Moreover, it has often been pointed out that Barth's picture seems to leave little room for continuity or progress in the moral life. While theologians like Calvin or Jonathan Edwards are hardly modern optimists, they do seem to assume that there is such a thing as 'growth in grace'. The point here is not some acquired capacity that makes believers independent of God, but precisely the perfecting work of the Holy Spirit. Thus Luther writes that the Spirit sanctifies believers 'not only through the forgiveness of sin acquired for them by Christ ... but also through the abolition, the purging, and the mortification of sins, on the basis of which they are called a holy people'.[2]

Barth is not without answers to most of these criticisms. He might say that while his ethics does stress God's eschatological disruption of our ordinary existence, this does not mean abandoning all talk of continuity. While continuities constructed purely 'from below' may be suspect, the God who summons human beings to obedience is also the faithful God; therefore the moral agent can make *some* reference to acquired history and experience – although never in such a way as to make the commandment itself redundant.[3] Likewise, it has been argued that Barth allows a greater role for considerations of context in ethics than is often assumed, and that in practice (as opposed to what he sometimes says in theory) he assumes that moral reasoning and deliberation are inevitable aspects of the moral life.[4] The best validation of this point is the discussion of particular moral issues that occurs in *CD* III/4, where Barth offers arguments for the positions he adopts. These arguments are made on the basis of Scripture, but they obviously also involve a reasoning *from* Scripture to general principles; and if there are principles there are sometimes also exceptions. 'Christians can never engage in war, except when …' 'Abortion is always wrong, but …' Barth thinks the principles exist because the witness of Scripture is clear. At the same time, he thinks these ellipses (and others like them) can be filled in because life is messy and complex, and because obedience to God in specific situations requires that we 'trump' even Scripture-derived principles. Moral reasoning is possible because God is constant; moral reasoning is necessary because the good thing is not always the obvious thing; and there comes a point when we can no longer rely on reasoning at all, but must simply venture forth in the obedience of faith.

These reflections might be summarized as follows. If one focuses simply on the inscrutable moral decision itself, as Barth himself sometimes does, one will come away with a picture of him as a kind of Christian existentialist or decisionist: we cannot *know* what is good, we can only *do* the right thing as we are summoned by God in the moment of choice. This broadly Kantian aspect of Barth's thought offers a tempting and easy target, and critics often focus on it. What the critics generally miss is how much more there is to Barth's ethics than a 'naked' encounter between divine command and human obedience. For in Barth's view, ethics is not first of all about human beings, but about God. Recall once again that the account of the divine commandment occurs as the culmination of the doctrine of God, and seeks to articulate the gospel of grace – the law as a form of the gospel. What might seem like a 'naked' encounter is in fact clothed in grace. To grasp Barth's understanding of the moral life, one must attend to the ways in which he locates ethical reflection in a trinitarian and Christological context (and to a lesser extent, in an ecclesiological context; more on this below). Thus John Webster speaks of Barth's 'moral ontology', his attempt to construct an account of the real – God's grace engaging us in the realms of creation, reconciliation, and eschatological redemption – that will help us make sense of our lives as moral beings.[5]

Talk of Barth's ontology may help to turn back the charge that his account of ethics is sheerly irrational and voluntarist; it is surely neither of those things. It does not change the fact that Christian ethics for Barth has more to do with surprises than with certainties, more to do with the drama of a live lived in history than with a neat calculus worked out in advance. This is because the ontology in question is that of the triune God, who calls each of us to a uniquely responsible life in response to his abundant grace.

Life in Freedom: The Ethics of Creation

In light of what we have just said, it is perhaps not surprising to learn that Barth organizes his ethics of creation around the notion of 'freedom'. A quintessentially Pauline and Reformation notion, freedom was also a major concern of Enlightenment thought. Barth does not so much deny Enlightenment understandings of freedom, as attempt to show how the 'freedom with which Christ has set us free' anticipates and exceeds them. In III/4 he considers four aspects of created freedom: freedom before God, freedom in fellowship, freedom for life, and freedom in limitation. These topics correspond to the basic categories of Barth's theological anthropology, set forth in III/2: relatedness to God, to the fellow human, to one's own embodied agency, and to time.

In a sense, everything Barth has to say about ethics is implied in the thesis that introduces paragraph 53:

> It is the will of God the Creator that man, as his creature, shall be responsible before him. In particular, his command says that man is to keep his day holy as a day of worship, freedom and joy, that he is to confess him in his heart and with his mouth and that he is to come before him with his requests. (III/4, 47)

Barth's emphasis on the holy day hearkens back to his discussion of the Sabbath earlier in the doctrine of creation (III/1, 213 ff.). There, the Sabbath stands as the sign that the gift of creation is more than simply the work of creation; creation is perfect in so far as God takes delight in it, enters into fellowship with it. The creaturely 'correspondence' to this seventh day is the human observance of the Sabbath. Interrupting the rhythms of everyday life, the Sabbath sets this time apart – a concrete reminder that human life and action have their end only in God. This vertical reference is primary in Barth's account of the Sabbath. Even worship and rest, important secondary goods that God commands as part of the Sabbath observance, are subordinated to the sheer setting apart of time for God.

Already in these early pages of creation ethics, we begin to see the interplay of form and freedom that characterizes Barth's ethics as a whole. Rather than lay down strict guidelines for how the Sabbath should be observed (the sort of legalism he abhorred), Barth is content to lay down certain broad guidelines, often suggesting a practical mean between extremes. While Sunday is to be a day of rest, it must not be the kind of enforced rest that becomes a chore; while worship and community are central, these exist for God's sake and not for utilitarian ends. It is not the job of theological ethics to anticipate the exact mode in which an individual obeys the commandment – that is precisely a matter of his or her freedom before God. What it can do is describe an overall pattern of life, and in a way that helps believers make well-formed judgments about what obedience entails.

As we saw earlier, Barth's view of the human creature is inherently social or covenantal: to be human is to exist in a relation of 'I' and 'You', a relation inscribed in human flesh in the complementarity of man and woman. In the section titled 'Freedom in Fellowship', Barth reflects on the male–female relation from the perspective of theological ethics. Readers of this paragraph often fasten on what he has to say about the subordination of wives to their husbands. There is an undoubted hierarchicalism in Barth's thinking; a traditionalist in such matters, he saw no reason to doubt that the pattern described in Ephesians 5:22 should be taken as normative. What is often ignored in this discussion is Barth's conviction that there is no necessity in Christians getting married: in the Messianic age marriage is a specific vocation, not a natural structure or 'order of creation' to which all must adhere. Christian marriage is precisely a calling of the two partners in Christ; hence the ultimate norm for their relation is Christological – a relation of mutual love and service to the other. One of the strengths of Barth's account is its unsentimental character; mutual forgiveness and patience are more important in a marriage than romantic love. 'Freedom in Fellowship' also covers the relation between parents and their children (the question of birth control arises in this context), as well as the obligations that bind us to our own national and cultural community and other such communities ('Near and Distant Neighbors', §54.3). The latter discussion is especially interesting for Barth's nuanced exegesis of the Babel story in Genesis 11, which neither allows us to treat human cultures as ends in themselves (nationalism, fascism), nor reduces them to an empty pluralism (if everyone is merely 'different', then every one is finally the same). Christians dealing with issues of so-called multiculturalism will find much stimulus in these pages.

The longest major portion of III/4 is paragraph 55, titled 'Freedom for Life'. This is the place where Barth engages many of the issues that people think of when they hear the word 'ethics': suicide, abortion, euthanasia, capital punishment, self-defence, war. In one way or another, each of these practices challenges the Christian understanding of life as a gift from God, which Barth – characteristically – interprets in terms of one's service to the neighbour:

> As God the Creator calls man to himself and turns him to his fellow-man, he orders him to honor his own life and that of every other man as a loan, and to secure it against all caprice, in order that it may be used in this service and in preparation for this service. (III/4, 324)

Life is not an end in itself. Christians honour life not because it is intrinsically sacred, but because God commands them to do so in light of the incarnation: 'We may confidently say that the birth of Jesus Christ as such is the revelation of the command as that of respect for life' (III/4, 339). But of course, no stronger warrant than this can be imagined. God's loan of life is extraordinarily precious; determining how life should be honoured in practice is the task of theological ethics.

How does one move from the command to respect and protect life to specific forms of moral guidance? Early in III/4, Barth makes clear that he is not interested in 'casuistry' – the Catholic tradition of reasoning about a general moral rule in light of specific cases (III/4, 6 ff.). There is a problem here, in that it is not at all clear that Barth understands the tradition he sets out to critique.[6] He argues that talk of rules and exceptions makes it seem as if everything can be worked out in advance; whereas in the actual living of the moral life, each individual must make his or her own answer before God. In point of fact, however, Barth engages in something very much like casuistry himself. As an example, take his discussion of suicide. The overall force of the biblical witness is clear: life is to be honoured and protected. 'You shall not kill'. Given that life is a loan from God, the Christian presumption must be strongly against the possibility of suicide. But is all self-destruction suicide? That is, do all forms of self-killing count as a rejection of God's gift? Not necessarily; one can imagine circumstances in which the needs of the community might come first. Thus, persons under torture might legitimately feel called on to kill themselves rather than betray their friends (III/4, 412). Barth notes that even in the Bible, Samson is clearly a different kind of figure from Saul, Ahitophel, or Judas; while he brought about his own destruction, 'the Old Testament sets him in the light rather than in the shadows' (III/4, 411).

Barth calls ambiguous examples like these *Grenzfälle*, literally 'borderline cases'. Acknowledgment of the *Grenzfall* does not mean a blank cheque. In relation to war, for instance, Barth sets an extraordinarily high bar against the use of violence, especially in light of what war has become in the modern era. Still, at the end of the day he does envisage certain carefully delimited cases in which Christians might participate in war. In relation to euthanasia, on the other hand, he finds it almost impossible to imagine exceptions to the rule. The weak, the sick, and the elderly deserve our special protection; here the command 'You shall not kill' erects a barrier that simply may not be crossed.

The final section of the ethics of creation is entitled 'Freedom in Limitation' (paragraph 56). Here he argues that the freedom given us by God is a finite freedom. Our life is but a temporary loan; we live with the knowledge that we must die; we are not called to realize all possibilities, but must devote ourselves to some while passing others by. The theme of *memento mori* ('remember that you must die') gives this part of the ethics a powerfully existentialist flavour. But here if anywhere, Barth makes clear that human freedom is not a choosing into the void. The very limitations and particularities of our lives are blessed by God. Thus I can venture with confidence into a particular vocation, not as a 'career', but as a form of service to God and neighbour. Moreover, to be an individual is to receive from God a unique dignity; Barth elaborates this in terms of the old-

fashioned notion of 'honour' – a discussion that says much about his sense
of moral character and relations in society. Receiving his honour from God,
a man 'can be honorable and have his glory only in pure thankfulness, in the
deepest humility, and – we say it openly – in free humor' (III/4, 664).
Throughout most of the ethics of creation, the church appears only in
passing, as when Barth notes its central role in worship and in the confession
of faith. But when he discusses 'The Active Life' (§55.3), the church comes
into its own in a very striking way. The paradigmatic instance of obedience
to God's command, and therefore of human action, is when one enters the
Christian community:

> But if there is a human action which, as an obedient step into freedom in answer
> to the call of God, fulfils the essence of human action and the active life, it is the
> simple but very strange action … of associating oneself with the community of
> the coming kingdom …. In other words, the obedient action of man consists
> basically in joining the community. We have only to grasp the range of this step
> to see that the life of man cannot be more active than in this simplest basic form.
> (III/4, 493)

This passage takes us to the threshold of themes Barth develops at greater
length in his ethics of reconciliation. But to see why the church is so
important for ethics, we must spend some time on the ecclesiology
developed in *CD* IV/1–3.

The Body of Christ: The Church as Event

Two initial points will help orient us in Barth's thinking on the church. First,
the church exists wholly and exclusively for the sake of its witness to Jesus
Christ. Barth firmly secures this point by grounding ecclesiology in the
doctrine of election. In electing Christ, God also elects Israel and the church
to be witnesses of his grace. No more than Israel is the church an
afterthought; it is integral to the history for which God 'determines' himself
in choosing to be God-with-us. The actual unfolding of that history is
subsequently described in the doctrine of reconciliation, where Barth
chooses to locate his major treatment of ecclesiology.

Second, the church's witness originates in and is empowered by the action
of the Holy Spirit. Indeed, witness is the defining characteristic of the Spirit;
he is the self-effacing member of the Trinity, fulfilling his mission by
pointing to Another. It should be stressed from the outset that the Spirit's
witness to Christ does not require any human means or media. The Spirit's
attestation of Christ is a miracle, exceeding any merely natural human
possibilities. Nonetheless, the Spirit *also* enlists human beings in this task,
fulfilling in history that for which they were eternally elected: their
membership in the Christian community, as the 'provisional representation
of the whole world of humanity reconciled in [Christ]'.

Rowan Williams has argued that two models have historically dominated discussion of the Spirit's work.[7] In the first, the Spirit appears as a revelational 'bridge', whose function is to impart knowledge of God to finite creatures. As the Word mediates God to the world, so the Spirit can be said to mediate the Word himself – the Spirit as revealer of the revelation, so to speak. The problem with this view is that it tends either to reduplicate Christ's work (for how can one mediate the Mediator?), or to make the Spirit's role far too important (the Spirit as source of a secret wisdom, available only to an elite).

In the second kind of pneumatology, which Williams himself endorses, the Spirit's role is that of drawing men and women into communion with the triune God and with each other. Rather than a scource of knowledge, the Spirit fashions persons into a sacramental community that is itself a participation in Christ. 'The bread that we break, is it not a communion in the body of Christ?' On this model, the Spirit stands in closest connection to the concrete means of communion.

It is very difficult to range Barth's pneumatology within the two options laid out by Williams. He would obviously reject the first view as implicitly gnostic. While Barth often uses the term 'knowledge of God' to describe the Spirit's work, he uses the term as Calvin would have used it: to describe the effective power (*virtus*) of Christ's communication to us. The Spirit bears witness to Christ not by a naked recitation of facts, but by effecting participation in Christ: 'the relationship, the fellowship, indeed the unity between him and the community, between him and the individual Christian' (IV/1, 648). The Spirit does not so much impart information about Christ as give us Christ himself (one thinks of the cry 'preacher, give us Jesus', heard in African-American churches). Membership in the community is an integral part of that gift.

On the other hand, neither would Barth sit easily with Williams's second option: the Spirit as effecting communion with Christ through the embodied forms of the church's own life (it is clear that Williams does not mean by this simply 'the sacraments' in a narrow sense). Partly this has to do with Barth's extreme reluctance to grant any role to human mediation or means of grace: that a person becomes a Christian is never anything less than a miracle, an act that only the Spirit can perform. But it also has to do with his conception of the church as a history constituted by divine and human action. Barth wants us never to treat the church as a given, a safe refuge where we may tend to our religious needs. The church originates in God's action. And by the logic of 'correspondence', that action unleashes human activity:

> As the work of the Holy Spirit the Christian community, Christendom, the Church is a work which takes place among human beings in the form of a human activity. Therefore it not only has a history, but – like the human being (CD III, 2 §44) – it exists only as a definite history takes place, that is to say, only as it is gathered by the living Jesus Christ through the Holy Spirit, lets itself be gathered, gathers itself. (IV/1, 650, rev.)

Barth has a penchant for triadic formulas; the one in that last phrase above is an attempt to capture the complexity of the church as a divine–human reality. It is the living Jesus Christ who gathers his church through the Spirit, and not human beings who make it by their own initiative. Christ, however, does not gather his people by violent means. The church 'lets itself be gathered', freely opening itself to God's gracious action. Nor does this receptive moment imply passivity. The church 'gathers itself'; it engages in visible, public forms of activity that are its concrete witness. We might summarize these points by saying that the church's being is *sola gratia* – it is not a 'voluntary' community – that it lives a liturgical existence, and that it is called to a life of freedom.

In Barth's first treatment of the church in *CD* IV, the emphasis falls mainly on the 'is gathered' – God's action in constituting the church (paragraph 60, 'The Holy Spirit and the Gathering of the Christian Community'). To be sure, the human element is everywhere presupposed. Barth harshly criticizes all attempts to render the church as an inward, completely invisible reality. The church does not exist except as a real human institution, a creature of existing in history. The church's visible aspects are as essential to its identity as the body is to that of the real human being. We may not be 'ecclesiastical Docetists' (IV/1, 653). As Colm O'Grady points out, the church's visibility is for Barth already a function of its election: 'As surely as Jesus Christ was elected from and to all eternity … in His concrete humanity and visibility, so surely in the same Jesus Christ God has elected His community from and to all eternity in its very being *ad extra*, in its visibility and worldliness.'[8] Moreover, this visibility means that the church can be analyzed in historical, sociological, or cultural terms, as one religious institution among others. It is simply that these disciplines can never capture what constitutes the church's identity *as church*.

What does constitute the church is God's action, which Barth refers to in a variety of ways. Sometimes he speaks of the church's 'invisibility' or 'hiddenness' as the necessary corollary of its visibility. More usually, he employs his characteristic vocabulary of actualism. The church 'takes place' or 'happens' (*geschieht*) as God draws human beings into a particular history (*Geschichte*). The church's reality is not static, but dynamic: 'The church *is* when it happens to these human beings in common that they may receive the verdict … pronounced in the resurrection of Jesus Christ from the dead' (IV/1, 651). In other contexts, Barth will speak even more straightforwardly of the church as an event, an *Ereignis*.[9]

The language of 'event' has sometimes been taken to mean that Barth denies the church's existence as a continuous, visible institution; the Spirit irrupts in a church-event and then withdraws. This is certainly a misreading. The point of event-language is not presence or absence along a time line, but the divine mystery of the church's existence at every moment of its life. 'Event' simply means that talk about God's action can never be reduced to terms of this-worldly causality.[10] God does not 'cause' the church in the sense of acting as one finite agent upon other agents; God sets people free to be his community, by the mysterious action of the Holy Spirit. The eventfulness of the church unleashes human action rather than constraining it. Thus the visible and historical elements of the church are essential for Barth, and within limits he will even venture description of its typical forms (for example, worship in IV/2, forms of ministry in IV/3, baptism and the Lord's Supper in IV/4). It is simply that such practices are not to be seen as constitutive of the church's identity. They cannot be that, because Barth regards them as human works which can never be a substitute for the grace of God. A result of this is that he is reluctant to affirm the inherent holiness or sacramentality of any ecclesial action – a major issue in ecumenical dialogue, especially where Roman Catholic theology is concerned.

Barth's description of the church as event is a remark about the 'how' of its existence. It reminds us that the church is never less than a miraculous creation of the Holy Spirit. But can we say something more substantive about the church's identity? Barth makes a characteristically bold, though also problematic, assertion at this point: the church is the body of Christ. This is no mere image or figure of speech, but an ontological claim: the church is the 'earthly-historical form of existence of Jesus Christ' (IV/1, 661). If we combine this with the 'event' language just examined, we arrive at the following result: the church's being is nothing more nor less than Christ's activity of uniting himself with it by the Spirit. It is only because Christ is present by his promise that we can speak of the church as one, holy, catholic, and apostolic. Without him it is not one but divided, not holy but radically sinful, not catholic but subject to every passing shift of the cultural wind, not apostolic but sadly forgetful of its mission. But by God's grace the church is precisely not these things. Its identity as church is constituted by Christ's ever-new action, forming one history with this frail human institution.

The church's life is thus a history on both the divine and the human sides. On God's side, the history is simply the identity of Jesus, which includes the church's story within it. To use Augustine's language, the full reality of Jesus is that of the *totus Christus*, Christ-united-with-his-people. But this reality is precisely eschatological; we do not yet 'have' Christ as we will in the fullness of the kingdom. We must constantly pray for him. And this prayer is what sets the church in motion:

> As the true church it would always die and perish if he [Christ] did not speak to it, if it did not hear his voice, summoning it to watch and pray: to watch over its being in all its dimensions, in its preaching and doctrine and theology, but also in its constitution and order and various ministries ... and to pray that in all these things it may remain with him and in love to Him ... For what is the good of all its watching if it does not pray that this may take place, that it may, therefore, be or be again a Christian community? (IV/1, 711)

Watch *and* pray; watch, because the church on earth is called to constant action and vigilance; pray, because no human action is sufficient to guarantee the fidelity of the church's witness; and do both with confidence, because in the end the gospel does not stand or fall with what we do.

A Holy People: The Church as Congregation

In the previous chapter we saw that IV/2 is devoted to the exaltation of human nature in Jesus – an exaltation already accomplished in his suffering and death, and revealed in his resurrection. These themes are carried through in the ecclesiological part of the text as well (paragraph 67, 'The Holy Spirit and the Upbuilding of the Christian Community'). Just as Jesus perfectly sanctifies human existence, so the church is the community that forms 'a provisional representation of the sanctification of all humanity ... as it has taken place in him' (IV/2, 614).

The language of 'representation' takes us back to our basic move. In its human action the church represents, mirrors, or bears witness to the new and sanctified humanity effected in Jesus Christ. This is not any virtue or quality of its own; if we fasten abstractly on the church as a human performance, we will encounter only a *Scheinkirche*, a mere 'apparent church'. Only through the Spirit's action does the sinful *Scheinkirche* become *die wirkliche Kirche*, the 'real' or 'actual' church – an effective sign of Christ's sanctifying work. The church can only pray that this will happen, yet in prayer believers may be confident that it will happen.

The church carries out its task of witness through its 'upbuilding', or to use the more traditional term, its 'edification' (*oikodome*). The term comes from New Testament texts like Ephesians 4:12–15, which speaks of God's bestowing gifts in order to 'equip the saints for the work of ministry, for building up the body of Christ' (*eis oikodomen tou somatos tou Christou*). The term *oikodome* trades on building-metaphors, evoking notions of the church as spiritual building or as temple of the Spirit (see Eph. 2:19–22, 1 Cor. 3:16–17). We are not surprised to learn that Barth stresses the eschatological character of this temple. While the temple that Jesus vowed to build in three days certainly denotes the Christian community, he writes, what this means is 'the community in its eternal form which is still hidden and awaits a future manifestation' (IV/2, 630). Clearly the church in this sense can be built by God alone.

But once again, divine action does not exclude human action. Just as the church is both gathered and gathers itself, so the community is an active participant in its own edification:

Even if only in faith and not in sight, to say 'Christ' is to say 'Christ and his own' – Christ in and with his fulness, which is his community. As his community (his body), this cannot be merely a passive object or spectator of its upbuilding. It builds itself. And as we are forced to say that as its upbuilding is wholly and utterly the work of God or Christ, so it is wholly and utterly its own work. (IV/2, 634)

The church's upbuilding is a task for both the individual believer and the social body. It happens as individual members become integrated or harmonized with one another, yet not in such a way that the individual gets lost in the collective. Rather, believers are to respond to each other's needs in actions of mutual consolation, admonishment, forgiveness, hospitality, and the sharing burdens. This also involves discernment about what sorts of actions do and do not build up the church. This implies that Christian congregations are, by their very nature, committed to forms of practical moral reflection; here again, no strict line can be drawn between ecclesiology and ethics. 'Christian ethics is never concerned only with the requirement of an abstract private morality, but always with instructions for the edifying of the community' (IV/2, 637).

The church as seen in IV/2, therefore, is the church in its tangible and human form – the local *Gemeinde* in all its specificity and concreteness. At the heart of its common life is the activity of worship, which – viewed 'from below' – forms the key to the church's identity. We might say that worship is to Barth's ecclesiology what prayer is to his ethics: the Spirit-enabled human action corresponding to the self-witness of Jesus himself. In worship, it becomes utterly clear that the church is no human project, but a community ecstatically swept up in the activity of the Holy Spirit. Yet worship, no less than prayer, is unthinkable apart from human agency; here once again we see the familiar logic of analogy or correspondence at work.

Barth's theology of the congregation in IV/2 does not entirely evade the charge that his thinking on the church remains at an abstract level. His reflections on worship furnish a good example: despite insisting on the utter centrality of worship, he fails to say anything specific about what worship should look like. Is it possible to speak of worship without discussing ritual, gesture, image, and music – the concrete elements of an actual liturgy? Surely this lacuna reflects Barth's own experience in Reformed worship, perhaps especially as practised in Switzerland in the late nineteenth and early twentieth centuries. This makes it all the more striking that he acknowledges a connection between worship and the church's existence as a moral and political community. Here we have yet another instance of Barth's gesturing to a more robustly historical understanding of the church, which he nonetheless fails to fill for fear of precluding both divine and human freedom. If the 'essence' of the church is Jesus Christ, he argues in effect, then the precise form of liturgy does not matter all that much. One might agree with him about the importance of diversity in Christian worship, yet disagree that such matters fall outside the legitimate scope of dogmatics.

To say that the church lives doxologically is not, however, to say that it lives anarchically. A political community cannot help being a community governed by laws. This is the theme of the final subsection of paragraph 67,

'The Order of the Community', where Barth argues that the church requires some form of structured governance. In contrast to Emil Brunner, who denied that the church's outward structures have anything to do with its inner truth, Barth insists that polity is more than a practical requirement. He quotes Calvin's words in the Gallican Confession: 'As to the true church, we believe that she must be governed according to the polity established by our Lord Jesus Christ' (IV/2, 681). Polity is a Christological necessity, since the divine–human Jesus Christ chooses to have a genuinely embodied life in his community.

What does this mean in practice? While Barth (unlike some parts of the Reformed tradition) clearly does not believe the New Testament dictates a single normative pattern of governance, neither does he think decisions about governance should be left purely to chance. He suggests a set of criteria for bringing church polity into line with the 'Christological–ecclesiological concept of the community' (IV/2, 680). These are four: Church law must be (1) a law of service, in which authority is exercised exclusively for the sake of God and the neighbour; it must be (2) liturgical law, in that worship is the protypical action by which the church orients itself to its Lord; it must be (3) living law, because the church must always be open to reform and renewal by the Holy Spirit; finally, it must be (4) exemplary law, because by its testimony to Christ's lordship, the church reminds the nations of the One to whom all power is ultimately responsible (IV/2, 690–726).

What Barth offers, then, is a set of criteria for judging good and bad law in the church. What he does not give us are actual prescriptions for worship, authority, discipline, moral formation, all the things that make up the life of the visible church. This reluctance precisely reflects the situation in Barth's ethics, where he refuses to anticipate God's concrete command. In the present case, too, he adopts a kind of middle ground – for example, arguing that church law must be grounded in worship, but not (as we saw earlier) telling us what an actual liturgy should look like. In theory, any church polity is acceptable that adheres to the guidelines offered above. In practice, Barth believed these principles were best honoured by some form of congrega-tionalism, in so far as this polity presents 'the least possible resistance to the renewal of the Church by its living Lord', and so ensures 'the maximum degree of being, open, free, and at the disposal of Him and the reformation which he accomplishes'."

The World's True History: The Church as Witness

The ecclesiology of *CD* IV culminates in paragraph 72, 'The Holy Spirit and the Sending of the Christian Community'. Having described what the church is (the body of Christ), and how it lives (as a community of mutual upbuilding), Barth now addresses the question of what the church is for – the question of teleology. The answer is that the church exists solely for the sake of its mission of witness and service. If there is any theme that recurs again and again in Barth's ecclesiology, it is that the church never lives for itself alone, but for the sake of the world that 'does not yet or no longer believes'.

Like its parallels in IV/1 and IV/2, paragraph 72 must be understood in its particular context within the doctrine of reconciliation. *CD* IV/3 is devoted to the work of Christ the Prophet. Jesus Christ not only enacts the reconciliation of the world, but proclaims his own victory: as the Risen One, he bathes all of human life and history with his light. It is not the case, therefore, that Jesus' triumph 'back there' in first-century Palestine needs to be actualized by us. Jesus is not 'back there' at all; the Father's verdict has made him contemporaneous to all times and places; this in itself is a sufficient guarantee of his presence.

This raises an interesting question: does God need the church? In an important sense, the answer must be 'no'. Only God can save; the church, its sacraments, and its moral life can at best be witnesses to that salvation. As Barth states it bluntly, 'the world would not necessarily be lost if there were no church' (IV/3, 826). But, paradoxically, that does not mean that the church is redundant. While God might have chosen to save the world otherwise, God has, in fact, chosen to make the church a participant in Christ's prophetic ministry. Because human history is in fact Jesus-history (recall what we said in the previous chapter about the inclusion of all history in the cross–resurrection event), it is also inevitably ecclesial history. The church reflects the eventfulness of the light of Christ as it shines in the world. A question that might be raised for Barth – it will be relevant to our discussion of Henri de Lubac later in the chapter – is what relation the church bears specifically to Christ's humanity. Does the church, precisely as it participates in Christ's human body, already anticipate the healing and renewal of creation in him? Or does the church simply bear witness to an eschatological renewal that has taken place in him, but whose reality in us is yet hidden from view? It seems clear that for Barth the latter is the case. The church participates in, precisely, the *prophetic* activity of Jesus Christ – a testimony to his accomplished work; it does not 'embody' him in any significant sense.

In any event, the Christian community is not called to dwell even on its relative necessity in God's scheme of things. The world does not need the church so much as it needs to hear the gospel, and it is the world that should be the community's focus of attention. As the light of Christ the Prophet moves out into human history, so the church – itself a 'historical' quantity – is called to engage the world both in its unbelief and in its promise. The church is called to be 'the provisional representation of the calling of all humanity' in Jesus Christ. Christ incorporates the church in his prophetic work

... by sending it among the peoples as his own people, ordained for its part to confess him before all human beings, to call them to him and thus to make known to the whole world that the covenant between God and man concluded in him is the first and final meaning of its history, and that his future manifestation is already here and now its great, effective, and living hope. (IV/3, 681, rev.)

The ecclesiology of paragraph 72, therefore, has largely to do with the mysterious interaction between the church and the world. Both are integral to God's plan of salvation. Neither can exist without the other. Indeed, their common history takes place within the one history of Jesus Christ. While his history cannot be 'read off' of either the church or the world, the church knows (as the world does not) that all events have him as their inner secret. It is the church's calling as a missionary community to let its light shine, so that the world may come to a saving awareness of 'the light of life', Christ himself.

The Christian community's attitude toward the world is marked on the one hand by a sense of the church's difference, its 'otherness' from the world, and on the other hand by a sense of solidarity. These two aspects of the church correspond to God's freedom on the one hand, God's love on the other. The church must remain other than the world if it is to be an effective witness; but witness to Christ is always for the sake of the other, not against him or her. A good example of this dialectic occurs when Barth discusses the marginal character of the Christian community in the midst of the nations. Typologically, the church's situation is that of Cain, a vagabond and wanderer on earth (Gen. 4:12). The church's Cain-like existence, however, exposes the truth about humanity as a whole, wandering and alienated from God. Note how the church's 'otherness' here serves precisely as a parable of a deep kinship between Christian and non-Christian. The church is not a self-satisfied community of the 'saved', but a people that bears witness to Cain's hope, and its own:

> In the discipleship of Jesus Christ the community must confess its *solidarity* with this Cainite humanity, which is still loved and preserved by God like its ancestor. It does this by accepting without complaint its status as an alien and the great weakness of its visible existence. By virtue of its invisible nature the community will here too be an example; precisely in its life as an alien it will hear and witness the Word of God in the midst of world occurrence, claiming already a share in the peace granted to Cainite humanity. To that extent the community will be far ahead of other peoples in being truly safe and secure in world occurrence, at home in the Father's house. By its existence it will thus attest the true homeland that also awaits these others.[12]

Barth assumes that the church's existence in the world will in some sense be marginal; indeed, paragraph 67 may be read as a set of 'notes toward a post-Christendom ecclesiology'. It is crucial to note, however, that this conviction is the very opposite of sectarianism. The church does not choose to be set apart from other peoples. Its identity as Christ's body is given to it, and this identity requires that the church be both set apart from the unbelieving world and completely 'available' to the world, not adopting a suspicious or hostile attitude toward it, but seeing it as the world for which Christ died. The community exists wholly for God and therefore wholly for the world. Nowhere does the overall hopeful character of Barth's theology come across more clearly than in this treatment of the task of witness.

The Politics of Baptism: Barth's Ethics of Reconciliation

Barth's ethics of reconciliation are in many ways a continuation of the themes we have just been examining. While they do not deal explicitly with the church, these lectures – which remain, alas, incomplete – set forth a vision of human agency as set free for service of God in the world. The one part of the work Barth was able to edit for publication is the opening treatise on baptism, published in 1967 as 'The Foundation of the Christian Life' (*CD* IV/4). The book caused a major theological uproar. Barth here rejected not only the practice of infant baptism, but the traditional understanding of baptism as a sacrament. Indeed, by this point in his career he had come to reject the notion of sacraments altogether. He insisted, however, that these denials must be read in light of the work's positive teaching: that baptism is the responsible human action corresponding to the Yes of God's grace.

The special link between reconciliation ethics and the church is implied by the subject matter. As *CD* III/4 had described the command of God the Creator, so *CD* IV/4 would describe the command of God the Reconciler. What does God require of us not in so far as we are creatures, but in so far as we are reconciled through the death of his Son? Reconciliation ethics is thus 'Christian' ethics in the most proper sense: an account of the moral existence of the community of faith. The work opens with a theology of baptism as the foundation of the Christian life – the act in which one claims one's identity as a a child of God. It was intended to conclude with a treatise on the Lord's Supper, understood as the renewal or continuation of the Christian life; it denotes 'the thanksgiving which responds to the presence of Jesus Christ in his self-sacrifice and looks forward to his future' (IV/4, ix–x). Both baptism and eucharist are to be seen as quintessentially moral practices, undertaken in the freedom of human obedience to God. While Barth denies the sacramental character of these actions, he could hardly be more emphatic in affirming their centrality for the life of discipleship.

Between these two markers, Barth planned to unfold his ethics of the Christian life itself. As its unifying theme he chose the rubric 'the invocation of God', analogous to the role played by 'freedom' in the ethics of creation. Why invocation? In an earlier draft, he had proposed 'faithfulness' as this central concept. Yet Barth came to believe that while faithfulness connotes the temporal character of life under the covenant, it does not suggest action; invocation does. When human beings call upon God, they are already embarked on the moral adventure, already actively responding to the divine grace; note the parallel to Barth's treatment of prayer in III/4. Moreover, invocation neatly combines the vertical and horizontal aspects of ethics. Ethics begins with the divine command 'Call upon me!' – the vertical dimension; obedience to the command prompts us to call upon God for help – the horizontal dimension; and precisely this act marks a person's liberation for joyful service of God and neighbour – the Christian life.

The notion of 'invocation' suggested to Barth the possibility of organizing the work around the petitions of the Lord's Prayer, beginning with its opening cry of 'Our Father!' This is an intriguing move in itself. For one thing, it helps to recover the original location of this prayer in the context of Jesus' moral instruction to his disciples: the prayer is an outline for a communal ethos.[13] Moreover, the eschatological character of the prayer provides Barth with an opportunity to explore the connections between eschatology and ethics. He accomplishes this in part by exploiting the New Testament's language concerning the 'principalities and powers', those created structures that, in the present evil aeon, act to oppress and enslave human beings. The theme of the powers allows Barth to avoid both utopianism and pessimism in his ethics. Christians know that they cannot either save themselves or the world at large; that is why they pray 'Thy kingdom come!' At the same time, this does not mean there is nothing at all believers can do when confronting oppression. While we cannot defeat the powers on our own, we can at least resist them. Human action bears witness to the One who alone can deliver us from evil; it may also render concrete service to our neighbour, who is also the object of God's concern.

While the theme of correspondence between divine and human action runs throughout *The Christian Life*, it is most clearly exemplified in the fragment on baptism. Where does human faithfulness to God originate? In the history of Jesus Christ, in whom one's identity as a child of God is an accomplished fact. But it is intrinsic to this history that it does not remain external to a person. As Christ encounters us in the Spirit, his history *pro nobis* becomes *in nobis*, a personally 'subjective' factor in his or her life story. Barth calls this divine, recreating action 'baptism with the Holy Spirit', a term that appears several times in the the gospels and Acts (cf. Mark. 1:8, Acts 1:5, 11:16). This action is totally and exclusively the work of Jesus Christ; it claims one personally, demanding a life of gratitude and free obedience; it is always a new thing, never completed, implicating the believer in a life of constant conversion. In sum, Barth describes baptism with the Spirit as the divine action that makes a person a Christian.

But one thing baptism with the Spirit is not: baptism with water! Baptism with the Spirit is purely a divine action, with no enabling or mediating human component involved. Baptism with water is a human action, the 'yes' of the individual to God's grace, as he or she seeks admission to the Christian community. While this human action is indispensable for the life of faith –

only the individual believer can assume responsibility for her own confession – it is nonetheless not to be confused with the work of the Spirit. The fact that baptism with water is 'merely' human is by no means to discredit it. On the contrary, Barth argues that the paradigm of water baptism is Jesus himself. Just as Jesus' obedience to the Father caused him to seek baptism by John, so the believer's baptism with the Spirit inevitably binds him or her to the public act of confession that is water baptism. The Christian thus becomes a witness to Jesus Christ by imitating him, entering into a way of life that corresponds to his own gracious existence.

Barth's denial of the sacramental character of baptism (and indeed, of the Lord's Supper) must be seen in this light. His constructive intention was not to denigrate baptism by water, but to underscore its significance for discipleship. He believed that to treat water baptism as a sacrament was to treat it docetically – i.e., in such a way that the human act is 'overshadowed and obscured' by a supposed divine act. On the sacramental view, Christian baptism

> is divested of its character as the water baptism which is distinct from the baptism of the Spirit, as the human decision which corresponds to the divine turning to man. It thus ceases to be a truly human work and word which proceeds from that basis, which hastens to that goal, and which is done in the freedom that God has given to human beings. At the commencement of the Christian life there is, then, no free human answer to the act and call of the free God ... It is a strangely competitive duplication of the history of Jesus Christ, of his Resurrection, of the outpouring of the Holy Spirit. (IV/4, 102)

It has been wisely said that thinkers are frequently right in what they affirm and wrong in what they deny. Who would wish to quarrel with Barth's affirmation of the enormous responsibility involved in baptism, of its significance as an act of personal confession? What theologian would seek to locate it other than as the first step in the life of discipleship? Moreover, one can hardly deny that in the context of Christendom baptism has often been understood in quasi-magical terms, as an inoculation against going to hell. Much of what Barth has to say needs to be read against the background of his scathing critique of European Protestantism, with its cavalier attitude toward the responsibilities that go with baptism.

But does affirmation of the human act of baptism necessarily mean a denial of its character as a sacrament? Not only Roman Catholics, but the heirs of Luther and Calvin have always thought one could have both. It is not only Barth's results that need to be questioned here; one could argue that his systematic distinction between water baptism and baptism in the Spirit has, so to speak, been invented in order to maintain a maximum separation between divine and human action. Despite what Barth suggests, the mere 'baptism with water' performed by John is precisely *not* Christian baptism, even if Jesus himself humbly submitted to it. Paul, for example, clearly saw baptism as a rite of communal entry that effectively unites a person with

Christ's death. It is telling that the emphasis in Barth's account falls on the synoptic accounts of Jesus' baptism, rather than on the great commission in Matthew 28 – a commission directed not to the candidate for baptism, but to the community that baptizes.

Whatever one makes of Barth's theology of baptism, it is important to see how it draws together important themes from both his ecclesiology and his ethics. It highlights the primacy of divine grace for the moral life. It emphasizes the centrality of human action and freedom, which, though not identical with God's grace, nonetheless forms a likeness or correspondence to it. Moreover, while Barth's understanding of baptism might be seen as fostering a low ecclesiology, one could argue that his intention was just the opposite. To the extent that the church simply becomes a mirror of its host culture (and this is what happens when indiscriminate baptism is the norm), then it forfeits its claim to being the body of Christ or the temple of the Holy Spirit. The church, Barth tells us, is the 'earthly-historical form of existence of Jesus Christ'. But if so, then its human practices of baptism and eucharist must be distinctive practices that set it apart from other communities – not for the sake of being different, but for the sake of witness to the gospel. Christ unites himself with a people whose whole way of life is constituted by witness. Barth foresaw a day when the church of Christendom would yield to a church of the 'living congregation', a church that by that very fact would be more rather than less catholic.

Barth in Dialogue: Henri de Lubac on the Church

Criticism of Barth's ecclesiology has largely focused on his understanding of the church as event, and on the way this seems to split the church into two realities, one visible and all too human, the other divine. In one sense, 'church' refers to an assembly of people with their potluck dinners, Bible studies, youth groups, and Sunday worship; at a more profound level, 'church' means the divine decision of grace, which may transform this array of human practices into Christ's body ... or then again it may not. The visible, empirical church can only ever *become* the body of Christ; it can never simply be identified with that body as such.

Yet to state matters this way is to begin from the wrong end. If one starts with the human, empirical community, one is inevitably driven to ask whether the social reality one now confronts is 'really the church'. Barth, however, begins with the divine promise, acknowledged in the confession *credo unam sanctam catholicam ecclesiam*. God being faithful, we need not doubt the presence of this *unam sanctam* in the particular ecclesial communities to which we belong. The divine gift of the church calls forth the church as a human reality, as lightning calls forth thunder. Consider the following exchange between Barth and one of his students, culled from the *Table Talk*:

Student: Does 'Body of Christ' have any sociological meaning for you?

Barth: Yes, if seen Christologically. The Church is *indirectly* identical with Jesus Christ. He is not without his Body. We *believe* in the *totus Christus*, and that includes His Body on earth. But it is a living body, so we come back to the notion of event.

Student: Is the 'body' an event?

Barth: Yes, bodily existence is an event.

Student: Is it not dangerous to say '*totus Christus*'?

Barth: No. We are only Christ's Body, not the Head. This means that we can never have a 'head' of the Church on earth; this is the Roman Catholic heresy.

Student: But should we say that his Body is not yet perfect?

Barth: I would rather say, 'His Body is not yet *revealed*.' What we see is imperfection, but what we need is *apokalypsis*.[14]

Christ and the church constitute a single reality – Barth is not afraid to say *totus Christus*, the whole Christ, so long as it remains clear that Christ is the subject and the church the predicate, Christ the giver and the church the receiver of gifts. The language of event and of apocalypse serves as a stark reminder of this. While the church is an ordinary human community in many respects, its ontological status is nonetheless strange, enacted by grace and 'unreadable' except in light of the prayed-for apocalypse. Moreover, Barth's rhetoric of event has paranetic force: it draws attention to believers' responsibility to live as the church in their own situation. Of course, even such activity takes place under the overarching bow of covenant grace.

Of all modern theologians, perhaps none has developed the theme of the *totus Christus* with as much passion and persistence as the French Jesuit Henri de Lubac (1896–1991). De Lubac is one of the towering figures in twentieth-century Roman Catholic theology. Primarily a historian rather than a systematic theologian, he was a pioneer in the retrieval of patristic and medieval exegesis and in the theology of the eucharist. His single greatest achievement was his attempt to overcome the mechanical distinction between 'nature' and 'grace' that had become standard in modern Catholicism, and to replace it with the Church Fathers' vision of the divine image at work in all human beings, drawing them toward a common supernatural destiny. De Lubac's efforts in this direction earned him a great deal of suspicion, both among his fellow theologians and at the Vatican; for a brief period in the early 1950s he retired from his teaching activities at Lyons. But by the time of the papacy of John XXIII, Père de Lubac had become widely recognized as one of the most brilliant minds in Catholicism. A *peritus* or theological advisor at the Second Vatican Council, he was named a Cardinal by Pope John Paul II in 1983.

The church stands at the very centre of De Lubac's theological vision. While he never developed a systematic ecclesiology, certain enduring themes can be traced through his major writings on the church. In what follows, I will examine three of these: (1) the social destiny of humankind as a function of grace; (2) the church as the *totus Christus*, a theme closely tied to de Lubac's program of exegesis; and (3) the eucharist as 'the heart of the church', the action in which the church realizes its identity as Christ's body in the world. I will be drawing chiefly on de Lubac's *Catholicism: The Social Aspects of Dogma* (1938), his first major work and one of his most influential, as well as his *The Splendour of the Church* (1953).[15]

The rather dry subtitle of *Catholicism* fails to convey the author's far-ranging intention, which is nothing less than to justify a social, communal approach to Catholicism on specifically theological grounds. (The subtitle of the English translation better captures the spirit of the work: *Christ and the Common Destiny of Man*.) De Lubac seeks to situate the church – 'Catholicism' – within a grand Christocentric interpretation of human history, stretching from God's eternal plan for creation to the beatific vision. Arguing against the idea that Christianity is a religion of private salvation, a view held not only by the church's atheist critics, but by many Catholics themselves, de Lubac argues that Christian faith is irreducibly social. He makes this point by citing an extraordinary range of biblical and patristic texts – the approach known as *ressourcement*, which would have such a deep impact on the thought of Vatican II. Appealing to thinkers such as Paul, Augustine, and Origen, de Lubac endeavours to show that the individualist spirit is foreign to the thought of early Christianity. The Fathers conceived of salvation in universal, even cosmic, terms; their concern was the 'new human being' (the *kainos anthropos*, Eph. 2:15, 4:24), not simply the soul of the individual.

The human race, then, is joined in solidarity at both the beginning and the end. Or should we say, the Alpha and the Omega? – because de Lubac is adamant that the unity of the race derives from its teleological orientation toward Christ. To be created in God's image means to be destined for inclusion in Christ's Mystical Body, the *totus Christus*. Moreover – and here we come close to the heart of de Lubac's project – this Mystical Body is indirectly identical with the historical church, the pilgrim people of God stretching from Adam to the Eschaton. The church is not a mere voluntary association of individuals, who happen to hold certain beliefs in common. The church is precisely 'catholic' Christianity, embodied in a complex variety of historical and institutional forms, but with an unmistakeable identity one would not confuse with, say, Buddhism or modern humanism. De Lubac has no need to talk about the church as an 'event' (although we will have reason to qualify this remark in a moment). The church is the Catholic Church, the visible body of the faithful in communion with the bishop of Rome.

It is important to emphasize that de Lubac's goal in *Catholicism* is precisely not to depict the church as a sectarian enclave, shut off from the wider world of human aspirations. Quite the opposite. The church is humanity's hope because, in a certain sense, she is herself the summing-up of all human history: 'For definitely the Church is nothing else than humanity itself, enlivened, unified by the Spirit of Christ' (*Catholicism*,

279). While de Lubac says that *Catholicism* is addressed to believers, the work clearly serves as a quasi-apologetic theology of history. It is surely no accident that one of de Lubac's closest friends was his fellow Jesuit, Teilhard de Chardin, who spoke of the entire cosmos as moving toward the Omega Point that is Christ.

I said above that the church for de Lubac is 'indirectly' identical with the Mystical Body, the eschatological destiny of all the saved. This qualification is crucial. The church is on the way to this goal, but it is not yet there. *Catholicism* contains some surprisingly strong language about the church as an imperfect and sinful community. Characteristically, de Lubac makes a distinction between the church in its 'transitory, imperfect state' and in its 'complete, spiritual, definitive state'. Cast in terms of the biblical metaphor of the church as Bride:

> The one metaphor of the Bride conjures up two contrary visions, both founded on Scripture and both frequently portrayed: the wretched being on whom the Word took pity and whom he came to save from prostitution at his Incarnation; on the other hand, the new Jerusalem, the bride of the Lamb, 'coming out of heaven from God': the daughter of strangers or the daughter of the king. On the one hand we see an assembly of sinners, a mixed herd, wheat gathered from the straw, a field with tares growing in it: *Corpus Christi mixtum* ... on the other we have an unspotted virgin, mother of saints, born on Calvary from the pierced side of Jesus, or else the very Assembly she has made holy: *Ecclesia in sanctisi, virgo mater*. (*Catholicism*, 68–9)

Considered in her historical imperfection, the church is but a means, destined to pass away in the eschaton; considered in her perfected unity with Christ, the church is herself the goal of all God's works.

But de Lubac's care in distinguishing the church's two aspects should not lead us to imagine any dichotomizing of the church, as if the two aspects could be neatly parsed into two realities. There is but one church. And the reality of the church is such that she is at once human and divine, the way and the goal. De Lubac ranges both dimensions of the church under the description 'the body of Christ'. Unlike Barth, who interprets 'body' in terms of event and action, de Lubac takes it in an organic sense. Christ and the church are one body in that they constitute a single historical reality: 'No one who reads St. Paul's Epistles can miss the fact that by this metaphorical expression he means a certain organism which he thinks of as real ... and whose members are at one and the same time diverse and united' (*Splendour*, 70). Thus de Lubac can write that the church is 'the unity of a totality', and that the Head is 'of one nature with his members' – so much so that 'the two names "Church" and "Christ" would seem to be interchangeable, as we can see as early as St. Paul' (*Splendour*, 71).

De Lubac is not unaware of the dangers of such language. Not only can talk of organic unities submerge the person within a collective – something the anti-Nazi and anti-Communist de Lubac clearly wishes to avoid – but it threatens to obliterate a necessary distinction between the Head and the Body, Christ and Christians. As Susan Wood points out, de Lubac especially runs this risk when he interprets 'body of Christ' in light of the Chalcedonian definition, as if to suggest that the church (rather than the historical Jesus of Nazareth) is the locus of incarnation.[16] This would be a disastrous inference, and one that falls short of de Lubac's own best insights.

Both the strengths and weaknesses of de Lubac's ecclesiology come into sharp focus in his theology of the eucharist. Once again, the issue is what we mean by Christ's 'body'. De Lubac's reading of patristic sources convinced him that, in the early church, the term *corpus mysticum* (mystical body) referred to believers as united with Christ in the eucharistic assembly.[17] For complicated reasons, this understanding was lost somewhere around the twelfth century. Ecclesiology ceased to take its bearings from Scripture and the sacraments, and instead drew its inspiration from secular models of power: as the emperor is to the empire, so the pope is to the church. At the same time, the doctrine of the eucharist was treated more and more in isolation, leading to a focus on the miracle of transubstantiation. For the Fathers, the locus of mystery lay in Christ's life-giving union with his people; for the medieval Scholastics, the locus of mystery lay in the transformation of bread and wine into Christ's 'true body'.

De Lubac had no wish to deny Christ's real presence in the sacrament. He did, however, seek to overcome the highly privatized understandings of the church that had grown up in modern Catholicism. He hoped to do this by recovering something of the Father's rich vision of the eucharistic mystery. Church and eucharist, he argued, are each the cause of the other, having been 'entrusted' to each other by Christ himself. In a famous formula, de Lubac wrote that 'the Church produces the Eucharist, but the Eucharist also produces the Church' (*Splendour*, 78).

One of the striking things about this phrase is the way in which it points to the reciprocal character of divine and human action: 'The Church produces the eucharist.' By itself, this assertion could be taken as describing an abstract power God bestows on certain human beings – precisely the view de Lubac was arguing against! But in fact, the claim stands under a double qualification. First, de Lubac views the church's agency as a function not of the clergy only, but of the entire body of Christ. The Christian priesthood is first of all the priesthood of the entire Church, a participation in the priesthood of Christ himself. While de Lubac certainly has a high doctrine of ordained ministry – he makes clear, for instance, that the sacerdotal priesthood does not derive from the common priesthood, but is directly given by God – his overall approach accords a high degree of dignity to the laity. This strand of thought is common to the *nouvelle théologie*, and would bear rich fruit at the Second Vatican Council.

But the more important qualification comes with the second half of the formula: 'The eucharist produces the Church.' It is worth pondering the fact that this sentence appears in the present tense, and that within it the church is passive. The church here is no mere hierarchical structure, instituted by Christ but then proceeding along on its own course. To put it in terms Barth would find congenial, the church 'happens' – precisely in that the Agent and Host of the Lord's Supper comes among his own:

> And thus the social body of the Church, the *corpus christianorum*, united its visible pastors for the Lord's Supper, really does become the Mystical Body of Christ; it is really Christ who assimilates it to Himself, so that the Church is then truly the 'Corpus Christ *effecta*'... The Head makes the unity of the Body, and that is how it is that the *mysterium fidei* [mystery of the faith] is also the *mysterium Ecclesiae* [mystery of the church] *par excellence*. (*Splendour*, 88)

De Lubac's way of thinking about the eucharist sounded a new note in modern Catholic thought. Unlike the picture implied by modern neo-scholastic theology, the church does not simply drop down from heaven. In so far as the church serves God's universal, historical plan of salvation, she must herself possess a historical character. Moreover, the formula 'the eucharist makes the church' decisively relocates the centre of ecclesiology: away from formal claims about hierarchy and dogma, and toward the liturgy, as the activity in which the church is most truly herself.

De Lubac's ecclesiology is an attempt to re-orient Catholic thinking about the church in two directions at once. His is a passionately Christocentric theology. His whole programme of patristic exegesis has Christ at its centre, looking backward to the Old Covenant that prefigures Christ, and to the New Covenant in which Christ gathers his mystical body, the church. At the same time, de Lubac seeks to overcome early twentieth-century Catholicism's suspicious attitude toward the secular world. The church serves not herself, but the 'common destiny of mankind'. Indeed, he even quotes Barth approvingly on this point: 'As Karl Barth has pointed out, if the Church has no end other than service of herself, she carries upon her the stigmata of death; and every Catholic will agree with him' (*Splendour*, 135).

Would Barth have repaid the compliment? He would certainly have appreciated such de Lubacian themes as human solidarity in Christ, the unity of the two Covenants, and the importance of reading Scripture in conversation with the Church Fathers. He would also have found much to approve in de Lubac's focus on the liturgy. (Recall that in *CD* IV/2, Barth argues that worship is central to the church's activity of 'building herself up' as a witness to God's grace.) Above all, he would have welcomed de Lubac's Christocentrism, a feature he associated with the overall renewal of Catholic theology in the post-World War Two era.[18]

For all this, one can imagine Barth directing some sharp questions to his Jesuit theological companion. I will suggest only three:

1. De Lubac's whole 'system' revolves around the idea of the *totus Christus*, Christ united with the body of the faithful. But does de Lubac

adequately distinguish between Christ and the church? Does his organic conception of their unity allow for any possibility of Christ's judging the church? De Lubac does, to be sure, acknowledge the church's failings and shortcomings during its earthly pilgrimage: the church does not claim to have achieved its eschatological perfection. Nonetheless, one wonders if de Lubac doesn't systematically undermine this point by treating the church as the embodiment of an essence (Christ himself) rather than as a people joined to Christ in covenant fellowship. Commenting on the 1943 papal encyclical *Mystici Corporis*, Barth asks whether it doesn't imply an 'unconditional identification of the mystery of the Church as created and maintained and ruled by Christ through the Holy Spirit with its historical action and juridical organization' (IV/1, 659). Now De Lubac's thinking on the church is certainly far more nuanced than *Mystici Corporis*. As Susan Wood points out, his use of the ascription 'Bride of Christ' has the potential to display Christ's intimate union with his church, without compromising the difference in their identities. Unfortunately, de Lubac does not exploit this language nearly as much as he might; in an odd mirror image of Barth's own ecclesiology, the concept of the church as Christ's body seems to crowd out other options.

2. A second question Barth might pose is closely related to the first: does de Lubac adequately distinguish divine from human agency? The claim that 'the church makes the eucharist, and the eucharist makes the church', helps us get to the heart of this concern. On the one hand, the double form of the claim might be taken to suggest a distinction between God's action and our own; the church makes the eucharist (a human act expressing gratitude) in response to the eucharist's making the church (a divine act of grace). De Lubac lends some support to this reading when he relates the two moments to the church's active and passive aspects. On the other hand, de Lubac's theology simply will not accommodate Barth's desire for a 'clean' distinction between divine and human action. Thus he describes the church's active role not simply as that of witness, but as an exercise of the church's 'sanctifying power'; the divine and human elements of the church co-inhere, as the one Body 'builds itself up through this mysterious interaction … up to the day of its consummation' (*Splendour*, 78).

To some extent, the difference between Barth and de Lubac in this area has to do with different conceptions of grace, with Barth emphasizing the church's own poverty and need of redemption, de Lubac the church's mysterious co-operation with God – a classic Protestant/Catholic debate. But neither should we overlook the significance of this disagreement for Christian ethics. Central to Barth's concern in distinguishing divine and human action is, as we have seen, to safeguard the integrity of the *human* as a responsible moral agent. Barth thinks that human agency should not be asked to assume a burden for which it is unsuited, namely securing grace; and that once this illusion is abandoned, we can focus our attention on what grace sets us free to do – serving the needs of our neighbour. In short, a too religious and ecclesial conception of salvation may tend to eclipse the true dignity of the human being as God's covenant partner.

But one can also imagine de Lubac offering a riposte to Barth at this point. While he did not write Christian ethics, de Lubac everywhere presupposes the complex array of practices by which Catholic Christians seek to be sanctified as followers of Jesus Christ: prayer, fasting, confession, imitation of the saints, and above all baptism and eucharist. In a sense, his vision of the church helps recover precisely the corporate dimension of these practices. 'The eucharist makes the church' so that the church may be a *community* of disciples, and not simply an institution that mediates grace and salvation to the individual. However far de Lubac's ecclesiology may seem from believers' church models, his insistence that it is the gathered assembly that constitutes 'the body of Christ' forges a link with traditions that likewise emphasize the corporate nature of discipleship. The distance between de Lubac and free church theologians such as John Howard Yoder or Miroslav Volf may not be as great as might first appear.

By contrast, one might wonder if Barth's ecclesiology, with its strongly vertical emphasis on the church as event, does not encourage a rather one-dimensional picture of ethics as obedience to divine command. While I have tried to suggest in this chapter that Barth has a richer understanding of the moral journey than is often supposed, the fact remains that he views both church and ethics consistently in terms of a divine disruption coming down from above. Even the 'great passion' for the kingdom described in *The Christian Life* comes as the response to the command 'Call upon me!' The issue is not whether Christian ethics does not need some account of the moral life that takes us beyond the 'Thou shall' language of deontology.

3. In our imagined conversation between Barth and de Lubac, one can also imagine Barth raising questions about the Catholic understanding of the church as such. Specifically, one can imagine him worrying about the claim 'The eucharist makes the church'. Even setting aside the issues this raises for the theology of grace, Barth might ask why the claim should be restricted to the eucharist. Why not say 'baptism makes the church', 'preaching makes the church', or even 'mission makes the church'? (a theme Barth develops extensively in IV/3). Is not the church's life as a community constituted by this whole range of activities, and not simply by the Mass? In his little book on Vatican II, Barth poses precisely this question to the document titled *Lumen Gentium*, the dogmatic constitution on the church: 'Why is it that among the four marks of the church in Acts 2:42 (devotion to the apostles' teaching, fellowship, breaking of bread, and prayers), it is the third (Eucharist) that is designated as constitutive for the life of the church?'[19]

A reasonable answer to this question might be: because Henri de Lubac helped deepen the council's appreciation of this truth. De Lubac's legacy to modern Catholicism is sometimes taken to be his emphasis on the communal, corporate nature of the church's life, especially as focused in the eucharist: 'we who are many are one body, for we all partake of the one bread' (1 Cor. 10:17). His writings are indeed filled with references to the notion of the church as *koinonia*, a communion or participation in holy things.

At the same time, de Lubac never lost sight of the mystery that stands at the centre of such communion. In a telling passage in *The Splendour of the Church*, he worries that renewed focus on the liturgy might lead to an all-too-human fascination with worship itself, as the act that unites believers in a common spirit. Worship is not an end in itself, but our chief means of access to the Crucified:

> The Catholic liturgy is luminous in its very mysteries, balanced and reposeful in its very magnificence; everything in it is ordered, and even that which calls most strongly to our being at the level of the senses come by its meaning only through faith ... [The] sacrifice at its center is 'a symbol and representation of the passion of the Lord', and sacrament of his sacrifice, and the memorial of his death. (*Splendour*, 89)

De Lubac might respond to Barth's question by arguing that the eucharist is the church at its most evangelical, sacramentally 'proclaiming the Lord's death, until he comes'. The answer would doubtless lead to further discussion of the church's relation to Christ's death, the meaning of his priestly work, and the sense in which that work is or is not complete. Surely both Barth and de Lubac would find it fitting that a debate on the church should ultimately return to Jesus Christ, the living Lord of the living congregation.

Notes

1   Martin Luther, W.A. 54, 470, present author's translation. This extract is part of a passage used by Barth 'instead of a foreword' to *CD* I/2 in 1938. The implications for the German Church Struggle should be apparent.
2   Martin Luther, 'On the Councils and the Church', in *Martin Luther's Basic Theological Writings*, ed. Timothy F. Lull (Minneapolis: Fortress Press, 1989), 540–41.
3   The case has been classically made by William Werpehowski, 'Command and History in the Ethics of Karl Barth', *Journal of Religious Ethics* 9/2 (Fall 1981), 298–320.
4   This point has been well argued by Nigel Biggar in *The Hastening That Waits: Karl Barth's Ethics* (Oxford: Clarendon Press, 1993). See especially chapter I, 'Ethics as an Aid to Hearing'.
5   See John Webster, '"The Grammar of Doing": Luther and Barth on Human Agency', in *Barth's Moral Theology: Human Action in Barth's Thought* (Grand Rapids: Eerdmans, 1998).
6   See Biggar, 'Barth's Trinitarian Ethic', in *The Cambridge Companion to Karl Barth*, ed. John Webster (Cambridge: Cambridge University Press, 2000).
7   Rowan Williams, 'Word and Spirit', in *On Christian Theology* (Oxford: Basil Blackwell, 2000).
8   Colm O'Grady, *The Church in the Theology of Karl Barth* (London: Geoffrey Chapman, 1968), 254.
9   See 'The Church: the Living Congregation of the Lord Jesus Christ,' in Barth, *God Here*

and Now, ed. and trans. Paul van Buren (New York: Harper and Row, 1964).

10 I am grateful to Stanley Hauerwas for this way of formulating the matter.

11 See 'The Church: the Living Congregation of the Lord Jesus Christ', 76; cf. 84.

12 *KD* IV/3, 853, present author's translation, emphasis in original; *CD* IV/1, 745.

13 See Gerhard Lohfink, *Jesus and Community: The Social Dimension of Christian Faith*, trans. John Galvin (Philadelphia: Fortress Press, 1984).

14 *Karl Barth's Table Talk*, ed. John Godsey (Edinburgh: Oliver and Boyd, 1963), 42.

15 Henri de Lubac, *Catholicism: Christ and the Common Destiny of Man*, trans. Lancelot Sheppherd and Sister Elizabeth Englund, OCD (San Francisco: Ignatius Press, 1988); idem, *The Splendour of the Church* (Glen Rock, NJ: Paulist Press, 1963). References to both works will be cited in the text.

16 See Susan Wood, *Spiritual Exegesis and the Church in the Theology of Henri de Lubac* (Grand Rapids: Eerdmans, 1998), 85 ff. This book offers an excellent introduction to de Lubac's thought, and especially to his ecclesiology.

17 The book in which de Lubac argued this case is *Corpus Mysticum: L'Eucharistie et l'Église au Moyen Age* (Paris: Aubier-Montaigne, 1944). A condensed version of the argument can be found in *Splendour*, chapter 4.

18 See IV/1, 768. Aside from this brief allusion to the *nouvelle théologie*, I can find no reference to de Lubac in Barth's writings.

19 Barth, *Ad Limina Apostolorum: An Appraisal of Vatican II* (Richmond, VA: John Knox Press, 1968), 24.

Chapter 7

The Finger of the Baptist:
Barth and the Christian Witness

> In all the riches of his divine being the God who reconciled the world with himself in Jesus Christ is one. Jesus Christ, elected the head of all human beings and as such their representative who includes them all … in his risen and crucified body is one. The Holy Spirit in the fullness and diversity of his gifts is one. In the same way his community as the gathering of the people who know and confess him can only be one.
> – Barth, *CD* IV/1[1]

On Being Theologically One-sided

The Second Assembly of the World Council of Churches met in the Chicago suburb of Evanston in 1954. As part of its preparatory work, a select group of Protestant theologians was invited to help draw up a report on the theme 'Jesus Christ, the Hope of the World'.[2] This committee was composed of twenty-five of the most distinguished names in contemporary theology, including Donald Baillie, Karl Barth, Emil Brunner, Robert Calhoun, Reinhold Niebuhr, Edmund Schlink, and Gustav Wingren. The 'Committee of Twenty-Five' first convened in Geneva in July 1951.

This high-minded enterprise almost ended in disaster, as the group quickly polarized into warring camps of European and American scholars. Barth and his allies insisted that hope be interpreted in radically Christological and eschatological terms: the crucified Jesus Christ alone is the world's hope. The Americans found this a recipe for social and political irrelevance on the part of Christians, in so far as it said nothing about the human quest for justice; indeed, Reinhold Niebuhr even suggested dropping the word 'hope' from the Assembly's theme. Barth and Niebuhr could not abide each other, and at various points each threatened to bolt the conference. But somehow the committee held together, in part due to the patient efforts of Bishop Lesslie Newbigin of the Church of South India, whom the group would eventually elect as its chair.

In the end, Barth got his way: the committee's final report in 1953 was marked by a strongly eschatological thrust.[3] Newbigin prevailed on Barth to help draft the text of this version at a meeting in Bossey, Switzerland. He records the following vivid scene in his autobiography:

My last memory is of Karl Barth, to whom I had assigned the job of writing the final section. I found him sitting surrounded by papers in the middle of the Bossey lawn, looking much disheveled. 'You look as if you are in trouble', I said. 'I am', he replied. 'This is a task for some great ecumenical theologian.'[4]

The classic model of ecumenical theology has emphasized dialogue, exchange, openness, as each participant patiently tries to hear his or her own faith expressed in the language of the other. It is easy to see why Barth would be impatient with this kind of approach. For him, the heart of Christian dogmatics lay in the theologian's wrestling with Holy Scripture – a personal, engaged, and in some respects lonely activity. (One of the chapters in *Evangelical Theology: An Introduction* is titled 'Solitude'.) Ecumenical theology is usually theology done by committee, and this simply was not Barth's style. Moreover, he was bound to be suspicious of a theological method so inherently oriented toward consensus and compromise, fearing that this might mean a blunting of the hard edges of Christian faith. Barth saw theological existence not primarily as a matter of dialogue, but of witness – the offering of testimony to God's victory in the cross of Jesus Christ. The theologian is like the 'impossible' finger of John the Baptist as depicted by Grünewald, directing the viewer's gaze to the figure of the Crucified. Ideas of balance, compromise, mediation are finally out of place here; Christ throws things off balance, and a theology oriented toward him will inevitably appear as extreme and one-sided. It is this rhetoric of one-sidedness that sounds so clearly, for example, in the Barmen Declaration, with its uncompromising *solo Christo*: 'Jesus Christ, as he is attested in all of Scripture, is the one Word of God, whom we must hear, whom we must trust and obey in life and in death.'

This was Barth's image of the theological task, and of his own vocation: to be the pointing finger of John the Baptist. Such an uncompromising summons to Christian witness may rightly be called a 'radical theology'. For Barth, an authentic Christian radicalism means not being as up-to-date as possible, newness for newness' sake, but simply being as faithful as possible. This is why his radicality of outlook went hand in hand with his obvious love and respect for the Christian tradition. Beyond his specific agreements and disagreements with Augustine, Aquinas, Calvin, or Luther, the fact is that they were all looking in the same direction: toward the cross. If Jesus Christ is the one Word of God, then patristic debates about Christology are obviously relevant in a way they were not for a theologian like Adolf Harnack, who thought that the Enlightenment marked the end of the road for 'dogma'. Barth, to be sure, never simply repeats what the tradition has to say – but neither did the great representatives of the tradition itself. Like Aquinas and Luther, Barth makes startling innovations *within* the received faith of historic Christianity. Just so does he help to carry on the 'historically extended, socially embodied argument' that constitutes the Christian tradition itself.[5]

Barth's Catholic Evangelicalism

Barth's particular form of radicalism must be distinguished from another strategy widely employed in modern Protestant thought. In this model, theology gains its critical edge by emphasizing the human propensity to construct idols – a common enough theme in the sixteenth-century Reformers. Thus Paul Tillich argued that genuine religion has to do with ultimate concern, whereas idolatry involves 'the elevation of a preliminary concern to ultimacy'.[6] In a similar way, H. Richard Niebuhr contrasts the biblical God of 'radical monotheism' with the false gods of class, nation, race, or political ideology.[7] Among the most important idols to be resisted are those of institutional religion, which often seeks to manipulate God in service of its own self-interest. The hedge against idolatry is found in what Tillich calls the 'Protestant principle', and in what Niebuhr called the stance of 'radical faith'. In both cases, the protest consists in a refusal to give allegiance to anything less than the One God.

On the surface, these themes sound a great deal like Barth, whose critique of religion in *The Epistle to the Romans* had much to say about idols, and who also treated the first commandment as a theological axiom. But there are also some crucial differences. Perhaps the primary difference is in the underlying picture of God. The God of the Protestant principle tends to lack the concreteness and terrible intimacy of Barth's God, who distinguishes himself from the idol not, in the end, by being transcendent, but by becoming incarnate in Jesus Christ. Moreover, while Tillich, Niebuhr, and other critical liberals were certainly Christocentric on their own terms – as we saw in chapter one, this was a defining mark of nineteenth-century liberalism – the overall vision they proffered might better be described as 'theocentric'. Willing to say that the Christ-event reveals God, they resisted Barth's claim that God enacts his being in the events leading from Galilee to Jerusalem, in such a way that the very term 'God' is bound up with *this* story. In the liberal construal such a claim sounds too narrowly particularist. In a certain sense, traditional Christian claims about Jesus here fall victim to the Protestant principle, setting God's transcendence over against God's enfleshment in Christ.[8] In the blunt words of Niebuhr's student James Gustafson, 'Jesus is not God.'[9] It is a theme echoed in various ways throughout modernist Protestantism, including some forms of feminist theology.

Now as we have seen throughout this book, Karl Barth likewise conceives of theology as a critical enterprise: he defines dogmatics as 'the scientific self-examination of the Christian church with respect to the content of its distinctive talk about God' (I/1, 3). But rather than employing a Protestant principle, he appeals to the event of God's lordly freedom, in which the Most High stoops down to be with his creatures as one of them. For Barth it is not finally the human subject who exercises critique, but God who criticizes – or in biblical terms, judges – the world in Christ's cross and resurrection. Moreover, even this act of judgment is at its heart an affirmation. Both the substance and the overall tenor of Christian theology are governed by the triumphant 'Yes' of God, making it a joyous exploration of God's ways in light of the accomplished (but at the same time ever new and fresh) action of God in Jesus Christ.

All this has enormous implications for Barth's attitude toward the larger Christian tradition. It means that however questionable he finds particular aspects of the tradition, he never approaches it from a fundamental stance of suspicion or distrust. In turning to the writings of the prophets and apostles, we expect to hear testimony to Jesus Christ. In attending to the fragile and imperfect witness of the church, we expect to hear echoes of the apostolic witness. This confidence is born neither of the text in the abstract (even the biblical writings are, after all, human and imperfect), nor of trust in tradition and institution (earthen vessels all). Rather, what might be called Barth's 'hermeneutics of assent' is ultimately a *Christological* claim. Because God in Christ has bound himself to us in covenant love, we may – and must! – turn to Scripture, and we may – with a less binding, but still definite, 'must' – read Scripture in the company of those who have gone before us. Barth makes this point in the talk he was writing in the night before he died, titled 'Starting Out, Turning Round, Confessing'.[10] He reminds his ecumenical audience that theology is always a matter of 'starting out', as the Israelites ventured forth from Egypt into the promised future; 'turning round' to the past – not out of nostalgia, but in hope of encountering the same promise in the witness of our forbears; and all toward the end of 'confessing' Christ in the present moment. The historical and traditioned aspects of Christian faith do not contradict its consistently eschatological character. Rather, the two are held together in Jesus Christ, who is himself the Alpha and the Omega, the beginning and the end.

The radicalism of Barth's thought thus stems not from an abstract principle of 'protest', but from the concrete event of God's self-giving in the risen Lord. It is because the risen Jesus is, and remains, Lord that we can never achieve doctrinal 'closure', as if the church could ever afford to stop listening anew for the word of truth. And it is also because Jesus is Lord that we may inhabit the great tradition of the church in a non-alienated way, without feeling that we need to re-invent the gospel simply because times have changed. Times are, indeed, always changing: Barth had nothing but scorn for those who seek to flee modernity in search of a pristine religious past. But those who cut themselves off from the past show themselves to be ungrateful – an attitude ill-befitting a people who live by God's gifts. While conversion does not only mean a conversion to the past, it *also* means that. For the One who makes all things new is free to disclose himself in the witness of the old:

> Seeing that the starting out of the church is a starting out to its origin [Christ], the turning round of the church that takes place in and with it is always an act of respect and gratitude in relation to the old which for its part has proceeded in

some sense from this origin: not because it is old, not in relation to everything that is old, but in relation to much of the old in which the new, closely viewed, already intimates itself.[11]

All this suggests that there is a strong case to be made for Barth as an 'evangelically catholic' theologian – or perhaps more accurately, as a 'catholic evangelical'.[12] He is evangelical in his constant orientation toward the gospel, toward its Christological content and its soteriological thrust. The church is precisely not a self-sustaining community, but lives in continual conversion to its Lord. This is the Barth of the *Veni Creator Spiritus!*, the partisan of God's 'disruptive grace'. But this evangelical theologian is in his own way also deeply catholic. He is catholic in his conviction that the God of the gospel is faithful, and does not leave the church without resources for faithfulness in 'correspondence' to God's own. It is this conviction that guided his grateful appropriation of insights from both classical and modern Christian theology. 'In the church that is in the process of turning round the saying is true that "God is not the God of the dead but of the living." "All live to him," from the apostles to the earlier and later fathers.'[13] The church would not be the church in conversion if it failed to listen to them, or if it sought to insulate itself from their testimony.

To the Threshold of the Apostles

The ecumenical relevance of Barth's thought is nowhere better seen than in his complex attitude toward Roman Catholicism, rightly described by Avery Dulles as 'an ambivalent love–hate relationship'.[14] Early in Barth's career, he laid out the basic terms of his dialogue with Catholicism. On the one hand, he argued that Catholicism constitutes a probing 'question to the Evangelical Church', in the sense that it challenges Protestantism to take itself seriously *as* church (and not simply as a voluntary religious association). Not surprisingly, Barth equates this challenge with Catholicism's profound convictions about the presence and activity of God in the church:

> Catholicism testifies and affirms a sure knowledge that he who really and primarily acts in the Church is absolutely and primarily God himself in Jesus Christ. Continually through its liturgy and dogma, Catholicism attests: *God's* presence makes the Church to be the Church, *he* preaches, *he* is the sacrificer and the sacrifice, *he* prays, *he* believes, *he* is the real *I* of the Church.[15]

On the other hand, Barth goes on to argue that Catholicism betrays these very convictions by claiming various human surrogates for this 'divine I' – the Pope, the sacrificing priest, the collective visibility of the church itself. Catholicism's impressiveness does not change the fact that it is disastrously wrong on matters like these. Nonetheless, at the material level Catholicism offers a powerful, undeniable witness to the God of grace. 'Here is churchly *substance*. Here is imbedded the knowledge that the Church is the house of God. The substance may perhaps be distorted and perverted, but it is not lost.'[16]

This dialectic may fairly be said to characterize Barth's whole relationship to Catholicism. He values Catholicism for its witness to the substance of the gospel, especially in comparison to Protestantism in its sad state of modern decay. But he also believes that Catholicism distorts this substance by exalting the role of human action, thereby effectively denying God's free grace. As a religious system, Catholicism is – again according to Barth – marked by the formal principle of the *analogia entis* (analogy of being), which sets God and creatures within a common frame of reference. He argues that such an 'analogy' can only issue in the domestication of God – but if so, then the God of which Catholicism speaks is not the God of the gospel. Little wonder that Barth, in his preface to *CD* I/1, describes the *analogia entis* as '*the* invention of Antichrist', and in this respect the only good reason not to become a Roman Catholic – 'all other reasons for not doing so being to my mind short-sighted and trivial' (I/1, xiii).

It is important to see that Barth's lover's quarrel with Catholicism is carried out largely at this systematic level. For all intents and purposes, he views the domestication of grace by the *analogia entis* as the inner principle of Catholicism – so much so that when he encountered a Catholic theologian who argued that God's activity must precede our knowledge of God, Barth questioned whether such a doctrine could really be Roman Catholic! (II/1, 82). Other aspects of Catholicism, for example Mariology or the teaching concerning the sacrifice of the Mass, were to be viewed as the inevitable workings-out of this basic principle: the heresy of human cooperation with God's electing grace. This tendency to treat Catholic as a system served a dogmatic necessity. In some ways, Barth needed the Catholicism of *analogia entis* as a foil for his own teaching on grace, just as he needed liberal Protestantism for the same purpose. Looking back, we can wonder if Barth did not 'construct' the Catholicism he needed as a means of avoiding a detailed engagement with the complexities of actual Catholic theology. To be sure, Catholic theologians have often been guilty of similar caricatures of Protestant thought; but that does not justify Barth's schematic treatment of his Roman counterparts.

Nonetheless, Barth was open to correction, even quite late in life. A shift in attitude is apparent in a series of writings, conversations, and interviews in the 1950s and 1960s. For example, in a 1964 conversation held with theological students in Tübingen, he acknowledged that the *analogia entis* was no longer the source of concern it had once been for him.[17] This seems to have been due in large part to an argument set forth by Hans Urs von Balthasar, who claimed that 'Barth's way of understanding God's revelation in Christ includes the analogy of being within the analogy of faith.'[18] God 'is' as Father, Son, and Holy Spirit, and the creature 'is' in correspondence to God's gracious action; if this is so, are not both sides of the analogy concerned with 'being'? Barth seems to have had no particular quarrel with this proposal. Positively, what mattered to him was that the relation between Creator and creature unfold in the form of a history, a living relationship, so excluding any static notion of 'being' that would domesticate God's grace. God's being is in act, but his act is truly being – and in Jesus Christ God shares his being with us. It is not that Barth's convictions had changed; rather, he seems to have become convinced that the *analogia entis* as taught by contemporary Catholics was quite different from the teaching he had once condemned. When asked about his earlier claim that *analogia entis* is 'the invention of Antichrist', Barth made clear that he did not want to be bound to his own polemical outbursts (*Spritzer*) made decades before. Indeed, he seems to have become thoroughly bored by the entire discussion.[19]

Barth's greater openness to Catholicism in the postwar period can be attributed to developments on both sides. On the Catholic side, there was of course the extraordinary theological ferment leading up to the Second Vatican Council (1962–65). One small part of this ferment were the Catholic thinkers who produced sympathetic yet critical commentaries on Barth's own work; this group included such names as Balthasar, Hans Küng, and Henri Bouillard. None of them turned out to be 'Barthians'. Even Balthasar, who was clearly captivated by Barth's universalist vision of creation elected and redeemed in Jesus Christ, held back when it came to church and sacraments. And most Catholic commentators criticized Barth (wrongly, I would argue) for treating human beings as mere passive spectators of God's redeeming work. Yet despite the disagreements, he welcomed the new atmosphere that marked Roman Catholic theology in the postwar era, including the *nouvelle théologie* represented by de Lubac. As Barth commented in a 1964 interview:

> I believe that the possibilities and long-term effects of the Council cannot be seen at present. Things are completely in flux. Wait and see! … Actually, I am less interested in the Council than in the movement that has become evident in the past ten years within the Catholic Church, as also within Catholic theology. A strangely powerful movement. Yes, I say strangely, though I might also say: a wonderfully powerful movement toward the center of the common Christian faith, simply stated, a movement toward Jesus Christ.[20]

Yet if Catholic theology had undergone a movement, so had Barth's own thinking. This movement will be misunderstood if one thinks of it in terms of a softening of basic convictions. When Barth wrote *The Humanity of God* in the late 1950s he was not substituting a kinder, gentler deity for the righteous God of *Romans*; indeed, in the title essay of *Humanity* he explicitly denies that this is the case. The urgent reminder that 'God is God' is still in force.

What had changed for Barth, rather, was a move from relatively more formal determinations of God's identity (the infinite qualitative distance, God as wholly other, even the theme of 'revelation') to a set of more material determinations (election, covenant, grace, reconciliation). In his earlier writings, Barth is at pains to emphasize that the God of whom the gospel speaks is truly *God*, a reality far removed from the fears and longings of ordinary religion. Having made this point, he goes on in later volumes of the *Dogmatics* to talk about the actual communion that God establishes with human beings in Christ. God proves himself wholly other not in keeping distance from the world, but by humbly giving himself for the world at the cross. The theme that comes through more and more strongly in the later Barth is the togetherness of God and his human partner, the history they share in Him who is both fully God and fully man. This is not so much a new theme as the making explicit of something that had been there all along. It is, one might say, the full fruit borne of his radical concentration on Jesus Christ.

The remarkable conversation between Barth and Catholic theology was possible because both were talking about the same thing: the 'Word made flesh', in whom God 'addresses human beings as his friends … in order to invite and receive them into his own company'.[21] The encounter had moved beyond argument about formal principles such as *analogia entis*, to a far more fruitful and interesting dialogue on material theological questions. Thus Barth's engagement with the Council in *Ad Limina Apostolorum* is marked by a constructively critical reading of the conciliar texts themselves. He does not mount an attack, but poses questions. The approach is respectful throughout, even as Barth never makes any secret of his own evangelical views – which would have been hard to disguise in any case.

It is fair to say that in the years since Barth's death, his encounter with Catholicism has been overshadowed by the broader dialogue that has taken shape between Roman Catholics and other Christian communions. He would certainly have been astonished by the breadth and seriousness of these dialogues. He would have welcomed them, while at the same cautioning that ecumenical agreement cannot rest on consensus or fraternal goodwill alone. Agreement in faith must reflect a 'movement toward Jesus Christ'. Would he have found such a movement in, say, the *Joint Declaration on the Doctrine of Justification*, signed by the Lutheran and Catholic Churches in 1999? One suspects that he would have offered a typically nuanced – that is to say, dialectical – response to this document. On the one hand, Barth would have taken to heart the Declaration's affirmations that the 'foundation and presupposition of justification is the incarnation, death, and resurrection of Christ', and that 'by grace alone, in faith in Christ's saving work and not because of any merit on our part, we are accepted by God and receive the Holy Spirit' (*JD* 15). Barth's own account of justification in IV/1 sets the accent squarely on Christ's faithfulness, and only secondarily on the human act of faith – precisely the strategy employed by the *Joint Declaration*. In so far as Christ grounds both our unmerited justification (Protestant emphasis) and the new life in the Spirit (Catholic emphasis), the sixteenth-century divisions no longer seem so final.[22]

On the other hand, one can imagine Barth being none too happy with much of the explanatory material accompanying the declaration. He would find the statement strongest at those places where it sounds most like a confession; weakest where it tries to fashion a common language uniting Catholic and Evangelical approaches to justification. The danger with this approach, of course, is that the new language will turn out to be an Esperanto reflecting the deepest convictions of neither community. Moreover, one can imagine Barth becoming impatient with the text's unremitting focus on the churches themselves. Lutherans and Catholics affirm that justification need no longer divide them, a good thing. But what about the world to which the message of God's righteousness is preached? What about the implications of God's righteousness for the church's battle against the principalities and powers? – as we have seen, a theme that plays a prominent role in *The Christian Life*. While the text does stress the renewal of believers' lives in the Spirit, Barth might argue that the document is too much concerned with maintaining ecclesial identities, too little concerned with the church's task of proclaiming the good news to a suffering world.

The Politics of Election

Barth's great exploration into the reality of God is titled *Die kirchliche Dogmatik*. Though translated as *Church Dogmatics*, it might just as well be rendered *Ecclesial Theology*.[23] Christian theology is an activity of the *ekklesia*, the elect people of God. With this bold and simple stroke, Barth released theology from what might be called its modern academic captivity, and reclaimed it for the community entrusted by God with the task of witness.

A quick review of the five dialogue partners we have examined will show that, like Barth – in some cases in direct dependence on Barth – each one 'begins in the church'. This is clearly true of George Lindbeck, for whom the church, that story-shaped people, practises theology as integral to the tasks of catechesis and moral formation. It is likewise true of Michael Wyschogrod, who 'begins in the synagogue' with the carnal election of Israel by YHWH. Stanley Hauerwas's whole theological corpus is a clear and at times defiant 'beginning in the church', although in the work we examined, the community appears primarily as the place where believers (and perhaps skeptics and atheists as well) come together to name the silences of their suffering. Robert Jenson begins in the church as the community set free to proclaim – and embody, as liturgy and politics in one – the good news of God's gracious future. Finally, Henri de Lubac obviously begins in the church as the visible, social reality of Christ's body, assembled around the eucharist that forms the very heart of the *ekklesia*.

The owl of Minerva, Hegel said, flies only when it is dusk. It is ironic that the ecclesial character of theology should become a commonplace at a time when communal ties among Christians have been severely weakened, especially in North Atlantic societies. Since Barth's time the forces of voluntarist individualism have continued to erode ecclesial identities, in ways he might have found difficult to imagine. Thus the authors of a contemporary ecumenical proposal cite modern consumer religion as a major – though certainly not the only – factor working against Christian unity. If membership in the church is simply an expression of one's lifestyle, why not allow denominational 'flavours' to multiply, so as to expand the range of available choices? How can doctrine bind or discipline be exercised in a situation where 'anyone who is offended can simply walk down the street to another church'?[24]

While Barth might not have been able to envisage the extremes of contemporary 'church shopping', he clearly perceived the larger forces that have shaped our current situation. In an address of 1925 titled 'Church and Theology' he acknowledged that modern Protestantism is shaped by the forces of 'the Rationalism and the Pietism which have so successfully infiltrated us'.[25] In modernity, the individual subject reigns supreme. Given this fact, Barth cautions Protestants from throwing stones at Roman Catholics, with their insistence on the objective givenness of church and dogma. While Protestants cannot, he argues, accept Catholic answers at face value, they must respect the Catholic intention of setting God ahead of human choices. One way of reading Barth's whole project is as an attempt to solve, in a resolutely evangelical and Christological way, the peculiarly modern question concerning the church. As has often been pointed out, the modern discipline of 'ecclesiology' assumes a situation in which the church itself has become a problem for Christians.

Does Barth's theology provide us with resources for addressing this set of concerns? Or for redefining them, so that we might see that the questions themselves are skewed? The evidence seems mixed. As we saw in chapter 6, Barth offers what is in many ways a deeply attractive picture of Christian life in community. From his earliest work onward, he makes clear that the church is not simply the sum of our individual choices, but is God's *ekklesia*, a people set apart for witness to the gospel. Moreover, Barth strongly resists the kind of sociological reduction of the community that is a constant temptation in the modern world. The church is neither a glorified social-service agency, nor, in reaction to this, a purely religious or sacramental zone of individual piety. As the 'living congregation of the Lord Jesus Christ', the church's primary responsibility is to serve him as his body. But it turns out that service to *this* lord draws Christians into a common life in which they are responsible to and for each other (that is what *oikodome*, 'edification', means), and also responsible for the concrete needs of the neighbour – not an object of our charity, but merely as the 'Good Samaritan' in whom we surprisingly encounter Christ himself (I/2, 420 ff.). Barth's account of the community in *CD* IV/1–4 keeps theological descriptions of the church primary, even while constantly reminding us that the event of the church is realized in concrete forms of communal life – what might be called an 'ecclesial politics'. It is hard to imagine the author of the Barmen Declaration saying less than that.

Nonetheless, as I hinted in the previous chapter, Barth's ecclesiology has been heavily criticized for being abstract – a formal affirmation of divine eventfulness with insufficient human content. Nicholas Healey has thus argued that while Barth tries hard to hold together the church's theological identity (for example, as the body of Christ) with its identity as a visible and concrete community, the two identifications ultimately fail to cohere.[26] Only by virtue of divine action is the church *die wahre Kirche*, the true church; by contrast, the activity of sinful human beings can produce only a *Scheinkirche*, a false or merely apparent church. Healey argues that since human activity never constitutes the church, this part of the description does no 'work', with the result that Barth simply ends up neglecting the human side of things: his local congregation remains an abstraction. He can therefore contribute little to helping us think about those practices needed for maintaining the church's identity in a post-Christian world. Healy suggests moving toward a model of 'practical–prophetic ecclesiology', with a decided stress on the visible, the local, and the concrete – a view of the church no less theological than Barth's, but constructed at least partly from below.[27]

Similar worries appear among Christian writers engaged in reflection on the people Israel. As we saw in chapter three, the irony of Barth's account of Israel is that while he in one sense accords it the highest possible dignity – it is the irrevocably elect people of God – he fails to honour the material, embodied existence of the Jewish people in history. While Israel remains beloved of God, her 'carnal' existence in the lives of generations of Jews has no theological significance, except perhaps to illustrate God's faithfulness in the face of Jewish unbelief. Both Kendall Soulen and Scott Bader-Saye have suggested a reason for this: Barth's doctrine of election, which tends to absorb and dissolve Jewish history into the reality of Jesus Christ.[28] If covenant history in the significant sense concludes at the cross, then Jews outside the church no longer constitutes a blessing to the nations, but merely a riddle of world history – 'your majesty, the Jews!' It is surely a sign of Barth's deeply biblical imagination that he cannot shake these figures from his mind, even as he insists on seeing them as the 'joyless synagogue'.

The force of both Soulen's and Bader-Saye's argument is that this sheerly Christological construction of election leads to an evasion of history. (This is, indeed, perhaps the most common of all charges levelled against Barth.) Jesus Christ as the electing God elects persons *in* eternity, *for* membership in the community, whether Israel or the church gathered from among Jews and Gentiles). Barth thus has no difficulty saying that the community mediates or mirrors election; it is God's chosen instrument for bringing men and women to a knowledge of God's grace. But while the community may be said to mediate election, that is all that it does. Bader-Saye thus argues that while the doctrine of election in II/2 is superficially communal, in the sense that the paragraph on the election of the community precedes that on the individual, it is in fact the individual who claims Barth's attention; the *telos* of election is the individual believer rather than the formation of a people. Bader-Saye concludes that while Barth performed a crucial service in resisting the Nazis' de-Judaizing of the gospel, the means he employed in fact tended to reinforce the marginalization of Israel in Christian theology. Barth's rich theology of electing grace falls short of offering a politics of election – an account of the material existence of Jews and Christians in their conflicted historical existence.

While the case made by Soulen and by Bader-Saye has to do with Israel, *mutatis mutandi* it applies to the church as well. Jesus Christ is the reality of election, just as he is the 'being of the church' (we encounter this claim as early as *CD* I/1, 4). Because he is an inclusive reality, we need not worry that the church, too, is real. Christ sustains the church by his promise, calling it to a life of responsible witness and service. But one can argue that what theology needs is less than an ontology of the church, as an account of Christian congregations and movements in all their messy, historical complexity. Without such an account we lack the resources for strengthening those communal ties that are essential to authentic Christian witness. In short, Barth's identification of the church with Christ's own being fails to stem the tide of modern privatized religion. Even if it is ultimately true that Christ's being includes that of the church – the idea of the *totus Christus*, touched on briefly in the previous chapter – one still needs to say far more than Barth does about the *ekklesia* in its lived historical reality. To use Bader-Saye's language, ecclesiology must be willing to engage in debate over 'the politics of election'. While he employs this language to speak of the conflicted relation between Judaism on the one hand and Gentile Christianity on the other, we might well extend it to include the internal divisions among Christians themselves.

In recent literature, there has been a good deal of discussion of 'church practices' as a helpful focus for theological inquiry into the Christian life. Not only does an appeal to practices such as liturgy, baptism, the eucharist, or the reading of Scripture promise to render ecclesiology maximally concrete; it also promises to be ecumenically useful. Thus the editors of a recent work on church practices write:

> If the Church is understood in this way primarily in terms of the singular practices through which it is formed and bound to God, then theology which is oriented to these practices can share in that which unifies the Church even when the Church is divided ... Such theology may even hope to be an unpretentiously prophetic theology of and for the one Church in the midst of the divided churches.[29]

While the idiom of 'practices' is clearly quite different from that of Barth, I doubt very much that he would simply dismiss it out of hand. Just as the proof of the pudding is in the eating, so the proof of church practices is in their capacity to direct us to the One who alone can unite the church, and who prays to the Father 'that they may be one, even as we are one' (John 17:11). Barth himself is not above reflecting on church practices from time to time; the treatise on baptism in *CD* IV/4 is one long exercise in just that. While I suggested in chapter 6 that Barth unnecessarily dichotomizes the divine act of 'baptism with the Holy Spirit' and the human act of 'baptism with water', the fact remains that he devotes the bulk of IV/4 to an analysis of the human practice. The work is itself an 'unpretentiously prophetic theology', calling on Protestants and Catholics alike – though in Barth's context, mainly Protestants – to rethink the tradition of infant baptism in a post-Christendom world.

Barth would no doubt offer a vigorous response to the charge that he lacks an ecclesial politics. He might well begin by saying that the place to look for such a politics is not his ecclesiology proper, or even his doctrine of election, but the writings on ethics and sanctification that pervade the *Church Dogmatics*. No one, reading this body of work, could doubt that Barth intends the church's witness to be a visible, public manifestation of Christian holiness, in an implicit and explicit rebuke to the 'lordless powers' who claim to govern this world.[30] Moreover, he might point to his substantial writings addressing the Christian witness to the state, both in the Nazi period and in the era of cold war and nuclear armaments. Barth certainly did not think that a Christian political ethic should simply mimic the response of the Confessing Church in the 1930s. Indeed, he was all too keenly aware of the failure of that body. Nonetheless, there is a sense in which he believed the church must always be a *bekennende Kirche*, a church that boldly proclaims the lordship of Jesus Christ in the face of present needs. Such a church cannot rely on its practices or past performance, but must simply be willing to assume the responsibilities of discipleship. As Barth wrote in the preface to *CD* I/1, 'I believe that to the very day of judgment we shall wait in vain for an Evangelical Church which takes itself seriously unless we are prepared to attempt in all modesty to take the risk of being such a Church in our own situation and to the best of our ability' (I/1, xv).

One then imagines Barth going on the offensive, posing some sharp questions to theologians advocating the 'church practices' approach. He might ask whether it is really true that the church can be identified primarily through a relatively stable matrix of practices. He would warn against seeking the church in the 'abstract visibility' of its outward forms – even when these outward forms are connected with Jesus of Nazareth, as they are in Schleiermacher's *The Christian Faith* (IV/1, 656). The alternative to an abstract visibility is a concrete visibility, defined less by practice than by the complex Trinitarian relations in which the community finds itself. While these relations clearly demand to be articulated in outward form – recall Barth's insistence that the church as an institution is never without law – the forms must always be subservient to the Christological substance. The church is not a project we engage in, but a history happening in our midst, the Spirit's activity of shaping our lives for witness. Finally, Barth might ask whether the current emphasis on the church's materiality and visibility is not overly governed by a reaction to consumer privatization. He was himself a democratic socialist, and would surely have joined in the protest against late-modern society's reduction of all relations to commodity exchanges. This moral protest has profound affinities with the gospel; but it is not after all the gospel. Here as always, Barth would insist on the priority of grace over even the best of our works.

This imagined Barthian riposte does not end the debate. Many Christians understand the church's identity to be constituted *at least* by such things as baptism and the eucharist, not in competition with God's gifts, but as the very form those gifts take in our midst. Some communions would add other elements as well, such as the ordained ministry. Yet even for those inclined to see baptism, eucharist, or ministry as constitutive of the church's being, one might ask whether the language of 'practices' really does justice to these mysteries of *koinonia*. Might it not be more important to ground each such mystery directly in the trinitarian–Christological heart of the faith? The discussion thus ends after all with Barth having the final word.

Barth's Ecumenical Promise

The character of Barth's legacy for the divided church in our time depends on how one reads him. Is he simply of interest to a particular tendency or tradition within modern Protestant thought? Or is he of enduring significance for the ecumenical Christian church as a whole? This book clearly advocates the latter view. As a way of concluding, I think it worth dwelling on what this significance might be.

If Barth is seen as a typical, mid-twentieth-century neo-orthodox theologian, then his usefulness will be restricted by the limitations of this paradigm. To be sure, thinkers like Bultmann, Tillich, and H. Richard and Reinhold Niebuhr were often rich in insight, and the student of theology ignores them at her peril. But like its liberal Protestant parent, neo-orthodoxy assumed a church that simply no longer exists – the church of official or semi-official establishment, struggling to be relevant amid the ruins of Christendom. In the 1940s and 1950s there was still enough residual Christianity in Western culture that theologians could see themselves as blowing on the dull embers of 'religion', hoping to coax them into flame. The apologetic strategies of the day thus stressed seeking points of contact with the search for meaning, or with the quest for personal authenticity in the face of death. While traces of these strategies are still with us – often in much diluted form, as in the contemporary vogue for spirituality – it is hard to see how these will sustain a vigorous Christian faith and practice in the long term. Whatever the church of the twenty-first century looks like, it will not resemble the 'main line' Protestant establishment of the twentieth.

I hope this book has shown that Barth far transcends any such narrow classification. He is not 'neo-orthodox' in either of the two accepted uses of that phrase: he seeks neither a return to premodern certainties, nor simply a more radical and self-critical version of liberalism.[31] Rather, he seeks to re-orient Christian theology toward its proper end, the reality or subject matter (*die Sache*) to which the gospel points – the self-giving love-in-freedom of God. This proposal outbids modernity by directing the theologian's gaze away from the modern – but also universally human – conceit that human beings are their own self-makers, to the point where this illusion is exposed. This is the meaning Barth finds in Grünewald's great altarpiece depicting the crucifixion. Only on the surface is this scene 'negative', in the sense of dwelling on the suffering of Jesus. The painting is the *Johannine* version of the crucifixion – the presence of Mary with the beloved disciple, as well as the words attributed to John the Baptist make that quite clear – in which the death of God's Son is itself a triumph: 'It is accomplished!' (John 19:30) In this action, the world as we know it is unmade, but even more importantly, recreated by the *agnus dei, qui tollis peccata mundi*.

There is something undeniably Protestant about this scene, or at least about Barth's reading of it. Here we behold not nature reaching upward toward grace, but the descent of grace into our midst. Here we see not so much creation perfected, but creation remade. Does this mean that Barth's vision is incompatible with more Catholic understandings of grace, which stress the healing (as opposed to the remaking) of the world? Do we perhaps even see here the 'basic difference' dividing Catholicism and the Reformation, which some theologians have proposed as a way of explaining intractable divisions in the church?

A case along these lines has been made by Bruce McCormack, in a powerful essay on Barth's doctrine of election.[32] McCormack argues that this doctrine implies a radical ontology, in which all things – persons, galaxies, the cat next door, our family's car – are what they are only by virtue of God's electing grace. This view would seem incompatible with traditional ontologies in which things have a stable nature or essence simply by virtue of being created. Thus McCormack calls into question Hans Urs von Balthasar's claim to have found an 'analogy of being' at the heart of Barth's 'analogy of faith'. He argues that the traditional Catholic *analogia entis* presupposes that grace finds a stable nature already 'there', a reliable counterpart for God; whereas in Barth's view, grace has no presupposition in the creature whatsoever. He sees the human act of faith and obedience as real only in response to God's own being in act in the person of Jesus Christ. In short, a 'basic difference' obtains between the ontology of Catholicism and Barth's own covenant ontology.[33]

McCormack's analysis is rich and insightful. Still, one cannot help wondering if he overstates the contrast between two schools of thought on 'being', one classical and essentialist, the other modern and historical. This reading seems to set the conceptual cart before the theological horse. Surely one reason Barth himself stopped worrying about the *analogia entis* is that he saw Catholic practice moving in different directions from that of neo-scholastic thought. In the work of thinkers like Balthasar and de Lubac, and in the documents of Vatican II, Barth could recognize the essential contours of the Christian mystery – just as Catholics could discern something of the same in him. This material convergence overshadowed continuing disagreements over the thought-form proper to Christian theology. Finally, one could argue that focusing too strongly on Barth's actualism risks turning the latter into a mere Protestant principle, a dissent against the very idea of 'natures'. But Barth's own practice was to find the whole world of creation inscribed in the reality of Jesus Christ. It is this that gives his thinking its cosmic breadth of vision, and that makes it possible even to speak of a qualified 'natural theology' in the *Church Dogmatics*.

If Barth is not neo-orthodox, neither is he simply a confessional Protestant. Rather, his insistence on Jesus Christ as 'the beginning of all the ways and works of God' is ecumenically Christian. This view of him does not blunt the sharp edges of his often uncomfortable witness. As I suggested at the beginning of this chapter, Barth became restive whenever ecumenism threatened to elevate mere consensus above questions of truth. In his brief involvement with the Faith and Order movement, he seems to have learned that genuine ecumenism need not mean easy compromises of this sort. Indeed, it has often been pointed out that the classic ecumenical movement of the twentieth century was deeply Christocentric. It was on the basis of the unity already existing in Jesus Christ that believers from various confessions could come together and work toward visible unity – precisely Barth's view of the matter in his ecclesiology (cf. IV/1, 668 ff.). More recently, the 'Christocentric universalism' of this style of ecumenism has come under attack, as being perhaps not relevant in a post-Christian, post-colonial era in world history.[34]

If Karl Barth were suddenly to appear in our midst, what prophetic word might he speak to our fragmented churches? Many things, no doubt; but I imagine him saying five things in particular.

First, he would remind us that Christian faith involves not adherence to a principle, but fidelity to a person – the crucified and risen Jesus, who is the very Word of God made flesh. No principle can *guarantee* the truth of the church's communion with him. This caveat applies equally to Catholic structures, Protestant doctrines, and Pentecostal experiences. Yet while there are no guarantees, there is the eschatological promise by which the church lives. The church's communion-relationship with Christ is always deeply marked by this promise, causing it to cry out: *Veni Creator Spiritus!* – a motto from Barth's earliest writings, which he took up again toward the very end of his career.[35] This eschatological dimension to the faith prevents the church from sliding into self-satisfied complacency. On the contrary, eschatology always serves as a summons to action; the church is caught up in a hastening that waits. Here opens up that space for prayer, sanctification, and active engagement with the world that is one of the hallmarks of Barth's theology. It is in the midst of such activity that divided Christians may begin to discover that they have more in common than they had realized.

Second, Barth would remind us that the ecumenical agenda is incomplete unless it also includes that first 'schism', the separation of church from the synagogue. This was the message he sought to convey prior to the Evanston assembly of the World Council in 1954. As we saw in chapter three, his own understanding of Israel's place in the economy of salvation is problematic. Nonetheless, it is to his credit that he pursued the question of Israel as a pressing issue for Christian theology. This is not simply a matter of pluralism or of guilt induced by the Shoah, but an issue of central *theological* importance. Here, indeed, the politics of election must take precedence over the easy accommodations of consumer society, where each one can find his or her own religious niche. While Barth certainly would not discount the importance of Christian engagement with Muslims, especially in light of the current world situation, he would still insist that the encounter with Judaism is unique and demands our attention as no other; 'God has not rejected his people whom he foreknew' (Romans 11:2).

Third – and here Barth's deep roots in the Reformation come clearly into view – he would insist that any authentic ecumenism must derive from a renewed listening to Holy Scripture. If people know anything at all about Barth's thought, it is that he represents in some sense a 'return to the Bible'. I hope that in the course of this book I have been able to convey something of what that does – and does not – mean. Barth's approach to Scripture is characterized by an attitude of strict adherence to the text (to the consternation of some liberals) combined with an extraordinary freedom in interpretation (to the consternation of some conservative evangelicals). He has clearly learned the art of reading the Bible from the Reformers, and to a lesser extent from other voices in the Christian interpretive tradition. We are only beginning to unpack the implicit rules that guided his imaginative exegetical practice. But if interpretation is to happen, the Scriptures must be known – and preached from. Surely Barth would chastise 'main line' Christians in the West for their increasing alienation from (and sheer ignorance of) the biblical text. Surely he would once again summon us to 'exegesis, exegesis, exegesis', as he did his students in 1935.

Barth uttered those words as he was about to depart from Germany for Switzerland, following his dismisal from his post in Bonn. This brings us to a fourth point: an authentic ecumenism cannot be simply an intra-ecclesial affair, but must have its eyes open to the world to which the Christian witness is directed. This is easier said than done. Barth certainly does not advocate the kind of 'contextual' theology that would simply read the church's agenda off some political programme, whether of liberation or of restitution.[36] Himself a political progressive, Barth was wary of aligning the gospel with specific ideologies. The strange world of the Bible is far too complicated for that. Adherence to the first commandment means resisting the ideological captivity of the church.

Nonetheless, this does not mean that Christians are to hew to the safe middle, or withdraw altogether from the sphere of secular politics. That would mean avoiding confrontation with the 'lordless powers', and so of implicitly acknowledging their rule. Moreover, it would mean an abandonment of the neighbour in his or her concrete need. It is difficult to know, of course, how Barth might have addressed specific contemporary issues. Would he have counselled an international ban on human cloning? (Probably yes, I would imagine.) Would he have lent his support to the 'war on terror'? (The views on war he outlines in *CD* III/4 make this extremely doubtful.) But Barth's importance for such questions goes far beyond the specific positions he might have adopted. Two general principles stand out: (a) The God confessed by Christians is a God who is *for* the human being; any Christian politics will be tinged by a certain 'humanism', given the very nature of the gospel. The church should be less concerned with maintaining order in the world – though this is a not insignificant consideration – than with protecting the inherent dignity of human beings. It is worth noting that these are precisely themes one associates with the thought of another Christian critic of capitalism, Pope John Paul II – and what might Karl Barth have had to say about *him*?; and (b) The church must first of all be willing to practise what it preaches. While Barth does not describe the church itself as a 'politics', he certainly thinks of its gathered existence as a community in political terms. The gospel is not simply something we preach, but something we perform: a genuinely evangelical church must take the risk of 'being such a Church in our own situation and to the best of our ability' (I/1, xv).

This suggests that, in matters political as well as in matters ecumenical, Barth would have set a great premium on the activity of local congregations, relating to other such congregations on the basis of their unity in Christ and in response to common needs. This approach from 'below' need not exclude the possibility of ecumenism at the national or the international level. I am sure that Barth would have conceded the necessity and usefulness of bilateral dialogues, for example. Yet his writings on the church suggest that his instincts lay always with the local fellowship of believers, not because he celebrates voluntarism, but because it is at this level that each has a role to play in building up the body of Christ. When churches take themselves seriously *as* church, then they will inevitably be drawn into fellowship with other communities confessing a common Lord. Under the lordship of Christ, Barth writes, 'each particular Christian congregation and every grouping of the same in all their differences will know all these as only different forms of the *one* congregation, in which each will recognize itself in the others and the others in itself'.[37]

This makes it sound as if all it took to achieve unity was for each community to turn to the crucified and risen Lord, and in so doing turn to the Christian 'other' – and beyond that, to the world for which Christ died. That is, of course, exactly what Barth means. Here is Barth's fifth word of counsel for us. From the time of his theological conversion in the years after 1914 he was convinced that the Bible had a centre – Jesus Christ – and that this One was in fact the moving centre of all reality. It is not finally our approach to him that matters, but his approach to us; he is Emmanuel, 'God with us'. Yet his drawing near to creatures by becoming one of them has the most extraordinary consequences for the way we live our lives, both in the church and in the world. The doubly eccentric existence of the church means that it is drawn off-centre, first of all by the triune God who graciously invades and renews the lost creation, but secondly by the world God has loved.

Barth's orientation toward 'Jesus Christ, as he is attested in all of Scripture' is what makes him a great ecumenical theologian, a theologian who bears witness to the faith received once for all from the apostles and prophets. This faith is only provisionally against the world. At a more fundamental level it is for the world, as God is for the creatures to which he has bound himself in covenant. Part of Barth's greatness consists in the fact that, whatever the shadows and shortcomings of the modern world in which he found himself, he was able to take delight in it as God's world, created in Christ and destined for communion with him. If Grünewald's depiction of the Baptist is Barth's icon of the divine love, then the music of Mozart – that quintessentially modern composer – is his parable for creation, beloved of God, set free to be itself, owing nothing to its Creator except its offering of praise and gratitude. Willing nothing other than to be God with us, God wills us to share in his eternal joy – the joy of the Father's Yes to the Son in the *koinonia* of the Spirit.

Notes

1 *CD* IV/1, 668.
2 The account that follows draws on Busch, *Life*, 395–6; Lesslie Newbigin, *Unfinished Agenda: An Autobiography* (Grand Rapids: Eendmans, 1985), chapters 12–13; and Richard Fox, *Reinhold Niebuhr: A Biography* (New York: Pantheon Books, 1985), 243–4.
3 *Christ – the Hope of the World: Documents on the Main Theme of the Second Assembly, World Council of Churches, Evanston, August 15–31, 1954* (Geneva: World Council of Churches, 1954).
4 Newbigin, *Unfinished Agenda*, 140.
5 I here cite Alasdair MacIntyre's classic definition of a tradition. MacIntyre, *After Virtue: A Study in Moral Theory* (Notre Dame: University of Notre Dame Press, 1984), 222.
6 Paul Tillich, *Systematic Theology* I (Chicago: University of Chicago Press, 1951), 13. To be sure, Tillich also reminds us that God has a concrete as well as a universal or ultimate aspect. If God lacked concreteness, he could not manifest himself as power; *Systematic Theology* I, 227. Perhaps the question for Tillich is whether his Christology of the 'symbol' is really all that concrete.
7 H. Richard Niebuhr, *Radical Monotheism and Western Culture* (New York: Harper & Brothers, 1960); see 32.
8 This is not to say that liberal theology avoids incarnation-talk altogether. German Idealism had a rich tradition of reflection on incarnation, which made its way into

various forms of Protestant and Anglican liberalism. The issue always comes down to whether incarnation is tied to the particular self-enactment of God in Christ, or whether 'God-manhood' is simply a universal principle which Jesus exemplified. This is the gist of the debate between 'right-wing' and 'left-wing' Hegelians.

9 James Gustafson, 'The Sectarian Temptation: Reflections on Theology, the Church and the University,' *Proceedings of the Catholic Theological Society* 40 (1985), 93.

10 Barth, 'Starting Out, Turning Round, Confessing', in *Final Testimonies*, ed. Eberhard Busch, trans. Geoffrey W. Bromiley (Grand Rapids: Eerdmans, 1977).

11 Barth, 'Starting Out, Turning Round, Confessing', 59.

12 On this point see Reinhard Hütter, 'Karl Barth's Dialectical Catholicity: *Sic et Non*', *Modern Theology* 16:2 (April 2000), 139. I am indebted to Hütter for my overall account of Barth's relation to Catholicism.

13 Barth, 'Starting Out, Turning Round, Confessing', 60. The sentence that follows is Eberhard Busch's extrapolation of the thought; see *Final Testimonies*, 63.

14 Avery Dulles, 'Karl Barth: A Catholic Appreciation', *Christian Century* 86 (1969), 408–10.

15 'Roman Catholicism: A Question to the Protestant Church', in Barth, *Theology and Church: Shorter Writings 1920–1928*, trans. Louise P. Smith (New York: Harper and Row, 1962), 314; Barth's emphases.

16 Barth, *Theology and Church*, 315.

17 See the transcript of this discussion in Barth, Gespräche 1964–1968, ed. Eberhard Busch (Zürich: Evangelischer Verlag, 1997), 88 ff.

18 Hans Urs von Balthasar, *The Theology of Karl Barth: Exposition and Interpretation*, trans. Edward T. Oakes, S.J. (San Francisco: Ignatius Press, 1992), 382.

19 *Gespräche 1964–1968*, 89, 91.

20 *Gespräche 1964–1968*, 17.

21 *Dei Verbum*, Dogmatic Constitution on Divine Revelation, ch. I.2, in *Documents of Vatican II*, ed. Austin P. Flannery (Grand Rapids: Eerdmans, 1984), 750–51.

22 One of the groundbreaking efforts in ecumenical dialogue on justification was, in fact, a study of Barth's thought: Hans Küng's *Justification: the Doctrine of Karl Barth and a Catholic Reflection* (London: Burns and Oates, 1964). Küng here attempts both to expound Barth's teaching on justification, and to demonstrate that it does not, in fact, conflict with traditional Catholic doctrine. In an appreciative letter that serves as a preface to this volume, Barth concedes that Küng gets him right on justification ... but wonders whether other Catholic theologians will agree that this is the church's teaching.

23 I am grateful to George Hünsinger for this turn of phrase.

24 *In One Body Through the Cross: The Princeton Proposal for Christian Unity*, ed. Carl E. Braaten and Robert W. Jenson (Grand Rapids: Eerdmans, 2003), 35.

25 Barth, 'Church and Theology', in *Theology and Church: Shorter Writings 1920–1928*, trans. Louise P. Smith (New York: Harper and Row, 1962), 286.

26 Nicholas Healey, 'The Logic of Karl Barth's Ecclesiology: Analysis, Assessment, and Proposed Modifications', *Modern Theology* 10/3 (1994), 253–70.

27 Nicholas Healey, *Church, World, and the Christian Life: Practical–Prophetic Ecclesiology* (Cambridge: Cambridge University Press, 2001).

28 Kendall Soulen, *The God of Israel and Christian Theology* (Minneapolis: Fortress Press, 1996); Scott Bader-Saye, *Church and Israel after Christendom: the Politics of Election* (Boulder: Westview Press, 1999). I have borrowed the subtitle of Bader-Saye's work for the present section.

29 'Introduction: A Catholic and Evangelical Theology', in *Knowing the Triune God: The Work of the Spirit in the Practices of the Church*, ed. James Buckley and David Yeago (Grand Rapids: Eerdmans, 2001), especially 11.

30 One of the most acute interpreters of Barth as political theologian is John Howard Yoder. See the collection titled *Karl Barth and the Problem of War & Other Essays on Barth*, ed. Mark Thiessen Nation (Eugene, Oregon: Cascade Books, 2003).

31 Given the ways in which Barth was influenced by the theological traditions of the nineteenth century, there is a grain of truth in Gary Dorrien's assertion of the continuities that link him with his 'neo-orthodox' contemporaries (Gary Dorrien, *The Barthian Revolt in Modern Theology: Theology Without Weapons*, Westminster/John Knox Press, 2000). But the description is highly misleading when one views his authorship as a whole. As an aside, a whole essay could be written comparing the many 'Barths': Barthian, dialectical, neo-orthodox, evangelical, liberationist, narrative, and postmodern are just some of the labels that come to mind.

32 Bruce McCormack, 'Grace and Being: The Role of God's Gracious Election in Karl Barth's Theological Ontology', in *The Cambridge Companion to Karl Barth*, ed. John Webster (Cambridge: Cambridge University Press, 2000).

33 McCormack, 'Grace and Being', 109.

34 See the comments in *In One Body Through the Cross*, §17.

35 See *Evangelical Theology: An Introduction*, 58.

36 A thoughtful and sensitive treatment of the genuinely contextual element in Barth can be found in Timothy Gorringe, *Karl Barth: Against Hegemony* (Oxford: Oxford University Press, 1999).

37 Barth, 'The Church: The Living Congregation of the Lord Jesus Christ', in *God Here and Now*, trans. Paul van Buren (New York: Harper and Row, 1964), 73.

References

The *Church Dogmatics*

Barth's central work is *Die kirchliche Dogmatik* (1932–67), published by
Evangelischer Verlag, Zürich (abbreviated *KD*). The authorized English
translation is *Church Dogmatics* (1936–75) published by T & T Clark,
Edinburgh (abbreviated *CD*). For *CD* I/1, the student should consult the
1975 translation by Geoffrey Bromiley rather than the 1936 version, still
found in some older libraries. I have indicated places where I have altered
the standard English text as follows: (rev.). Occasionally I have provided
my own translation of passages from the *Kirchliche Dogmatik*.

Other Works by Karl Barth

The Word of God and the Word of Man (1928), trans. Douglas Horton,
London: Hodder and Stoughton.
The Epistle to the Romans (1933), trans. Edwyn C. Hoskyns, London:
Oxford University Press.
The Knowledge of God and the Service of God (1938), trans. J. L. M. Haire
and Ian Henderson, London: Hodder and Stoughton.
Dogmatics in Outline (1949), trans. G. T. Thomson, London: SCM Press.
Against the Stream: Shorter Postwar Writings, 1946–1952 (1954), ed. R. G.
Smith, trans. E. M. Delecour and S. Godman, London: SCM Press.
Protestant Theology in the Nineteenth Century: Its Background and History
(1959), trans. Brian Cozens and John Bowden, London: SCM Press.
A Shorter Commentary on Romans (1959), Richmond: John Knox Press.
*Anselm: Fides Quaerens Intellectum: Anselm's Proof for the Existence of
God in the Context of His Theological Scheme* (1960), London: SCM
Press.
The Humanity of God (1960), trans. J. N. Thomas and Thomas Wieser,
Atlanta: John Knox Press.
Theology and Church: Shorter Writings 1920–1928 (1962), trans. Louise P.
Smith, New York: Harper and Row.
Evangelical Theology: An Introduction (1963), New York: Holt, Rinehard,
and Winston.
Karl Barth's Table Talk (1963), ed. John D. Godsey, Edinburgh: Oliver and
Boyd.

'The Church: the Living Congregation of the Lord Jesus Christ' (1964), in *God Here and Now*, ed. and trans. Paul van Buren, New York: Harper and Row.

Ad Limina Apostolorum: An Appraisal of Vatican II (1968), trans. Keith R. Crim, Richmond, Virginia: John Knox Press.

Fragments Grave and Gay (1971), ed. Martin Rumscheidt, trans. Eric Mosbacher, London: Collins.

Gesamtausgabe (1971–), Zürich: EVZ. *Briefe 1961–1968* (1975), ed. Jürgen Fangmeier and Hinrich Stoevesandt, Zürich: Theologischer Verlag.

Final Testimonies (1977), ed. Eberhard Busch, trans. Geoffrey Bromiley, Grand Rapids: Eerdmans.

The Christian Life: Church Dogmatics, IV, 4, Lecture Fragments (1981), Edinburgh: T & T Clark.

Letters 1961–1968 (1981), ed. Jürgen Fangmeier and Hinrich Stoevesandt, trans. Geoffrey Bromiley, Grand Rapids: Eerdmans.

The Theology of Schleiermacher: Lectures at Göttingen, Winter Semester of 1923/24 (1982), ed. Dietrich Ritschl, trans. Geoffrey Bromiley, Grand Rapids: Eerdmans.

'The First Commandment as an Axiom of Theology' (1986), in H. Martin Rumscheidt (ed.), *The Way of Theology in Karl Barth: Essays and Comments*, Allison Park, Pennsylvania: Pickwick Publications, 25–60.

Wolfgang Amadeus Mozart (1986), trans. Clarence K. Pott, foreword by John Updike, Grand Rapids: Eerdmans.

Göttingen Dogmatics: Instruction in the Christian Religion (1991), vol. 1, trans. Geoffrey Bromiley, Grand Rapids: Eerdmans.

Gespräche 1964–68 (1997), ed. Eberhard Busch, Zürich: Theologischer Verlag.

Works by Other Authors

Algner, Caren (ed.) (2000), *Karl Barth–Eduard Thurneysen: Briefwechsel: Band 3 1930–1935*, Zürich: Theologischer Verlag.

Austin, J. L. (1960), *How to Do Things with Words*, Cambridge, Massachusetts: Harvard University Press.

Bader-Saye, Scott (1999), *Church and Israel After Christendom: The Politics of Election*, Boulder, Colorado: Westview Press.

Balthasar, Hans Urs von (1992), *The Theology of Karl Barth: Exposition and Interpretation*, trans. Edward T. Oakes, S.J., San Francisco: Ignatius.

Barth, Karl and Johannes Hamel (1959), *How to Serve God in a Marxist Land*, New York: Association Press.

Berkouwer, G. C. (1956), *The Triumph of Grace in the Theology of Karl Barth*, trans. Harry R. Boer, Grand Rapids: Eerdmans.

Biggar, Nigel (1993), *The Hastening that Waits: Karl Barth's Ethics*, Oxford: Clarendon Press.

Biggar, Nigel (2000), 'Barth's Trinitarian Ethic', in John Webster (ed.), *The Cambridge Companion to Karl Barth*, Cambridge: Cambridge University Press, 212–27.

Bluebond-Langner, Myra (1978), *The Private Worlds of Dying Children*, Princeton: Princeton University Press.

Bonhoeffer, Dietrich (1971), *Letters and Papers from Prison*, ed. Eberhard Bethge, London: SCM Press.

Bouillard, Henri (1957), *Karl Barth: Genèse et Evolution de la Théologie Dialéctique*. Aubier: Editions Montaigne.

Braaten, Carl E. and Robert W. Jenson (eds) (2003), *In One Body Through the Cross: The Princeton Proposal for Christian Unity*, Grand Rapids: Eerdmans.

Buckley, James and David Yeago, eds. (2001), *Knowing the Triune God: The Work of the Spirit in the Practices of the Church*, Grand Rapids: Eerdmans.

Bultmann, Rudolph (1951), *Theology of the New Testament*, vol. I, New York: Charles Scribner's Sons.

Busch, Eberhard (1994), *Karl Barth: His Life from Letters and Autobiographical Texts*, Grand Rapids: Eerdmans.

Casalis, George (1963), *Portrait of Karl Barth*, Garden City, New York: Doubleday and Company.

DeVries, Peter (1969), *The Blood of the Lamb*, Boston: Little, Brown & Co.

DiNoia, Joseph A. (2000), 'Religion and the Religious', in John Webster (ed.), *The Cambridge Companion to Karl Barth*, Cambridge: Cambridge University Press, 243–57.

Dorrien, Gary (2000), *The Barthian Revolt in Modern Theology: Theology Without Weapons*, Louisville, Kentucky, Westminster John Knox Press.

Dulles, Avery (1969), 'Karl Barth: A Catholic Appreciation', *Christian Century* 86, 408–10.

Farrer, Austin (1948), *The Glass of Vision*, Westminster: Dacre Press.

Feuerbach, Ludwig (1956), *The Essence of Christianity*, trans. George Eliot, foreword by H. Richard Niebuhr, intro. by Karl Barth, New York: Harper & Row.

Flannery, Austin P. (ed.) (1984), *Documents of Vatican II*, Grand Rapids: Eerdmans.

Ford, David (1981), *Barth and God's Story: Biblical Narrative and the Theological Method of Karl Barth in the 'Church Dogmatics'*, Frankfurt am Main: Lang.

Fox, Richard (1985), *Reinhold Niebuhr: A Biography*, New York: Pantheon Books.

Frei, Hans (1992), *Types of Christian Theology*, ed. George Hunsinger and William C. Placher, New Haven: Yale University Press.

Frymer-Kensky, Tikva, *et al.* (eds) (2000), *Christianity in Jewish Terms*, Boulder, Colorado: Westview Press.

Geertz, Clifford (1973), *The Interpretation of Cultures: Selected Essays*,

New York: Basic Books.

Gorringe, Timothy (1999), *Karl Barth: Against Hegemony*, Oxford: Oxford University Press.

Green, Clifford (ed.) (1989), *Karl Barth: Theologian of Freedom*, London: Collins.

Green, Garrett (1998), *Imagining God: Theology and the Religious Imagination*, Grand Rapids: Eerdmans.

Greene-McCreight, Kathryn (1997), 'Gender, Sin and Grace: Feminist Theologies Meet Karl Barth's Hamartiology', *Scottish Journal of Theology* 50 (4), 415–32.

Gunton, Colin (2000), 'Salvation', in John Webster (ed.), *The Cambridge Companion to Karl Barth*, Cambridge: Cambridge University Press, 143–58.

Gustafson, James (1985), 'The Sectarian Temptation: Reflections on Theology, the Church and the University', *Proceedings of the Catholic Theological Society* 40, 83–94.

Harink, Douglas (2002), *Paul Among the Postliberals: Pauline Theology Beyond Christendom and Modernity*, Grand Rapids: Brazos Press.

Hauerwas, Stanley (1988), 'Taking Time for Peace: The Ethical Significance of the Trivial', in Hauerwas, *Christian Existence Today*, Durham: Labyrinth Press, 253–66.

Hauerwas, Stanley (1990), *Naming the Silences: God, Medicine, and the Problem of Suffering*, Grand Rapids: Eerdmans.

Hauerwas, Stanley (2001), 'Salvation and Health: Why Medicine Needs the Church', in *The Hauerwas Reader*, ed. John Berkman and Michael Cartwright, Durham, North Carolina: Duke University Press, 539–55.

Hauerwas, Stanley (2001), 'Should Suffering Be Eliminated? What the Retarded Have to Teach Us', in *The Hauerwas Reader*, ed. John Berkman and Michael Cartwright, Durham, North Carolina: Duke University Press, 556–76.

Hauerwas, Stanley (2001), *With the Grain of the Universe: The Church's Witness and Natural Theology*, Grand Rapids: Brazos Press.

Hayum, Andrée (1989), *The Isenheim Altarpiece: God's Medicine and the Painter's Vision*, Princeton: Princeton University Press.

Healey, Nicholas (1994), 'The Logic of Karl Barth's Ecclesiology: Analysis, Assessment, and Proposed Modifications', *Modern Theology* 10 (3), 253–70.

Healey, Nichlolas (2001), *Church, World, and the Christian Life: Practical–Prophetic Ecclesiology*, Cambridge: Cambridge University Press.

Heppe, Hinrich (1978), *Reformed Domatics*, ed. Ernst Bizer, trans. G. T. Thomson, foreword by Karl Barth, Grand Rapids: Baker Book House.

Hoskyns, Sir Edwyn (1947), *The Fourth Gospel*, ed. Francis Noel Davey, London: Faber and Faber.

Hunsinger, George (1991), *How to Read Karl Barth: The Shape of His*

Theology, Oxford: Oxford University Press.

Hunsinger, George (2000), 'Beyond Literalism and Expressivism: Karl Barth's Hermeneutical Realism', in Hunsinger, *Disruptive Grace: Studies in the Theology of Karl Barth*, Grand Rapids: Eerdmans, 210–25.

Hütter, Reinhard (1993), *Evangelisce Ethik als Kirchliches Zeugnis*, Neukirchen-Vluyn: Neukirchener.

Hütter, Reinhard (2000), 'Karl Barth's Dialectical Catholicity: *Sic et Non*', *Modern Theology* 16 (2), 137–57.

Hütter, Reinhard (2000), *Suffering Divine Things: Theology as Church Practice*, Grand Rapids: Eerdmans.

Jenson, Robert (1963), *Alpha and Omega: A Study in the Theology of Karl Barth*, New York: Thomas Nelson.

Jenson, Robert (1997), *Systematic Theology: Volume I, The Triune God*, New York: Oxford University Press.

Johnson, William Stacey (1997), *The Mystery of God: Karl Barth and the Postmodern Foundations of Theology*, Louisville: Westminster/John Knox Press.

Jüngel, Eberhard (1986), *Karl Barth: A Theological Legacy*, Edinburgh: Scottish Academic Press.

Kerr, Fergus (1997), 'French Theology: Yves Congar and Henri de Lubac', in David Ford (ed.), *The Modern Theologians: An Introduction to Christian Theology in the Twentieth Century*, 2nd edn, Oxford: Blackwell Publishers, 105–17.

Kerr, Fergus (1997), *Immortal Longings: Versions of Transcending Humanity*, Notre Dame: University of Notre Dame Press.

Köbler, Renate (1989), *In the Shadow of Karl Barth: Charlotte von Kirschbaum*, trans. Keith Crim, Louisville, Kentucky: Westminster/John Knox Press.

Küng, Hans (1964), *Justification: The Doctrine of Karl Barth and a Catholic Reflection*, trans. Thomas Collins *et al.*, London: Burns & Oates.

Küng, Hans (1969), 'Tribute to Karl Barth', *Journal of Ecumenical Studies* 6, 233–6.

Lindbeck, George (1984), *The Nature of Doctrine: Religion and Theology in a Post*, Philadelphia: Westminster Press.

Lindbeck, George (1986), 'Barth and Textuality', *Theology Today* 43 (3), 361–76.

Lindbeck, George (2002), *The Church in a Postliberal Age*, ed. James J. Buckley, Grand Rapids: Eerdmans.

Lohfink, Gerhard (1984), *Jesus and Community: The Social Dimension of Christian Faith*, trans. John Galvin, Philadelphia: Fortress Press.

Lowe, Walter (1993), *Theology and Difference: The Wound of Reason*, Bloomington: Indiana University Press.

Lubac, Henri de (1944), *Corpus Mysticum: L'Eucharistie et l'Église au Moyen Age*, Paris: Aubier-Montaigne.

Lubac, Henri de (1963), *The Splendour of the Church*, Glen Rock, NJ:

Paulist Press.

Lubac, Henri de (1988), *Catholicism: Christ and the Common Destiny of Man*, trans. Lancelot Sheppherd and Sister Elizabeth Englund, OCD, San Francisco: Ignatius Press.

Luther, Martin (1989), 'On the Councils and the Church', in Timothy F. Lull (ed.), *Martin Luther's Basic Theological Writings*, Minneapolis: Fortress Press, 540–41.

MacCleod-Campbell, J. (1996), *The Nature of the Atonement*, reprint, Edinburgh: The Handsel Press.

MacDonald, Neil B. (2000), *Karl Barth and the Strange New World within the Bible: Barth, Wittgenstein, and the Metadilemmas of the Enlightenment*, Carlisle: Paternoster Press.

MacIntyre, Alasdair (1984), *After Virtue: A Study in Moral Theory*, Notre Dame: University of Notre Dame Press.

Mangina, Joseph (2001), *Karl Barth on the Christian Life: The Practical Knowledge of God*, New York and Frankfurt a.M.: Peter Lang.

Martyn, J. Louis (1997), *Galatians: A New Translation with Introduction and Commentary*, New York: Doubleday.

McCormack, Bruce (1995), *Karl Barth's Critically Realistic Dialectical Theology: Its Genesis and Development, 1909–1936*, Oxford and New York: Oxford University Press.

McCormack, Bruce (2000), 'Grace and Being: The Role of God's Gracious Election in Karl Barth's Theological Ontology', in John Webster (ed.), *The Cambridge Companion to Karl Barth*, Cambridge: Cambridge University Press, 92–110.

Milbank, John (1990), *Theology and Social Theory: Beyond Secular Reason*, Oxford: Blackwell Publishers.

Newbigin, Lesslie (1985), *Unfinished Agenda: An Autobiography*, Grand Rapids: Eerdmans.

Niebuhr, H. Richard (1960), *Radical Monotheism and Western Culture*, New York: Harper & Brothers.

Nygren, Anders (1954), *Agape and Eros*, London: SPCK.

O'Connor, Flannery (1988), *Collected Works*, New York: Library of America.

O'Grady, Colm (1968), *The Church in the Theology of Karl Barth*, London: Geoffrey Chapman.

Placher, William (1996), *The Domestication of Transcendence: How Modern Thinking About God Went Wrong*, Louisville, Kentucky: Westminster John Knox Press.

Robinson, James M. (ed.) (1968), *The Beginnings of Dialectical Theology*, Richmond, Virginia: John Knox Press.

Rogers, Eugene F. (1995), *Thomas Aquinas and Karl Barth: Sacred Doctrine and the Natural Knowledge of God*, Notre Dame: University of Notre Dame Press.

Rumscheidt, Martin (1971), 'Epilogue', in Karl Barth, *Fragments Grave and*

Gay, trans. Eric Mosbacher, London: Collins, 123–7.

Schleiermacher, Friedrich (1928), *The Christian Faith*, 2nd edn., ed. H. R. Mackintosh and J. S. Stewart, Philadelphia: Fortress Press.

Smart, James (ed.) (1964), *Revolutionary Theology in the Making: Barth–Thurneysen Correspondence, 1914–1925*, Richmond: John Knox Press.

Sonderegger, Katherine (1992), *That Jesus Christ Was Born a Jew: Karl Barth's 'Doctrine of Israel'*, University Park: Pennsylvania State University Press.

Soulen, Kendall (1996), *The God of Israel and Christian Theology*, Minneapolis: Fortress Press.

Tanner, Kathryn (2000), 'Creation and Providence', in John Webster (ed.), *The Cambridge Companion to Karl Barth*, Cambridge: Cambridge University Press, 111–26.

Taylor, Charles (1989), *Sources of the Self: the Making of Modern Identity*, Cambridge, Massachusetts: Harvard University Press.

Tillich, Paul (1951), *Systematic Theology* I, Chicago: University of Chicago Press.

Torrance, Thomas F. (1984), *Transformation and Convergence in the Frame of Knowledge: Explorations in the Interrelations of Scientific and Theological Enterprise*, Grand Rapids: Eerdmans.

Torrance, Thomas F. (1990), *Karl Barth: Biblical and Evangelical Theologian*, Edinburgh: T & T Clark.

Visser 't Hooft, W. A. (ed.) (1949), *The First Assembly of the World Council of Churches, Vol. 5 of Man's Disorder and God's Design*, London: SCM Press.

Ward, Graham (1995), *Barth, Derrida and the Language of Theology*, Cambridge: Cambridge University Press.

Weber, Otto (1953), *Karl Barth's Church Dogmatics: An Introductory Report on Volumes I:1 to III:4*, trans. Arthur C. Cochrane, Philadelphia: Westminster Press

Webster, John (1995), *Barth's Ethics of Reconciliation*, Cambridge: Cambridge University Press.

Webster, John (1998), *Barth's Moral Theology: Human Action in Barth's Thought*, Grand Rapids: Eerdmans.

Webster, John (2000), *Barth*, London and New York: Continuum.

Wells, Samuel (1998), *Transforming Fate Into Destiny: The Theological Ethics of Stanley Hauerwas*, Carlisle: Paternoster Press.

Werpehowski, William (1981), 'Command and History in the Ethics of Karl Barth', *Journal of Religious Ethics* 9/2, 298–320.

Williams, Rowan (2000), *On Christian Theology*, Oxford: Basil Blackwell.

Wittgenstein, Ludwig (1961), *Tractatus Logico-Philosophicus*, intro. by Bertrand Russell, London: Routledge.

Wood, Susan (1998), *Spiritual Exegesis and the Church in the Theology of Henri de Lubac*, Grand Rapids: Eerdmans.

World Council of Churches (1954), *Christ – the Hope of the World: Documents on the Main Theme of the Second Assembly, Evanston, August 15–31, 1954*, Geneva: World Council of Churches.

Wyschogrod, Michael (1974), 'Why Was and Is the Theology of Karl Barth of Interest to a Jewish Theologian?', in Martin Rumscheidt (ed.), *Footnotes to a Theology: the Karl Barth Colloquium of 1972*, Waterloo, Ontario: Studies in Religion/Sciences Religieuses.

Wyschogrod, Michael (1983), *The Body of Faith: Judaism as Corporeal Election*, Minneapolis: Seabury Press.

Wyschogrod, Michael (1986), 'A Jewish Perspective on Karl Barth', in *How Karl Barth Changed My Mind*, ed. Donald McKim, Grand Rapids: Eerdmans, 156–61.

Wyschogrod, Michael (1996), 'A Jewish Perspective on Incarnation', *Modern Theology* 12 (2), 195–209.

Wyschogrod, Michael (2004), *Abraham's Promise: Judaism and Jewish–Christian Relations*, ed. R. Kendall Soulen, Grand Rapids: Eerdmans.

Yoder, John Howard (2003), *Karl Barth and the Problem of War & Other Essays on Barth*, ed. Mark Thiessen Nation, Eugene, Oregon: Cascade Books.

Index